THE SWEENEY

To Peter –

Sincere best wishes from the author,

Dick Kirby 5"/13

This book is dedicated to all
Metropolitan Police CID Officers –
this is what it was like.

And to Ann –
'Til the stars fade from above.

THE SWEENEY

THE FIRST SIXTY YEARS OF SCOTLAND YARD'S
CRIMEBUSTING FLYING SQUAD 1919-1978

DICK KIRBY

First published in Great Britain in 2011 by
Wharncliffe Local History
an imprint of
Pen & Sword Books Ltd
47 Church Street
Barnsley
South Yorkshire
S70 2AS

Copyright © Dick Kirby 2011

ISBN 978 1 84884 390 5

The right of Dick Kirby to be identified as Author of this Work has
been asserted by him in accordance with the Copyright, Designs
and Patents Act 1988.

A CIP catalogue record for this book is available from the British
Library.

All rights reserved. No part of this book may be reproduced or
transmitted in any form or by any means, electronic or mechanical
including photocopying, recording or by any information storage
and retrieval system, without permission from the Publisher in
writing.

Typeset in 11/13pt Plantin by
Mac Style, Beverley, East Yorkshire

Printed and bound in the UK
by CPI Antony Rowe

Pen & Sword Books Ltd incorporates the Imprints of
Pen & Sword Aviation, Pen & Sword Maritime, Pen & Sword
Military, Wharncliffe Local History, Pen and Sword Select, Pen
and Sword Military Classics, Leo Cooper, Remember When,
Seaforth Publishing and Frontline Publishing.

For a complete list of Pen & Sword titles please contact
PEN & SWORD BOOKS LIMITED
47 Church Street, Barnsley, South Yorkshire, S70 2AS, England
E-mail: enquiries@pen-and-sword.co.uk
Website: www.pen-and-sword.co.uk

Contents

Contents

Acknowledgements

I
t was my son-in-law, Steve Cowper, who initially suggested researching for this book, shortly before I retired in 1993; in addition, he and my other son-in-law, Rich Jerreat have both been very kind in guiding me through the minefield of computer-land; my thanks to them both. However, I have always found writing the easy part; getting books published has posed the most insurmountable difficulties. Brigadier Henry Wilson of *Pen & Sword Books* had the foresight and courage to take this work on board, where many of his contemporaries in the world of publishing suffered from intellectual myopia and pusillanimity so I extend my grateful thanks to him.

Many people who worked at New Scotland Yard have been extraordinarily helpful with regards to research; the late Maggie Bird, Mary Clucas, Steve Earl, Robin Gillis, Joy Guest, Ellie Haynes, Julie Milstead, Alan Moss, Suzanna Parry and Ken Stone, plus many others.

Over the years, many people either assisted me considerably with my research or wrote, emailed and spoke to me with some wonderful stories which appear in this book. In alphabetical order, they are: Philip Atkins, Linda Bailey, John Bates, Les 'Dinger' Bell, the late Nick Benwell QPM, the late Nicky Birch, Chris Bird, Geoff 'Yorkie' Blanchard, the late Ernie Bond OBE, QPM, John Brinnand, the late Terry Brown GM, John Bunker, the late Henry Valentine Clark, Harry Clement BEM, Arnie Cooke BSc (Hons), Fred Cutts LL.B, John 'Dicky' Dawson BEM, Susanne Dowswell JP, Kenneth Edney, Bob Fenton QGM, Harry Forbes, Pauline Forrester, Michael 'Gerry' Germon, Stuart Giblin, Les Godman, Martin Gosling MBE, Russ Gray, Rudi Gross, David Hewett, the late Robert Higgins, John Jones, Peter Jones, the late Charles Kirby, Mark Kirby, the late Fred Lambert, Reg Leonard, Jenny Massey, Billy Milne, Stanley 'Steve' Moore, the late Terence O'Connell QPM, Michael

Pearce, Tim Phillips, the late George Price, Tony Purdy, Leonard 'Nipper' Read QPM, Bruce Reynolds, Bob Robinson, George Sharp, Laurie Sherwood QPM, LL.B, John Simmonds, Daphne Skillern QPM, Bill Smillie, John Swain QPM, the late Lou van Dyke, John Vaughan, Ian West and Pat Willey.

A number of others contributed, who wish to remain anonymous – my thanks to all of them. My thanks to the Metropolitan Police, John Dawson BEM, Tom MacMillan, John Vaughan, the late Terry O'Connell QPM, Rudi Gross, Elizabeth Moon and Bob Robinson for providing some of the photographs. Every effort has been made to contact copyright holders; the publishers and I apologize for any inadvertent omissions.

Last, and by no means least, my thanks to my family for their love, enthusiasm and support, particularly my wife, Ann, whose fight against cancer has the admiration of all who know her.

Dick Kirby

Foreword

by John O'Connor, Former Commander of the Flying Squad

This is the first book about the Flying Squad which goes beyond their towering operational achievements during their first sixty years. The Squad's involvement in dealing with all the major robberies in London and the Home Counties is well researched and is an accurate reflection of its impact on major crime. It is astonishing that such a comparatively small number of men and women could have achieved so much.

Tribute is paid to senior Squad officers, such as Ted Greeno, Reg Spooner, Bob Fabian, Ernie Millen and Tommy Butler who, by their exploits became household names. This illustrious list was joined in later years by Don Neesham and Jack Slipper.

Times were changing and Dick Kirby, to his credit, probes into the dark forces which set about the character assassination of the Squad's hierarchy. False rumours of alleged corruption were encouraged and both Slipper and Neesham had their careers curtailed and retired prematurely. The main weasel is named but those of us who lived through it know who the others are, and hope they hang their heads in shame. The author deals with the atmosphere of mistrust and backstabbing created by Operation 'Countryman' at the behest of professional criminals and bent lawyers – a shameful period of police history which those responsible would rather forget. We are allowed a worm's-eye view of the murky corners of police politics.

It is remarkable that even when the Squad was under attack, they were still performing at the highest level. Following a major robbery, one former commissioner was moved to state publicly, 'We can always rely on the Squad to bring home the bacon.' One wonders how much more could have been achieved if they had had the full backing of the police hierarchy.

This record is presented warts and all, and a balance has been achieved which recognizes the dedication and bravery of all the men and women involved. Whilst regretting what could have been, we must celebrate the achievements. The halcyon days may be over, the eagle has flown, but thanks to Dick Kirby, the memories linger on.

John O'Connor

Prologue: Heathrow, 1948

As he drove through the night towards Staines police station, perspiration beaded on the forehead of Donald Fish. This was not purely due to the humid weather in July 1948; he was a worried man and justifiably so. The former Scotland Yard detective was the head of the British Overseas Airways Corporation (BOAC) security at the newly opened London (Heathrow) Airport. Whilst the airport was operational, security was far from satisfactory; the only repository for the bullion and other valuables which were flown into the United Kingdom was nothing more than a corrugated iron converted aircraft hanger. Heathrow was fast becoming renowned as a centre point for every petty – and often not so petty – criminal in the country, at a time of severe post-war austerity when every saleable commodity required the production of ration coupons to legitimately acquire it. The area was patrolled by the private airport police, as opposed to the regular police and keeping it protected was causing the airport authorities considerable problems.

The second problem confronting Fish was far more pressing. Anthony Walsh, a warehouseman, had informed him that he had been approached by a notorious criminal who wanted his assistance to rob the custodians of the warehouse of a quantity of gold bullion, of which the arrival from South America was imminent. Walsh would be paid £500 for his cooperation. Everything that Walsh had told him checked out – and now Fish was losing no time getting to the local police station to impart the information to his friend, Divisional Detective Inspector Roberts of the Metropolitan Police's 'T' Division.

Roberts listened intently to Fish's story and quickly realized that with the calibre and number of the criminals concerned, his limited resources would be insufficient to deal with such a sophisticated gang. He reached for his telephone and asked to be connected to Scotland Yard's elite crime-busting unit, the Flying Squad.

★ ★ ★

Just one month previously the Squad had been detached from C1 Department, which hosted a number of different units, including the Murder Squad, and was given its own identity, C8 Department. With its new designation came a new leader, Detective Superintendent Bill Chapman, who was nicknamed 'The Cherub' because his smiling red face was framed with a halo of prematurely white hair. He arrived at just the right time. The *Sunday Empire News* had reported on 18 July 1948, 'The Flying Squad can't fly' and on behalf of the Squad men, the newspaper bemoaned the fact that vehicles were still being delivered to the Squad too slowly. Under Chapman's guidance the fleet started to improve:the Squad was expanded to 80 officers, 27 cars, 3 taxis and 4 vans.

Chapman handed operational control of the plan to thwart the robbers to his second-in-command, Detective Chief Inspector Bob 'Mr Memory' Lee – so called, because he possessed a phenomenal recollection for the faces, habits and associates of many of London's top villains.

The name of the criminal who had approached Walsh was one well-known to Lee – Alfred Roome (also known as 'Big Alfie' and 'The Ilford Kid') had gathered a formidable criminal record during his forty-two years. Lee then checked those of Roome's associates who possessed similarly impressive criminal pedigrees; firstly Edward William Hughes, who had carried out a robbery with Billy Hill and another man in July 1942. Convicted, Hughes had pleaded a weak heart, which precluded the flogging he so richly deserved, and was sentenced to three years' imprisonment. Hill figured with members of the gang again following his release; he, together with Sammy Ross (also known as Sammy Josephs) and Teddy Machin, carried out a £9,000 robbery in Manchester in September 1947 for which they were not caught. Hill was wanted for failing to appear at court on a charge of warehouse-breaking (he stoutly maintained he had been fitted-up) but he finally surrendered to police and was sentenced to three years' imprisonment. At the time of the intended raid at Heathrow, he was safely out of the way.

But the sallow-faced Teddy Machin was at liberty. He would play an important part in the raid to match his impressive underworld credentials; he was the 'chiv-man' for the organizer of the job, whose name was Jack Spot. In fact, the black Vauxhall Walsh had seen being driven off by Roome, and of which he had memorized the registration number, turned out to belong to Spot.

* * *

At this time, two men ruled London's underworld. One was Billy Hill, a brilliant criminal mastermind who meticulously researched his enterprises and was widely respected. When his men were caught carrying out one of his jobs, he provided their dependents with a 'pension' whilst they were incarcerated. He was charismatic but also utterly ruthless; his word was law and anybody who stepped out of line, whether they were on his or an opponent's side would be summarily dealt with by being 'striped' in the face with a razor, or 'chiv'.

The other was Jack Spot – he had been born Jacob Comacho – who was no thief; he had won his reputation as a ruthless gangster by running protection rackets in the East End of London, frightening money out of shop owners and stallholders; later, he would progress to blackmailing bookies at the racetracks. He used his fists to devastating effect and also, like Hill, the razor, ensuring that in striping an opponent the weapon never slipped far enough south to touch the 'jagular', as he described the four great veins at the side of the neck.

It seems likely that Spot was financing the robbery in return for a sizeable cut of the profits; in underworld jargon, he was known (though not to his face) as 'a thieves ponce'. Spot simply did not possess the intelligence to assist in the planning of the operation; these matters he left, with great confidence, in the hands of Messrs Hughes, Ross and Roome. The plan was as follows.

The gang had received information that bullion, valued at something in the region of a quarter-of-a-million pounds was going to be flown into Heathrow from South America, via Madrid. In addition, there was possibly a further prize of jewellery and other valuables in the warehouse which might well bring the total of the robbery up to half-a-million. And then the gang had an unbelievable stroke of luck. Whilst they were planning the job in a pub close to the airport, who should walk in but Anthony Walsh – and Alfred Roome immediately recognized him as being a former fellow POW in a German camp at Genshagen. Walsh had originally been a security guard at Heathrow but had been demoted and transferred to the warehouse, which had caused him considerable resentment. Roome decided to capitalize on Walsh's dissatisfaction with his employers. He suggested that Walsh's part in the venture would be that he would be passed a quantity of phenobarbitone tablets in order to drug the coffee for the three guards in the warehouse; while they were unconscious Walsh would open the doors of the warehouse and the gang would help themselves to the contents. This Walsh initially agreed to do, but later realizing the ramifications of the plot he decided to inform his employers.

On the evening of the raid, 28 July, Walsh came on duty, having accepted the phenobarbitone tablets from the gang; far from merely drugging the guards, their strength was quite sufficient to kill them. An hour later at nine o'clock, the aeroplane from South America landed and the bullion was off-loaded into the strongroom at the BOAC depot at Chiswick. Within the next hour the BOAC bullion van arrived at Heathrow, with the gang monitoring every movement, confident that all was going to plan. But the container which was unloaded into the warehouse from the van, and which should have contained the bullion, was empty. Behind the container and out of view of the gang fourteen Flying Squad officers clambered out of the van and secreted themselves behind the bales and packing cases inside the warehouse, where the lights had been turned down. Outside the warehouse were other detectives disguised as BOAC personnel and yet more were hidden inside a lorry in case they were needed to contain the situation. Flying Squad cars positioned up to two miles away waited in readiness.

The gold bullion had not arrived, but that did not mean there was nothing worth stealing inside the warehouse. Goods worth £224,000 were stocked in the building and the safe contained jewellery worth £13,900.

For their own safety (and to ensure the success of the operation) the three guards had been whisked away to secure accommodation; their place had been taken by Detective Sergeants Charlie Hewett, George Draper and John Mathews of the Flying Squad.

In a separate office, sat Donald Fish. His telephone was connected on an open line to Scotland Yard, so that when Fish whispered the code name of the operation – 'Nora', the name of one of the Squad officer's wives – word could be passed from the Yard by radio to the officers on the outside that the gang had

arrived. This would put them on stand-by; when the time came
to carry out the arrests, Fish would utter the words, 'In the bag.'

The hours ticked by. The heat was stifling inside the
warehouse. Eventually just before midnight the mobile canteen
arrived and Walsh went outside, obtained a jug full of coffee
which he brought back in to the three Squad officers. The coffee
was duly poured into three cups, which were tipped into a corner
of the warehouse, just in case the gang had a contingency plan
and had indeed doped the coffee, themselves. The Squad officers
knew – because Walsh had told them – that the gang anticipated
the drug would take twenty minutes to work.

The three sergeants now sprawled across the table, feigning
unconsciousness; one of the cups was left lying on its side as a
touch of authenticity, and now Walsh slid open the hanger's giant
double doors. The light from the warehouse, shining out into the
night, was the signal for the robbers to move in.

The first of the robbers stood in the opening. Sidney Cook
from Stratford had driven the lorry to be used by the gang up to
the warehouse doors. He was dressed in BOAC uniform and,
rather incongruously for one so attired, carried a car's starting
handle. Now, he looked carefully round at the hanger's silent
interior. He called to another gang member who also inspected
the premises and obviously satisfied the rest of the thieves, eleven
in all, trooped into the warehouse. All of them had their hands
covered, either with gloves or socks. But most unusual of all was
the fact that all of them (save Cook) were wearing stockings over
their heads – the first time this disguise had been used – and as
the men advanced into the premises, so the ends of the stockings
waved from side to side, inflating and deflating. They looked
rather like miniature elephants' trunks. It was then that Donald
Fish whispered the code word 'Nora' into the telephone receiver.

Alfred Roome surveyed the three supposedly unconscious
guards. Detective Sergeant Charlie Hewett, who due to his slim
build and short stature was much in demand for undercover
work, had posed as the security officer carrying the safe keys, and
Roome slapped him across the face. Satisfied that Hewett was
unconscious, Roome relieved him of the safe keys and kicked him
twice in the stomach, after which Hewett and the two other
officers had adhesive tape placed over their mouths and were tied
up. One of the other 'drugged' officers – John Matthews – failed
to fully convince the gang of his unconscious state and was

promptly cracked over the head with a starting handle, which produced a far more authentic effect.

As another of the gang produced a carafe of water and proceeded to wash out the coffee cups – it had been decided to remove the evidence so that this ploy could be used in the future – so Roome inserted the key into the safe. As soon as an audible 'click' had been heard, satisfying the requirements of the Larceny Act, DDI Roberts announced, 'We are police officers of the Flying Squad – stay where you are!' Donald Fish gave the Yard the signal, 'In the bag', the Flying Squad personnel emerged from their hiding places and as the gang leader shouted, 'Bring the guns out and let them have it – kill the bastards!' a battle royal commenced.

In fact, the gang had no guns – what they did have was a variety of murderous weapons. DCI Bob Lee had his scalp split open from a blow with an iron bar wielded by Alfred Roome, while the gang member who had been industriously washing out the cups now smashed the carafe and ground the jagged ends into Detective Sergeant Fred Allen's thigh. Blood poured from the wound, Allen cracked his opponent over the head with his truncheon and both men fell to the floor. Allen was grievously injured but conscious – his opponent was out cold. Draper had been untied and he now released Charlie Hewett who tore into Roome, inflicting serious injuries. Fifty years after the event, Hewett wrote, 'I did not feel guilty about what I did to "Big Alfie".' Detective Sergeant Donald MacMillan (he was Hewett's Flying Squad partner and they were known as 'Chas and Mac') had his nose badly broken as he defended Hewett from an attack by an assailant behind him.

The very popular and reliable officer, Detective Sergeant Mickey Dowse also waded into the fray: first he was hit with a giant pair of wire-cutters, then as one of the gang went to cosh him over the head and Dowse put up his arm to ward off the blow, his hand was shattered. In a similar way, Detective Inspector Peter Sinclair suffered a broken arm. As the fight spilled out of the warehouse, so the waiting Squad men rushed forward and eight of the gang soon lay unconscious on the tarmac.

Not all of them were caught. Billy Benstead and Bertie Saphir both escaped. Teddy Machin was chased by two officers and in the darkness lost both them and his balance. He fell into a ditch, passed out and was completely overlooked. (He was not quite so overlooked in 1970 when he received both barrels of a sawn-off shotgun through the window of his Canning Town home.)

Franny Daniels, a well-respected thief who had run with both Hill and Spot managed to crawl underneath a lorry and cling on to it as it moved off. He had intended to drop off at the first set of traffic lights; instead the lorry conveyed him to the yard at Harlington police station from where he made his escape. He carried the burns which he received from the underside of the vehicle for the rest of his life.

After some much-needed sleep, food and hospital treatment, the Squad officers accompanied the robbers to Uxbridge Magistrates' Court (all save Roome, who had been so badly beaten he was hospitalized) where the incredulous magistrate heard brief evidence of arrest – and seemed to differentiate with great difficulty between the bloodstained, bandaged robbers and their equally battered captors – before remanding the gang in custody.

Jack Spot was questioned about the matter, denied it and claimed that the car which had been seen and was registered in his name had been lent to a couple of pals for the evening. There was no evidence to the contrary and Spot was not even arrested. But it was the beginning of the end for him. Although, in the absence of Billy Hill he was still a very powerful gangland figure, the police paid so much attention to his gambling club in St Botolph's Row that it eventually closed. Then came a falling-out with Hill which led to a savage razor attack on Spot in 1956 and gradually his power receded and he died penniless, aged eighty-two, in 1995.

On 17 September, the gang appeared at the Old Bailey. They had previously pleaded guilty to conspiracy to rob and given the weight of the evidence against them, this was understandable. However, an added incentive was that this charge carried a maximum of two years' imprisonment. They had pleaded not guilty to assaulting the police but now, in a dramatic turnaround, they pleaded guilty to robbing Detective Sergeant Charlie Hewett of four keys, whilst armed. After listening to some fairly unconvincing mitigation, the Recorder of London, Sir Gerald Dodson told them:

One can only describe this as the battle of the BOAC, for that is what it degenerated into – a battle and nothing less. It is a thing honest people regard with terror and great abhorrence. All of you men set your minds and hands to this enterprise. You were, of course, playing for high stakes as there was nearly £14,000 worth of jewellery in the safe alone and thousands of pounds' worth of goods. You went there with a van to carry it and you went armed. It is a little difficult for me under those circumstances to accept the suggestion that the plan here did not involve violence. If that were so, why carry these weapons? If the drug had been successful no violence would be done, but if the drugging were not successful a different set of circumstances would arise. You made sure of your position by being ready for any situation with weapons of all kinds. This is the gravity of the offence. It does not matter that the actual property was some keys. Of course, that is what you were after first of all, the keys. They were the keys to the situation and to the safe. A raid on this scale profoundly shocks society. You went prepared for violence and you got it. You got the worst of it and you can hardly complain about that.

Telling Edward Hughes (the possessor of the weak heart) 'Corporal punishment is not now envisaged by the law, and so, strictly logically, the injuries you have received are no punishment at all – merely part of the risk you ran,' the Recorder imposed the heaviest sentence; twelve years' penal servitude. As women collapsed and became hysterical in the corridor, Hughes replied, 'Thank you for British Justice.'

Sammy Ross was sentenced to eleven years' penal servitude and two brothers, Jimmy and George Wood (the latter was also known as John Wallis) received nine and eight years, respectively. George Smith and Sidney Cook were each sentenced to eight years' penal servitude and William Henry Ainsworth, to five.

And what of the hard man Alfred Roome, 'Big Alfie' who had recruited Anthony Walsh and who had been responsible for the savage assault on DCI Bob Lee? As the Recorder sentenced him to ten years' penal servitude, Roome broke down, sank to his knees and sobbed piteously. It was an act which was to have a profound, far-reaching effect. For such a display, Sammy Ross, the gang's leader, ordered that Roome be ostracized in prison. Upon his release his former associates continued this exclusion and after his wife started an affair with a younger man, Roome became so unbalanced that he blamed the pair for everything. He launched a frenzied attack on them and then took poison. They survived – Roome did not.

Anthony Walsh, who positively identified four of the gang to the Flying Squad, was dealt with at a separate hearing; he was bound over to be of good behaviour for a period of two years.

It was a time of celebration for the Flying Squad; all of them were commended by the commissioner and – leaving aside a piece of doggerel composed by one of the personnel from 'Operation Nora' which drags on for eight excruciating verses and which ends with the words

> 'Twas a marvellous fight – while it lasted;
> The hopes of the 'geezers' truly blasted;
> The villains are grabbed and marched away –
> And so to the end of a perfect day.

and is best forgotten – so the case passed into Squad folklore.

The Flying Squad officers exhibited characteristic courage, cunning and resourcefulness and it was to deal with exactly this type of crime that the Squad was formed in the first place; but to find out why and how, we have to go back almost thirty years before the Battle of Heathrow …

Flying Squad – in the Beginning

London. Autumn, 1916

Britain was halfway through 'the war to end all wars'. Two months previously the battle of the Somme had commenced, with 57,000 casualties on the first day alone; by the time the offensive was over some four-and-a-half months later, with practically no ground at all being gained, the casualties numbered one million. The home front was suffering too. The destruction of supply ships had led to severe food shortages and rationing had been imposed. News of the men at the front was excruciatingly slow to get to their families and loved ones and now, with the casualty lists mounting, the initial rush of patriotism to enlist had worn somewhat thin and conscription was introduced. So was the practice of bestowing white feathers, to show disapproval of those who were thought to be seeking to avoid confrontation with the enemy. Coastal towns were shelled and, most frightening of all, German Zeppelin airships which had commenced bombing Paris on 29 January, now decided it was England's turn.

Lieutenant William Leefe Robinson was awarded the Victoria Cross for being the first airman to shoot down a German airship on the night of 2 September; alas no help to Detective Chief Inspector Alfred William Ward of New Scotland Yard who had earlier been killed as the result of a direct hit from a Zeppelin bomb.

The name of Ward's replacement was Frederick Porter Wensley and he was then in his twenty-eighth year of service; twenty-six of them spent in London's East End. When he was approached by the Assistant Commissioner (Crime), Basil Thomson and asked if he could devise a plan for the Criminal Investigation Department to become more adaptable, mobile and smoother running, Wensley replied that he could. What follows explains why the CID was in such a poor state and why Thomson could not have chosen a better person to resolve such a difficult problem. Wensley, who had been awarded the first of the King's Police Medals and showered with awards and commendations for catching criminals, was widely regarded as being the greatest detective of all time.

⋆　⋆　⋆

Following the creation of the Metropolitan Police in 1829, the Detective Branch was formed in 1842 and was initially comprised of two inspectors and six 'serjeants' who wore plain clothes and were based only at New Scotland Yard. No other detectives existed, either in the divisions of the Metropolitan Police, nor in any of the United Kingdom's constabularies and therefore these Scotland Yard detectives were called up to investigate crimes both at home and abroad, with varying degrees of success. The Commissioner, Sir Richard Mayne KCB suggested an increase in the Force generally and the Home Secretary formed a committee to address the matter. When the Secretary of State asked Mayne his opinion of how to strengthen the Detective Force, in a letter dated 27 January 1868, Mayne proposed an increase of personnel to twenty-eight, i.e. one chief inspector, three inspectors (first class), three inspectors (second class), eleven sergeants, nine additional sergeants and one clerk. Following Mayne's death, Colonel Sir Edmund Henderson KCB, RE, was appointed commissioner in 1869 and he introduced detectives to divisions for the first time – which should have been a step in the right direction, except that many divisional superintendents took this heaven-sent opportunity to fill the quota with some of their worse, most incompetent and barely-literate officers. They were often left to their own devices, supervised by sergeants whose educational capabilities were on a par with their own and when it was suggested that they become more accountable by keeping a daily diary, it prompted an 1871 report from the head of the Detective Department, Chief Inspector Adolphus 'Dolly' Williamson who, although noted for his benevolence to his subordinates, felt impelled to inform the commissioner:

> I am afraid the keeping of a daily journal by officers employed in investigating criminal matters is with the present stamp of men impracticable, as a number of them who are employed as divisional detectives would, from their want of education, find it impossible to make a daily comprehensible report of their proceedings.

Following what became known as 'The Trial of the Detectives' where three officers were each sent to prison for two years for corruption, and the strength of the divisional detectives was comprised of 20 sergeants and 197 constables, the Criminal Investigation Department was formed in 1878. It was bound by a network of pettifogging rules, regulations and restrictions which were so binding that unless a criminal both lived and committed crimes in the same police area, the detective in the case was virtually powerless to follow the criminals across the jealously guarded police boundaries. Pursuit and arrest of the criminal and the recovery of stolen property depended solely on the cooperation and goodwill of the divisional inspectors; sadly, assistance was not always forthcoming from many of these self-important little men. This defect in the system had not been so apparent in the days when the CID was smaller and before criminals had gathered the wit to rapidly travel from place to place.

★   ★   ★

This was the lamentable state of affairs when, on 16 January 1888, Wensley, who was a 23-year-old native of Taunton, Somerset, was one of forty-eight candidates to join the Metropolitan Police. Wensley was initially posted to Lambeth where a warm reception awaited him; a gang of drunken toughs threw him through a plate glass window. Next, he spent over three months off sick, having been seriously injured while tackling a group of hooligans and then following his return to duty, he disarmed and arrested a lunatic who had lunged at him with a swordstick. Wensley's tough apprenticeship continued when he was one of several hundred police officers drafted into Whitechapel in order to try to apprehend 'Jack the Ripper' and now, the embryo detective's shrewdness became apparent when he nailed strips of bicycle tyres to the soles of his boots to reduce the sound of his approach.

But as Wensley surveyed his surroundings, what he saw made him long for the tranquillity of Lambeth. Whitechapel was notable for its filth and squalor and for being a huge hot-bed of crime, fuelled by the enormous numbers of East Europeans who had flooded unchecked into the United Kingdom and would continue to do so until the introduction of the Aliens Act 1906.

The police had been given powers in 1851 to supervise the lodging houses of the area, which were interlinked by a series of cellars, courts and alleys, all of which made flight easy and pursuit almost impossible. Although the police shut down over 700 of these insanitary tenements and in 1894, the London County Council took over the supervision of these premises, it was not until 1902 that matters started to improve – but not by much.

Murders were often not treated as such and went undetected, while robberies, garrotting, and pickpocketing were commonplace and the whole polyglot cacophony must have made Wensley feel that he had stepped into a madhouse. But he hit the criminals head-on; he made arrests both on and off-duty and began to make a name for himself as a thief-taker which would last for the rest of his career. Wensley was appointed to the CID and within six months arrested a man for murder while he was off-duty. As the years passed, he rose through the ranks arresting a whole succession of murderers, robbers and burglars. When gang warfare flared up, Wensley took significant action – the members of two rival Russian gangs, 'The Bessarabians' and 'The Odessians' were each sentenced to long terms of penal servitude, while a home-grown variety of gangsters from Bethnal Green, 'The Vendettas' were sentenced to a total of twenty years' imprisonment. Wensley took a decisive role in the infamous 'Siege of Sidney Street' and, at the same time, assisted another division by arresting a man wanted for a murder which one of his contemporaries was investigating.

The name of his associate was Detective Chief Inspector Alfred Ward; it was with his demise that Wensley (who had been promoted to the rank of detective chief inspector four years previously) was posted to New Scotland Yard. And with the assistant commissioner's request for a more mobile group of detectives ringing in his ears, Wensley's fertile mind slowly began to devise a plan which would ultimately result in the formation of the Flying Squad.

* * *

Wensley's encouraging answer to the assistant commissioner, concerning the mobility and streamlining of detectives, met with Basil Thomson's approval but it seemed as though the idea might be stillborn. Thomson was heavily entrenched with wartime matters. He had become deeply involved with the Special Branch who had their hands full with the current Fenian investigations, following the Easter Rising that year in Dublin and after he was knighted in 1919, Thomson became director of intelligence within the Special Branch. He remained in post until his retirement in 1921, he never returned to the CID and the concept of detectives becoming more adaptable passed from his mind.

But although Wensley, too, was heavily involved in war work, detecting counterfeit coiners and prosecuting offences under the Defence of the Realm Act and the Military Service Act, he did not – *could* not – forget the matter. A skeleton plan, whereby detective superintendents of great experience might assume command of the detectives in each of the four districts, grew in his mind. They would coordinate the detectives in the divisions within their districts and be in touch with their counterparts working in other divisions. Wensley recalled that, in 1906, Chief Inspector Fred Fox of Scotland Yard had been given a small group of officers to detect a gang making counterfeit coins and in order to do so they were authorized to make their enquiries anywhere in the Metropolitan Police District. But after a year, the team was disbanded and the commission to act and travel carte blanche was rescinded. Although attempts were made to continue and systematically develop this idea, they failed. Much of the trouble stemmed from young, inexperienced officers being sent out to conduct enquiries without adequate supervision. This, resolved Wensley, would not happen again. His roving band of detectives would be strictly supervised and would be able to move rapidly and operate in a division where there was an epidemic of crime. They would be able to operate independently or in conjunction with their divisional counterparts. By the end of the war, Wensley was ready to seek authority to implement the scheme. However, events were about to overtake him.

★   ★   ★

Following the end of hostilities the crime figures, already high, had burst through the ceiling and were spiralling upwards out of control. Men who had fought bravely and patriotically through the carnage of the French and Belgian trenches, arrived home to hear that on 24 November 1918, the Liberal Prime Minister David Lloyd George had announced to a credulous crowd at Wolverhampton, 'What is our task? To make Britain a fit country for heroes to live in.'

Alas, they were to be bitterly disappointed. Politicians, whose main aim in life may appear to be bamboozling the public in every conceivable way, spoke just as much bloated rhetoric then, as they do now. The only difference was that the public of yesteryear were more prone to believe what their 'betters' told them.

It did not take long before the truth of the matter sank in – that the standard of housing was as poor as it was scarce and that employment was in an even worse state. By 1922–3, almost three million men, one quarter of the working population, were out of work. In addition world trade had all but collapsed and poverty was staring Londoners in the face; many of the men who had bravely defended their country turned to crime. The figures were swollen by young men who had known little discipline in the home, due to the absence of their fathers during the war years and also by many work-shy, larcenous and thoroughly dangerous immigrants.

Offices were broken into and their safes were cut open. Jewellers were forced to put up grilles on their premises, to protect their stock from the increasing number of 'smash and grab' gangs. Gang warfare flared to epidemic proportions. Cashiers of both sexes were knocked down and robbed, motorists were held up and their cars plus any other valuables they possessed were stolen and police officers were threatened and shot at with the enormous number of firearms which were flooding into the country – and which were increasingly being used in bank hold-ups and masked burglaries.

And if this breakdown in law and order was not enough, the influenza pandemic commonly known as 'Spanish 'Flu', which had started in March 1918, now gathered momentum. It is estimated that the disease which swept worldwide may have claimed the lives of 100 million people. It was a grim total, compared to the fifteen million people who died during the First World War, which lasted twice as long as the flu pandemic. A further 500 million were infected but recovered – 1,500 Metropolitan Police officers went sick on the same day – and it was not until June 1920 that the disease came under control.

Matters were not helped by the fact that the police themselves
were in disarray. Following the Police Strikes of 1872 and 1890,
policemen had struck again in 1918, and of the three this was the
most serious. Police pay was so low that many officers were in
debt and they and their families were suffering from
malnutrition. One third of the 18,000 personnel of the
Metropolitan Police went on strike and the Commissioner, Sir
Edward Henry, Bt, GCVO, KCB, CSI, who had thought this a
particularly suitable time to go on holiday to Ireland, was forced
to resign. The strike ended after pay and conditions were
improved but, incredibly, the following year the police went on
strike again. The headline of the *Daily Herald* for Friday, 1 August
1919, stated, 'London police defy the Government' – but it was
for the last time. On this occasion 1,056 Metropolitan Police
officers struck and all were immediately dismissed.

The welfare of the police was now in the capable hands of the
newly-formed Police Federation, but with regard to the state of
increasing lawlessness it was clear that decisive action would have
to be taken and the new Commissioner, General the Right
Honourable Sir Cecil Frederick Nevil Macready, Bt, GCMG,
KCB, acted. In a memorandum, dated 22 October 1919, he
adopted Wensley's plan and split the Metropolitan Police District
into four areas – until then, they had been referred to as districts
– for the appointment of detective superintendents on special
duty. To nobody's surprise (least of all his own) Wensley, having
been speedily promoted, was one of them.

Wensley now put the second part of his plan into operation.
From the four areas, he took the best of the detectives, purely, as
he stressed to their outraged senior officers, 'on loan'. Detective
Sergeant Clarke and Detective Constable Edwards, both from
West London's 'F' Division were first into Wensley's office,
followed by Detective Sergeant Selby and Detective Constable
Rutherford from 'G' Division, traditionally one of the toughest
areas in London's East End. Then came Detective Sergeant
Hayman and Detective Constables Humphrey and Dawkins
from, respectively 'M', 'P' and 'L' Divisions, all south of the River
Thames. Detective Constable Laven from the West End of
London, Detective Constables Croucher and Dance from North
London and Detective Sergeant Wiltshire completed the team.

And now, Wensley invited the men to sit down as he proceeded
to outline his game plan. They would work anywhere in London

that they were needed, he told them. The boundaries which had existed for them in the past were to be ignored. The gangs of criminals who were responsible for the crime wave were to be identified, then arrested and convicted. 'The success or not, of this mobile patrol scheme will depend on you,' said Wensley. 'But in twelve months' time, the commissioner must report to the Home Secretary. He will decide whether this experiment should either continue or be disbanded.'

The expression 'mobile patrol scheme' sent a ripple of excitement through the assembled detectives. But at this time the Metropolitan Police possessed only two motor cars; since 1903 only the commissioner and Scotland Yard's Receiver had the use of two 10hp Worseleys and although these vehicles were updated, the intervening sixteen years had done nothing to increase the Yard's motor vehicle fleet.

So the mobility given to Wensley's detectives at the end of 1919 was not mechanical; two horse-drawn wagons were leased from the Great Western Railway. As they trundled out of the Yard into Whitehall, they were unrecognizable from the thousands of similar horse-drawn vehicles roaming the city. The difference was that the boards gracing the sides of the wagons, giving the names and addresses of businesses, were fixed into slots – thus they were interchangeable so that businesses suitable for the area in which they were patrolling could be substituted. Then there was the cargo: the detectives hidden from view in the back, underneath the canvas hoods, peering through the spyholes cut in the sides.

As the horses ambled along, thieves, car stealers and pickpockets were astonished when they were seized, literally out of thin air, just as they were in the act of committing a crime.

Often the wagons would be used purely as a mode of transport, to convey officers to an area which was experiencing a particular outbreak of crime, where they would be dropped off to patrol and follow suspects on foot or to utilize public transport, in order to effect arrests.

By 1920, the 'Mobile Patrol Experiment' became permanent, having already started to make inroads into the arrest of London's criminal classes. However, the spiralling crime wave was exacerbated by the increasing prominence of the 'Motor Car Bandit', which the two horse-drawn wagons could not possibly contend with. The wagons were returned to the Great Western

Railway and the weary nags were undoubtedly directed to the nearest knacker's yard.

To further combat the rising crime figures, in July 1920 two Crossley Tenders, formerly the property of the Royal Flying Corps, were purchased. These heavy, ungainly 26 hp vehicles had no front brakes and it was only when their engines were specially modified that a top speed of almost 40 mph could be achieved. Their tyres were very narrow and it was with great difficulty that could they be controlled at speed or on wet roads. On the plus side, the tenders were initially considered to be reasonably mechanically sound and could contain up to a dozen men, hidden in the back under the khaki hood. Both Crossley Tenders had aerials fitted to their roofs which consisted of five parallel wires, mounted on adjustable arms which could be raised or lowered from inside the van – their extraordinary appearance led to the vehicles being dubbed 'bedsteads'.

At the time of their first mechanized patrol, Tender one was tasked to cover the area north of the Thames and Tender two, the south. In a wise, morale-inspiring move, the operational head of the Squad decided to lead his men from the front, and in so doing, set a pattern which would continue well into the Squad's future.

After this initial patrol, crime fighting would never be the same again.

The Squad Begins to Fly

Walter Hambrook had been undecided in 1898 whether or not he should join the Metropolitan Police; his mind was made up after his elder brother, Frederick, a police constable at south London's Deptford police station was attacked by a local tough, appropriately nicknamed 'Killer Tom' and received facial injuries which were so severe that he was unrecognizable for a week afterwards. But Frederick hung on to his attacker and later had the satisfaction of seeing his adversary sentenced to three months' hard labour. Suitably inspired, the younger Hambrook decided that the police would be his vocation, but despite making an impressive number of arrests whilst working in plain clothes as a 'Winter Patrol' his indecisiveness was still apparent. When the Chief Constable of the CID, Sir Melville McNaughton CB, sent for Hambrook to ask whether or not he wished to become a permanent member of the Criminal Investigation Department, Hambrook lamely replied, 'I don't know, sir.' Fortunately, Sir Melville was a sound judge of character – the Assistant Commissioner, Sir Basil Thomson later said that Sir Melville 'knew the official career of every one of his seven hundred men and his qualifications and abilities' – because he took the decision out of Hambrook's hands and appointed him a permanent patrol, to commence on Monday, 10 March 1902.

At nine o'clock on the evening of 15 September 1920, the uncertainty of Walter Hambrook's earlier days was long gone. For the past ten weeks he had been posted to the Flying Squad as one of the new detective inspectors (second class) – Charles Cooper was another – and had been put in charge of Tender two. He was utterly committed to his course of action; he intended to smash a gang of south London tearaways who had been terrorizing shopkeepers and carrying out smash and grab raids, with the aid of motor vehicles.

Hambrook was aware that the gang operated both in the north London area of Camden Town and also in the vicinity of south

London's Elephant and Castle. Therefore he dispatched Detective Inspector Charles Cooper and his men in Tender one, to search the Camden Town area for the gang, whilst Hambrook and half-a-dozen officers scoured the area south of the Thames, both initially without success.

But on the second night's patrol, Hambrook's team saw a known villain, a member of the gang, get into a ten-hundredweight covered van, which he drove away. It was the break that Hambrook had been waiting for. Following the van at a discreet distance, the Squad saw it stop close to the Elephant and Castle where six more men, three of whom they recognized as notorious tearaways, climbed aboard. The van rumbled away, shadowed by the Squad, to Tooting High Road, where the seven men got out and reconnoitred shops and flats in the area – but that was all they did. Climbing back into the van, the gang then drove slowly back to the Elephant and Castle, where the Squadmen located the shed where the gang's van would be garaged. In ones and twos the gang drifted away, and once the coast was clear Hambrook contacted Detective Inspector Cooper and his men. The whole complements of the two tenders were deputed to keep observation on the garage, in relays.

After thirty-one hours of observation, at four o'clock in the morning of 18 September, the patience of the Squad officers was rewarded by the arrival of members of the gang. All of them were carrying parcels and as they threw them into the back of the van a metallic clang rang out from a long, thin appliance, wrapped in newspaper; it would later transpire that this was an eight-sided jemmy. As the van started up, the watchers awoke their slumbering companions in the back of the tender and saw the van pull out into the Old Kent Road. But then, surprisingly, the van turned north away from the direction of Tooting and as it trundled across Westminster Bridge, Hambrook, anticipating that the gang would be heading towards Whitehall, ordered his driver, Police Constable King, to cut through the private road of Scotland Yard. In Whitehall, the gang's van was nowhere to be seen; but then Detective Constable Rutherford looked in the opposite direction down towards Parliament Square, and in Margaret Street, outside the Houses of Parliament, he spotted the van. As the tender edged closer, so three more men got into the van, which moved off and after a half-mile journey stopped in Victoria Street. Three of the gang got out and reconnoitred a silversmith's shop; perhaps they decided that it was too heavily fortified, but whatever the reason they rejoined the rest of their associates and the van moved off. Another half-mile drive brought the gang to Pimlico Road; here, at a clothier's shop, four of the gang took up look-out positions and the remaining three strode purposefully towards the premises.

Hambrook now decided that the time was right to make the arrests, but even as he gave the order the presence of the Squadmen was detected by one of the look-outs who shouted a warning to the gang. Sprinting back to their van they then tore off into Bourne Street, the Squad tender thundering in pursuit and as the van headed towards Cliveden Place the tender pulled in front of it, causing it to screech to a halt. The gang scrambled out of the van and Hambrook and his men leapt out of the tender, just as the late summer storm which had been threatening all night suddenly broke. A terrific flash of lightning, followed by an ear-shattering clap of thunder theatrically heralded the commencement of the first – but certainly not the last – pitched Flying Squad battle.

Hambrook and his men were under no illusions about the capabilities of the hoodlums they were about to tackle; desperate men indeed, armed with knuckledusters, life preservers and daggers, they rushed the Squad officers who lashed out left and right with their truncheons. Hambrook, who felled several of the gang with his treasured heavy ash walking stick, was in turn forced to his knees by one of the gang wielding a life preserver, who exultantly shouted, 'Let's kill the bastard!' Incensed at such immoderate language to his senior officer, Detective Sergeant Selby cracked Hambrook's attacker across the head with his truncheon so that he, too, crashed to the pavement as the rain poured down, soaking the two sets of adversaries alike. One by one, the gang were pounded into submission. Their van was found to contain jemmies, iron bars and wedges – a complete burglar's kit. The gang were put into the back of the tender and driven to nearby Gerald Road police station, where the rain-soaked and bloodstained villains were charged by their equally battered captors with possessing housebreaking implements by night and possessing offensive weapons.

During one of their remand hearings, three of the gang were positively identified by Police Constable 727'P' Nealon of Camberwell police station. A few nights prior to their arrest the constable, who had been off-duty, had seen the gang breaking into a shop. He single-handedly attempted to arrest the men, who savagely attacked him using the eight-sided jemmy which had been recovered from the gang's vehicle, and leaving him for dead.

In committing the gang for trial, the magistrate at Westminster police court praised the twelve officers for their skill, a commendation which was echoed some two months later by Sir Henry Dickens, the trial judge at the Old Bailey. Sentencing two of the gang (who had no previous convictions) each to twelve months' imprisonment and the others (one of whom was on licence from a ten-year sentence for shopbreaking and assaulting a police officer) to varying periods of penal servitude, Sir Henry called the Squad before him and highly commended them for their 'courage and ability in bringing the gang to justice.' The commissioner highly commended Hambrook and also PC Nealon, to whom he awarded five pounds (well worth having when one considers that at that time, a constable's weekly wage was £3 5s 0d (£3.25p)) and the other Squad officers were commended and received monetary rewards.

Sir Henry also dealt with another gang of smash and grab raiders who had been brought before him courtesy of the Flying Squad. The gang's driver had, on one occasion when he and his accomplices were fleeing from the scene of a crime, driven straight at a police constable who had tried to stop them; the officer was lucky to have escaped unscathed. The Flying Squad had ambushed them in Upper Brook Street, Mayfair and when the raiders unwisely put up a fierce resistance, they were enthusiastically belted with the Squad officers' truncheons. Sentencing them to terms of penal servitude, Sir Henry told them:

> These smash and grab raids have got to be put down. They have reached such a pass that nobody is safe. I recently had a case where a raid was carried out with a car in the middle of the day and another car was used to impede the traffic so that the raiders could get away. Something has to be done, and the only thing to be done is to be severe.

Not that Hambrook was inclined to rest upon his laurels. At the conclusion of the Autumn Sessions, he and Detective Sergeant Hayman, plus Detective Constables Edwards, Humphrey,

Dawkins and Dance were also commended by the judge and jury at the County of London Sessions for their conduct in a case of larceny.

There was a further, almost unnoticed commendation. Four days after Hambrook's arrests in Belgravia, the crime correspondent for the *Daily Mail*, Mr G. T. Crook recorded:

Flying squads of picked detectives with motor transport at their disposal were based at police headquarters, ready to go anywhere, at any time ... The result of these live operations have been remarkably successful .... scores of the most daring and dangerous criminals in London have been caught. They have been picked up by the flying squads at all hours of the day and night, some while actually engaged on a burglarious enterprise, while others have been stopped with housebreaking implements in their possession.

It was probably nothing more than an example of press hyperbole, a nickname; but it stuck. When the commissioner wrote in his annual report for Parliament in 1920,

Some excellent work has been done by a small centralised body of detective officers, working under the direction of superintendents of areas, in following up and arresting or dispersing gangs of criminals who are engaged in shop and warehouse breakings in different parts of the district

it was the Flying Squad to whom he was referring. The following year, without any sense of irony, the name 'The Flying Squad' was in common usage in official reports at the Yard. In time to come, the Flying Squad would also become known as 'The Heavy Mob', 'The Sweeney' or simply 'The Squad' – but in any event, the term 'Mobile Patrol Experiment' had been consigned to the dustbin.

*   *   *

The Squad continued to make massive inroads into the gangs infesting London. In *Police Orders*, dated 29 March 1923, the commissioner highly commended Detective Inspector Charles Cooper for 'ability in an extraordinarily intricate case of conspiracy to defraud', plus two other Squad officers for valuable assistance in the same case, as also did the Director of Public Prosecutions and the Common Serjeant at the Old Bailey. In addition, Detective Inspector Stevens of the Squad, plus four other officers, were commended by both the commissioner and the justices at Hendon Petty Sessions for their action in a case of shopbreaking.

Interestingly, in the same *Police Order*, a certain Detective Sergeant (Second Class) Dan Gooch from 'G' Division was also commended by the Chairman of the County of London Sessions, and the commissioner, and given a monetary award (as were three other officers) for ability and persistence in a case of larceny. Sergeant Gooch's abilities were being noted; it was not long before he was coopted into the Squad. Out patrolling in a Squad car, Gooch (now a detective sergeant (first class)) and his crew received a radio message regarding suspects at an auction at a house in Paddington. With the Squad car parked, his crew remained behind whilst Gooch stripped off his jacket, entered the house and emerged a few moments later wearing a green baize apron, helping to shift furniture. He had already recognized four gang members inside the house and kept them under observation while he moved furniture out of the auction house. The gang entered the room where the cashier was counting the takings, grabbed the money and dashed out of the building – where Gooch and his men were waiting for them. To nobody's surprise, a few years later Gooch became head of the Flying Squad.

★   ★   ★

Although two more tenders were purchased, their continued use was beginning to prove a hindrance. The tenders would go out on 'dawn patrols' (this habit would continue for the next sixty years), and were used to transport the Squad officers to race meetings in their war against the gangs who infested the tracks. They were also employed to assist Special Branch in their battle against the Fenian gangs; during the Sinn Féin elections in 1918 and the insertion of the British Black and Tans into Ireland, which had resulted in guerrilla warfare. The reason for the Squad's assistance was that, until 1929, the Flying Squad was the only arm of the Metropolitan Police to possess vehicles fitted with radio. By September 1923 excellent Morse code transmissions could be received by the three Squad wireless operators who, like the drivers, had been taken from the Yard's A3 Branch; and eighteen months later the number of wireless operators was increased to nine. The messages were transmitted in code and streets and districts were identified by numbers in order that they could not be intercepted by unauthorized listeners. The range of the transmission was initially over a distance of 17–18 miles from Room 210, the new secret communications centre situated on the top floor of Scotland Yard; later however, a note frequency oscillator would increase the range to 100 miles.

However, the tenders had by now become instantly recognizable to the very people whom the Squad were supposed to be keeping under clandestine surveillance and their appearance at the racetracks was regarded purely as a preventive measure against civil disorder. The tenders were ungainly and despite the initial high expectations as to their mechanical road-worthiness, they were flagging badly when it came to stopping the activities of the 'motor car bandit'.

Report after report was submitted in respect of this unsatisfactory state of affairs and after one such complaint had lain for months on the desk of the Assistant Commissioner (Crime), Sir Norman Kendall, he stated that he believed the tenders to be capable of speeds of up to 40 mph. 'Is this not as much as one can reasonably expect from a tender?' he enquired. 'They can hardly be regarded as "chasers",' he added with an exasperated air.

'If the tenders were capable of travelling at 40 mph,' acidly replied Hambrook, 'I, personally would be delighted.' Hambrook went on to state that due to a series of complaints he had tested the best of the tenders, and on level ground the best speed that had been achieved was 28 mph. He found the acceleration to be extremely poor and after stopping in Lower Regent Street and then driving off on the incline towards Piccadilly Circus, the tender covered the first 200 yards at a maximum speed of 5 mph. This vehicle, which Hambrook stressed again was the best of the bunch, had covered only 7,000 miles since its acquisition.

Then a cryptic report was submitted to the assistant commissioner, pointing out that if suggested repairs costing between £50 and £60 were to be carried out on a tender which during its two-and-a-half years service had covered 30,624 miles, this would scarcely be considered to be cost effective, since the market value of the tender would still be only £40. This sounded the death knell to the Crossley Tenders, and they would later be relegated to conveying large numbers of officers and shifting bulky property, neither of which, it can be assumed, would be in a particular hurry to reach their destination.

*   *   *

Major T. H. Vitty was in charge of the Engineering Department at the Yard and he was bombarded with requests from the Flying Squad for better and faster vehicles. In 1927, he sent a Squad driver, Police Constable 305'CO' George 'Jack' Frost to the Lea Francis factory in Coventry, to test their new 14 hp tourers, which had a top speed of almost 75 mph. Frost, who until then had been driving one of the Crossley Tenders, registration number XB 5706, was delighted to try out a vehicle with better capabilities. Permission was obtained from Brooklands Race Track (which had hosted the first British *Grand Prix* the previous year) to test the cars and over the period of a week, the club's experts measured the wind speed, tested the adhesion of the tyres on the track and operated electrical timing devices to ascertain the car's mean and maximum speeds. When the tests were satisfactorily concluded, the cars were fitted with an 'MP' sign which could be raised and illuminated and a Morse receiver was fitted underneath the seat of the wireless operator, who sat behind the driver. The transmissions were received through the operator's earphones but, should any call be received which required acknowledgement, the car had to head towards the nearest public telephone box. Experiments had been carried out with a view to using direct speech in radio communications, but had been unsuccessful and although there was one further attempt during the first two months of 1933, coded Morse transmissions were to remain until after the end of the Second World War.

It was not a sudden chill in the morning of 27 October 1927 which caused the Commissioner, Brigadier General Sir William Horwood GBE, KCB, DSO, to sniff sharply as he strode towards the entrance of New Scotland Yard. Having been in office since the success of Hambrook's motorized ambush in the Crossley Tender, he had held a paternal interest in the Flying Squad and it was the sight of the Squad's new Lea Francis tourers and vans in the parking bays which had caused his sudden annoyance. He lost no time in contacting Major Vitty who, until that very moment had been privately congratulating himself on augmenting the Flying Squad's fleet. 'There can be no doubt in the minds of criminals,' said the commissioner, frostily, 'that these vehicles belong to us.'

'But why, Sir William?' wailed the hapless major.

'Because for one thing, all the vans and the Lea Francis tourers are the same colour,' roared the commissioner, 'and for another, all of the registration numbers are consecutive!'

Major Vitty, driven to the verge of tears, suggested in a report that the identities of the vans could be disguised by putting manufacturers' names on the sides of the vehicles by means of transfers and that the colours of the Lea Francis tourers could be changed to blue or – er – crimson. The papers were passed to Wensley, who had been appointed chief constable of the CID three years previously, and who dealt with the matter in a characteristically straightforward manner.

The tourers should be painted in colours common to their make, said Wensley, bringing a touch of commonsense to the proceedings, and the registration numbers of both the vans and the cars should not, of course, be consecutive. In addition, Wensley recommended that a different form of ventilation for the vans be introduced and that mica screens should be supplied to the cabs of tenders, which would both afford protection for the driver and prevent the patrolling officers from being recognized, in common with the tourers. Finally, he urged that the new vans should be utilized in exactly the same way as the tenders had been used in the Squad's formative years – slots should be cut in the sides and boards with different names and businesses to suit the location should be inserted. 'Personally,' wrote Wensley, putting the finishing touches to his minute, dated 8 November 1927, 'I never knew it to fail.'

The papers were passed to the Assistant Commissioner (Crime), Major General Sir Wyndham Childs, KCMG, KBE, who sided with Vitty and thought that paper advertisements should be pasted onto the sides of the vans, but this suggestion was vetoed by the commissioner (Childs had outranked him when they served in the army) who agreed with Wensley's suggestion of slots and boards. However, the commissioner was adamant that sidescreens for the tenders would not be applied for and that officers who drove exposed to the elements would 'have to be suitably clad.' In addition, he decreed that Squad vehicles would not be left at the Yard on 'stand-by' – they would be garaged across the river, at Lambeth. (The commissioner's comments came as no surprise: during his eight years in office, he made no attempt to meet or receive the opinions of his men and was thoroughly disliked; he was once referred to as being 'an unattractive man who mistook arrogance for leadership'.)

The colours of the Lea Francis tourers (nicknamed 'Leafs') were quickly changed – one, repainted yellow, became known as 'the Canary' – and they achieved impressive results in tackling robberies at post offices and shops, payroll hold-ups and the gangs of pickpockets.

On one occasion when Police Constable Marley was driving a Lea Francis, the half-shaft sheared off the offside wheel which overtook the car, leaving it to come to a halt with a grinding bump. The concussion caused a fright, plus a severe jolt to the wireless operator's nether regions. An ex-signaller, formerly Royal Navy (as were many of his contemporaries), he had a large vocabulary of salty expletives, which he now shared with the rest of the Lea Francis crew.

By December 1928, the number of wireless operators had been increased to sixteen to man the tenders and the 'Leafs'. The detectives who crewed the cars were of high calibre, men such as Arthur Askew who had been on patrol in Oxford Street in October 1911 when he was shot through the arm after tackling a man who had carried out a smash and grab. The jury at the Old Bailey did not bother to retire before finding Harry de Vere guilty of attempted murder and he was sentenced to fourteen years' penal servitude. Six years later, Askew (by then a detective sergeant) was awarded the King's Police Medal for gallantry after arresting a man in a dark passageway who had shot and killed a police constable, and Askew completed his distinguished service by heading the Yard's Murder Squad, between 1934 and 1938.

Henry Arthur Finbar Corbett was never known as anything other than 'Chesty' – his nickname stemmed from his daily practice with a chest expander and dumb-bells. Juggling a 56lb weight in one hand he would remark, with some justification, that no lawbreaker could escape once he'd grabbed hold of him. Corbett, who was just one-eighth of an inch over the Force's minimum height of five foot eight (and appeared just as broad), had an encyclopaedic mind and a fanatical hatred of pickpockets. Astonishingly, he joined the Flying Squad as a uniformed constable, after just twelve months' service, something that has never been emulated since. His nights were spent carrying out lone patrols on foot, tracking down pickpockets; utterly without fear, he was repeatedly commended for arresting up to six pickpockets single-handedly.

The Dance brothers were equally tough. Frank, who was always referred to as 'Squibs' joined the Flying Squad almost as soon as it was formed. At just over five foot nine, fair-haired and grey-eyed, Squibs was mentioned in the first of the Flying Squad commendations and by the end of his career had collected sixty-eight such awards. He was an undercover officer, a master of disguise, and on one occasion when patrolling in a 'Leaf' with another officer, they followed a gang whom they suspected of being behind a series of raids on public houses and went to arrest them. For once the two detectives were in danger of being overpowered, until a resourceful Flying Squad driver fortuitously picked up a length of hard rubber which he used on the heads of the gang members with telling effect. Alf, the younger brother of Squibs stayed with the Flying Squad for twenty-three years and rose to the rank of divisional detective inspector. He was described as being both 'a big, florid-faced, jovial man' and 'a very, very tough egg'. Like his brother, Alf knew all there was to know about London pickpockets, but the reason why the brothers were so successful was because they mingled with criminals, and knew their wives and girlfriends. When a criminal lined up for his fish and chips, the Dance brothers would be in the same queue. They went to the same dances, the same pubs and were frequently invited to the same weddings, christenings and funerals that the criminals attended. They knew the criminal world inside-out; when a job was pulled, they invariably knew who was responsible, where they would secrete the swag and to whom they would fence it.

This is a small selection of the men who patrolled the haunts of thieves and pickpockets in the Lea Francis tourers, which were fitted with mica screens and hoods to conceal both the detectives inside and also to camouflage the 'chicken wire' aerial. The drivers were now officially issued with a variety of caps and jackets in order to 'avoid drawing attention to themselves'.

In 1927, Charles Cooper (who had been in charge of Tender one on the Squad's initial patrol, seven years earlier) became head of the Squad. He certainly had the patronage of Wensley, who had noticed him sixteen years previously, when he assisted Wensley and Alfred Ward on a murder investigation. Wensley described Cooper as 'a young and enterprising officer whom I met for the first time and who impressed me by his ability and energy.' In Cooper's first year in office, 300 arrests were made – a significant increase from 176 arrests in 1925 – and the press noted that the Flying Squad personnel were dubbed 'Cooper's Feared Forty'. This was a little exaggerated, since the increase in the Squad's strength would not reach that figure until two years later. But Cooper, who had the air of a benevolent bank manager and who seldom worked less than sixteen hours a day, was good copy for the newspapers and undeniably the Squad were making their presence felt, even when the arrests were not personally carried out by them.

When a Squad officer spotted a limousine containing six expensively dressed women in Kensington during a 'dawn patrol' there was no reason for it to have raised a question mark in his mind, bearing in mind the location, where well-dressed women in limousines regularly shopped – except it did. He followed the car all through the West End, the City of London and into the East End, all the way through to the boundaries with the Essex Constabulary. He had no excuse to stop the car and search it or its occupants. So he sent a radio message to Essex Constabulary, asking that the car be kept under observation. It was. Six extremely surprised members of the notorious 'Forty Thieves' from the Elephant and Castle area, all expert shoplifters who had decided to plunder some of the stores at Southend-on-Sea, found themselves in the charge-room at Southend police station. It was fortunate that the gang had been caught unawares. Their leader was Maggie, sister of the notorious gangster, Billy Hill. Known as 'Baby Face, the Queen of the Forty Elephants', she possessed a ferocious temper. Not content with putting out a woman's eye with a hat-pin, she also received a sentence of four years' penal servitude when she stabbed a police officer in the eye. 'Take her away,' said the judge dismissively and Maggie, ever defiant, screamed, 'You didn't say that when you was fucking me last night!'

But Maggie was not without her compassionate side. Her brother, Billy Hill had been sentenced to three years' borstal detention in 1929; he had escaped and attacked a maid who had disturbed him while he was burgling a house. For this, he had received an additional sentence of nine months' hard labour, plus twelve strokes of the cat o'nine tails. Following his release he discovered that Maggie (herself serving a prison term) had left him sufficient money to purchase a first-rate set of burgling implements. Hill carried out two successful burglaries in the week following his release; alas, he was spotted by Detective Constable Fred Narborough of the Flying Squad who was patrolling St Pancras Way in a Squad tender. Hill and two of his associates were busy attempting to steal a Sunbeam saloon and following his conviction at Clerkenwell police court as a 'suspected person, loitering with intent to commit a felony' under the Vagrancy Act, Hill was sentenced to twenty-one days' imprisonment – worse, his Borstal licence was revoked.

Under Cooper's leadership, the tearaways were rounded up like sheep and it is little wonder that in 1928, after the Squad's establishment had been increased to thirty-five, they were responsible for 429 arrests, of which 215 were for suspected persons, loitering with intent to pick pockets. In Wensley's words, 'Events have proved that my judgement of his [Cooper's] capacity was not wrong.'

Police officers in general were now instructed that if they had reason to believe that criminals had escaped in a motor vehicle, they should give all available information to C1, with the description of the car and criminals if possible, so that C1 could have 'the officers patrolling in motor cars warned by wireless.' This was demonstrated when Police Constable H. Grubb, posted to 'The Metropolitan Police Telephone' forwarded the following message, which he received at 3.30 in the morning on behalf of the superintendent at Walton Street police station, to Superintendent Central:

> Four men (no description) in a small brown four seater motor car, other particulars not known, attempted to force the door of a shop at Knightsbridge and in doing so, broke the window. Car now proceeding towards the Albert Hall. Repeated to wireless, immediately. Copy to Squad.

On this occasion, it was too little, too late. The thieves got clean away.

But the tenders were still being utilized by the Squad and still they produced results. On 7 February 1928, Detective Inspector Wood was patrolling in a Crossley Tender during night duty when he received a radio message that a car belonging to the eminent pathologist Sir Bernard Spillsbury had been stolen. The car was spotted at Golders Green and the three occupants, who were in possession of housebreaking implements, were arrested and all were convicted at the Middlesex Quarter Sessions.

When the Lea Francis tourers had first been acquired consideration had been given to strengthening the chassis, since the vehicles were very lightweight, but this would have meant a significant (and unacceptable) reduction in the speed of the car. This defect was brought to notice on several occasions when, attempting to stop the bandits' bigger, faster and heavier vehicles, the 'Leafs' were coming off second-best.

A classic case was when Squad officers received a tip-off regarding a gang leader who had fallen out with his former associates, who had shot him. He survived however, so when one of his previous colleagues heard that the gang leader had formed a new team and that they intended to go out on a safe-breaking expedition, it was far more satisfying to inform the Squad, receive a bursary from the Informants Fund and see his erstwhile boss go off to gaol for a few years. And that was what happened.

At 4.30 in the morning, the gang leader and four other men were seen in the Islington area and were kept under observation by the Squad. One of the gang was followed to a garage from where he drove off in a stolen car and picked up the other four men. At that point, two Flying Squad 'Leafs' approached the car: the gang leader who was also the driver, drove straight at one of the Squad cars, smashing the steering gear and buckling one of the wheels and then, mounting the pavement, drove into the second Squad car. The gang jumped out and attacked the Squad officers but were eventually subdued, and a search of the stolen car revealed jemmies, a wrench, a hacksaw, ropes and a carrier used for the removal of safes. Each of the gang received three years' penal servitude.

In addition to the vulnerability of the 'Leafs' chassis, after two years service they had seen so much service that it became virtually impossible to tune the worn engines. It was clear that heavier, faster vehicles would be needed to update the Squad's fleet. However, before that happened a very dark cloud indeed was cast over the Metropolitan Police – a scandal involving bribes being accepted on an outrageous scale, which threatened public confidence in the Force. Nowadays, a white-lipped Home Secretary would demand an investigation conducted by a senior officer from another Force. Then, the matter was put to Chief Constable Wensley and in characteristic, unflappable style, he simply selected the best man for the job. True, the investigator selected for this distasteful enquiry was only a detective sergeant (first class) but he had already acquired an impressive reputation and his name was Fred Sharpe of the Flying Squad.

*   *   *

Frederick Dew 'Nutty' Sharpe, born in 1890, was a hard-faced, hard-fisted ex-miner who joined the Metropolitan Police in 1911. His reputation for bravery was legendary; he frequently posed as a drunken seaman in docklands, waiting to arrest his assailants after he was attacked and robbed. When a warehouse suffered inexplicable losses from its stock, Sharpe had himself nailed up in a packing case, complete with eyeholes and was delivered to the premises thus concealed. He was snapped up for Flying Squad work, almost from the Squad's inception; on patrol in a Lea Francis tourer, Sharpe spotted nine pickpockets at work in Bethnal Green. After they boarded a bus, so too did Sharpe and arrested the lot, single-handedly. When Sharpe, with his traditional bowler hat set at a threatening angle, confronted the gangs of tearaways at the racetracks, his presence was usually enough to inspire immediate flight. This was due to a previous occasion when Sharpe met with forty of 'Darby' Sabini's feared 'Italian Mob', head-on; he curtly told them to 'Clear off' – one gang member who refused found himself flat on his back, courtesy of a right-hander from Nutty. It was clear that Sharpe would tolerate no nonsense from anybody; Wensley's choice was a wise one.

*   *   *

Kate Evelyn Meyrick *née* Nason was born in Dublin in 1875. She and her eight children were abandoned by her husband and, arriving in London, Mrs. Meyrick cashed in on the craze for nightclubs, where drinking continued illegally after restaurants

and pubs had closed for the night. During the 1920s she ran a
series of nightclubs in London, of which the most famous was
The Cecil Club – it was also known as 'The 43 Club' – in Soho's
Gerrard Street. She became very rich and was able to put two of
her eight children through public school, three of whom married
into the aristocracy. The clubs were enormously popular with the
glitterati of the day; Jack Buchanan, Tallulah Bankhead, Jessie
Matthews, Richard Tauber, Georges Carpentier, Rudolph
Valentino and the Prince of Wales were a small selection of the
celebrities who attended the clubs. However, Mrs Meyrick – or
'Ma' Meyrick as she became known – was constantly in trouble
with the police for infringement of the licensing laws, in
particular,selling drinks after hours, and in 1924 she received a
short prison sentence for doing so. What she needed was
someone to forewarn her of intended raids on her clubs. Enter
the very corrupt Station Police Sergeant George Goddard of 'C'
Division's Vine Street police station …

George Goddard was twenty-one years of age when he joined
the Metropolitan Police in 1900 and by 1928 he had spent fifteen
years in the Soho area. The finger of suspicion had been first
pointed at him in 1921, when Police Sergeant Horace Robert
Josling had reported him to the commissioner for accepting
bribes from bookmakers. But Goddard had just been appointed
the officer in charge for suppressing brothels and disorderly
houses, as well as strictly enforcing the licensing, gaming and
decency laws in the Soho area and the charge carried very serious
implications. Not only was Goddard completely exonerated,
Josling was required to resign and returned to his former
profession of schoolteacher.

But in September 1928, the commissioner received a letter
alleging corruption between Goddard and Mrs Meyrick, and
'Nutty' Sharpe got to work, carrying out a series of observations
on Goddard and uncovering a number of irregularities at the
Cecil Club. As a result, Mrs Meyrick was sentenced to six
months' imprisonment. Sharpe visited her at HMP Holloway,
inviting her to incriminate Goddard but she refused to answer
any of his questions. However, Sharpe had another string to his
bow. He questioned Police Constable 163 'C' John Wilkin, who
had been working under Goddard's supervision to keep
observation on nightclubs; Wilkin cracked and admitted taking
backhanders from the club owners, via Goddard. He agreed to

give evidence against Goddard, in return for immunity from prosecution for himself. Goddard was arrested and had a hard time explaining how he had acquired a house worth £2,000 – at that time, a man earning Goddard's weekly wage of £6 15s 0d (£6.75) could have afforded a house costing only around a fifth of that. Goddard also possessed an expensive Chrysler car and two bank accounts, containing funds totalling £2,700. He found it even more difficult to explain how he had managed to gather together £12,500 in a safe deposit box at Selfridges, which he rented in the name of Joseph Eagles (especially when some of the £10 notes therein were traced back to Mrs Meyrick) and a catalogue of corrupt dealings with several of Soho's inhabitants was uncovered. Goddard was dismissed from the Force, sentenced to eighteen months' hard labour, fined £2,000 and ordered to pay the costs of the prosecution; Mrs Meyrick was sentenced to fifteen months' hard labour. Although a concerted effort was made to sequestrate the contents of his safe deposit box, by an anomaly in the law Goddard managed to hang on to practically every penny he had corruptly obtained. Mrs. Meyrick went on to serve two more six-month sentences for infringing the licensing laws and lost most of her money in the 1929 Stock Market crash. In 1933 she wrote her memoirs, *Secrets of the 43 Club*. Since the book exposed the private lives of some of the great and the good who had frequented her club over the years, it was stillborn, having been banned immediately on publication and 'Ma' Meyrick died the same year. Goddard, on the other hand, completed his sentence and then retired to a very comfortable life in the country.

Following Goddard's conviction, the Home Secretary offered Josling his job back; he refused, continued to teach and was later awarded the large (and well-deserved) sum of £1,500 compensation, over £42,000 by today's standards. He died at the early age of fifty-one.

The case (which received enormous publicity) did the reputation of the Metropolitan Police immense harm. The superintendent of 'C' Division was reprimanded, fined and transferred to another division. Peter Beveridge, then a detective constable in Whitechapel (and who would later head the Flying Squad), remembered that hooligans would shout 'Goddard!' at him, from a prudently safe distance. They were later seen and quietly reminded of their manners; the practice ceased. Following the trial, Sharpe was promoted to detective inspector (second class) and returned to more conventional Flying Squad duties.

★   ★   ★

Back now, to the urgent matter of acquiring Flying Squad vehicles with a heavier chassis and a comparable speed to the cars used by 'the Motor Car Bandit.' It was also thought necessary to notify the public of every development, courtesy of the indefatigable Major Vitty, who on 4 July 1929 informed the readers of the *Daily Mail* that:

> The colour of those [vehicles] now in use is constantly being varied. Registration numbers are changed and special cowls are fitted to the radiator so that their shape can be altered. It is possible to change the colour in 24 hours.

It appeared – to readers of the *Daily Mail*, at least – that Major Vitty had worked all this out for himself, without the benefit of Wensley.

The first of the new, heavier cars chosen was a 4¼ litre Invicta, a beautiful looking 29.1 hp tourer, capable of reaching 90 mph and costing Sir John Moylan, the Receiver of the Metropolitan Police, £632; it was money well spent.

Again, Jack Frost tested this car at Brooklands race track and later on the public highway with the assistance of 'B' Division officers who, early one morning, closed off a section of the Thames embankment for him. Following the carburettors being altered, different types of racing and sports plugs being fitted, a high-speed coil and a special kind of racing magneto being tested and the compression-ratio of the engine being specially tested, the car was considered fit for service. On its first outing, the Invicta's ability was to be demonstrated in stunning style.

★   ★   ★

Detective Constable Bob White of the Flying Squad could scarcely believe his luck when, during the early hours of 24 July 1929, he spotted three known villains, strongly suspected of carrying out a series of smash and grab raids. Charles Lilley was the driver of the large, powerful 30.98 hp Vauxhall which was parked in Kennington, South London; his two passengers were Alfred John Head and Alfred Hayes. Leaving the three men deep in conversation, White telephoned the Yard.

Jack Frost immediately started up the Invicta. Into it got Detective Inspector Edward Ockey and Detective Sergeant Ball. Following, in a Lea Francis tourer were Detective Sergeant Jock Weir and Detective Constables Green and Coates.

Soon the gang were spotted and followed as they crossed Westminster Bridge and having circled Parliament Square, turned into Victoria Street, retracing almost exactly the route of Hambrook's drive of nine years earlier.

Stopping outside Studd & Millington's Tailors shop, Lilley reversed the big Vauxhall up on to the pavement, whilst Head and Hayes started to hitch chains to the steel grille of the tailor's window. As they went to attach the chains to the drag bar of the Vauxhall, Frost restarted the Invicta's engine, which caused the two men to leap back into their car and roar off into Tothill Street. Racing across the junction with Queen Anne's Gate, the Invicta drew level with the Vauxhall in Petty France and Ockey dropped the illuminated 'MP' sign and sounded the gong. Lilley ignored the order to stop so, as the cars slowed slightly to 50 mph to negotiate the bend into Buckingham Gate, Ockey leapt from the Invicta on to the running board of the Vauxhall and grabbed Lilley round the neck in an effort to wrest control of the car from him. But the speed of the Vauxhall actually increased and Lilley bellowed, 'Knock him off!' – one of the gang smashed a jemmy against Ockey's head, the other battered his knuckles with an iron bar. The pain caused Ockey to fall from the running board into the path of the Invicta, which was only ten yards behind. Frost, with immense skill, managed to brake and swerve around Ockey and the Invicta thundered after the Vauxhall, which had now entered Buckingham Palace Road. Lilley now pushed the Vauxhall's speed to 80 mph on this long stretch of the highway but the Invicta stayed right on its tail, the crew coldly furious in the knowledge that Ockey might well be dead.

Hardly slackening speed, the Vauxhall screeched into Pimlico Road and Frost waited until Lilley took a sudden right-hand turn into Ebury Street; then he rammed the Vauxhall, side-on. As one of the tyres exploded, so the Vauxhall, with a sickening crunch turned over against a wall and the chase was ended. Not so the conflict; Lilley was arrested immediately but Head and Hayes, wielding the jemmy and iron bar, decided to make a fight of it. It was an imprudent move. They were thoroughly subdued and dragged into Gerald Road police station, where the staff probably thought that bringing in battered prisoners during the early hours of the morning was going to become a Flying Squad tradition.

Ockey, meanwhile, had been found by a patrolling police officer and was taken to hospital. His injuries were severe enough to keep him on the sick list for two months, and when Sir Percival Clarke, representing the Director of Public Prosecutions at the Old Bailey, called on Dr A. M. Barlow, who had examined Ockey at the hospital, the doctor told the jury of Ockey's injuries and offered the opinion that it was only Ockey's extremely long, thick hair that had saved his life. That, and of course, Frost's exceptional driving skill.

Sentencing Lilley to three years' penal servitude and Head and Hayes to four and five years' penal servitude respectively, for possessing housebreaking implements by night and inflicting grievous bodily harm, the Recorder, Sir Ernest Wild, said:

> The police showed considerable enterprise while their leader, Inspector Ockey, displayed great heroism. It is well that those who thought it right to undermine our police force should know what sort of man they were attacking. It is fortunate that the prisoner is not standing in the dock charged with murder. Had Ockey been killed, the prisoner would undoubtedly been hanged.

It was the first of several commendations that Ockey would receive. The Recorder's congratulations were echoed by the jury foreman and the rest of the jury and three months after his ordeal, Ockey was highly commended by the commissioner. Commendations and monetary awards also went to the rest of the Squad personnel and two weeks later Ockey was awarded a cheque for £15 from the Bow Street Police Court Reward Fund. In the New Years Honours list for 1930, Ockey was one of eleven recipients of the King's Police Medal.

*   *   *

Wensley had brought about the creation of the Flying Squad at a time in his service when most police officers had already retired.

In 1921, he was appointed superintendent of Central Branch and still he supervised the investigation of murders, including the highly controversial case in which star-crossed lovers Frederick Bywaters and Edith Thompson were both hanged on the same day for the murder of Mrs Thompson's husband. When he was appointed chief constable of the CID, Wensley took a paternal interest in his brainchild, the Flying Squad and did everything he could to help and promote them.

After over forty years of police service, Wensley left the Yard for the last time. The following entry appeared in *Police Orders*, dated Wednesday, 31 July 1929:

> The Commissioner has much pleasure in notifying the appointment of Mr. John H Ashley (Superintendent C.I. Department) *vice* Mr. Frederick P. Wensley OBE, retiring on pension: to date from 1st August. Mr. Wensley joined the Metropolitan Police on 16th January 1888, and was appointed to the Criminal Investigation Department on 3rd October 1895. He became Chief Constable of the CID in December 1924.
>
> His ability and devotion to the work of his Department has been a notable feature in its history. The Secretary of State has expressed his appreciation of Mr. Wensley's long and exceptionally distinguished service, and with this expression, the Commissioner wishes to be heartily associated.

It was a fitting tribute and an extraordinary one. Nothing like it had been seen before and it has never been repeated since.

*   *   *

Before the close of the decade, the fast cars of the Squad were in the process of being updated – an Alvis, Lagonda, MG Star, Talbot and a Vauxhall were added to the fleet – and the vehicles were fitted with Marconi radio equipment, some of which were capable of both receiving and transmitting. Flying Squad arrests for 1929 now rose to 515, and the *Daily Mail* informed its readers that 'the Flying Squad of Scotland Yard is to be strengthened', on 6 August 1929. In fact the Squad was completely reorganized under a detective superintendent from C1 Department: Walter Hambrook, who had been promoted from his post of divisional detective inspector at Albany Street police station, returned to the Flying Squad as its new chief inspector and with the Secretary of State's approval the Squad was increased to forty men.

After ten short years, the name of a small, dedicated section of the Metropolitan Police was on everybody's lips. J. Ord Hume had composed *The Flying Squad Quick March* for both military and brass band, the author, Edgar Wallace, had added a play to his already famous book, *Flying Squad*, which was turned into film of the same name directed by Arthur Maude, and the hero of one of Alfred Hitchcock's films was a Flying Squad detective. The Flying Squad was crowned with success.

The Racetrack Gangs

One of the biggest threats to public tranquillity is, and always has been, gangs of organized criminals. Although their confrontations are aimed at opposing gangs, the disorder which follows often involves many innocent people and this leads to a lack of confidence in the police who, the public rightly aver, should be protecting them. One such group of gangsters during the 1920s and 30s were known as 'the Racetrack Gangs'. They merit a chapter on their own; their behaviour brought about a series of confrontations with the Flying Squad. As a result, the gangs never recovered and were dispersed; the Squad's reputation was enhanced.

The English have had a passion for horseracing since the 1800s, through all levels of society; the wealthy purchased, bred and raced horses, the working classes toiled in the stables and the different social classes all turned out for a day at the races to enjoy 'a flutter on the gee-gees'. And as the popularity of horseracing grew, more and more racecourses opened across the country and the punters flocked to them, often in charabancs or special excursion trains. Enormous sums of money changed hands; it is estimated that between the two world wars, the annual turnover in racing circles amounted to £500,000,000.

Following the end of World War One, there came a boom period in racing and wherever there is wealth and enjoyment, it is not too long before crime and corruption surfaces. At that time, hardly any control was exercised at race meetings; in fact, practically anybody could set up business as a bookmaker and many of them would only pay out when they could afford it. They hired bodyguards to protect them from enraged punters who were the victims of welshing. Punters, in turn were bullied into buying worthless raffle tickets 'for a mate who's gone to prison' by the racetrack thugs. And if this were not enough, the tracks were infested by large, organized gangs of card-sharpers and pickpockets, not only from all parts of the United Kingdom, but also from France, Italy, Switzerland and Poland. The pickpockets – colloquially known as 'whizzers' or 'dips' – turned up by the coach-load at the tracks; the worst of them was probably 'The Nile Mob', who originated from the Nile district of Shoreditch in East London. The bookmakers themselves were prey to gangs who travelled round the country's racetracks – Epsom and Ascot were considered the most lawless – demanding protection money, and in turn the bookmakers turned to rival gangs to protect them from their tormentors.

The Bethnal Green Mob, the Hoxton Gang, the Italian Mob, the Birmingham Boys and the Leeds Crowd were some of the most ruthless. Billy Kimber, the head of the Birmingham Boys – they were also known as 'The Brummagem Hammers' – was a clever strategist who controlled the courses in the Midlands and the North, and had formed a coalition with the Leeds Crowd. In fact, Kimber had also taken over the unofficial excises imposed on the racetracks in the south of England, established a secondary headquarters in Islington, North London and formed an alliance, albeit an uneasy one, with the Hoxton Gang. The reason for this was simple: both factions shared a loathing for the Italian Mob.

The leader of the Italian Mob was Charles 'Darby' Sabini, a near-illiterate but cunning thug who, from his headquarters in Clerkenwell, ran a series of protection rackets together with his brothers, George, Fred, Harryboy and Joe. All were immensely tough and Darby, who had boxed professionally as a middleweight, invariably carried a loaded automatic pistol. It soon became clear to Sabini that the racetracks were a lucrative source of income and because he could call on the services of several hundred men at an hour's notice, he decided to encroach upon Kimber's territory.

It took no time at all for the rival faction's tempers to boil over and at a race meeting at Alexandra Park in 1921 there was a pitched battle between the Birmingham Boys and their Italian counterparts. Shots were fired and terrible injuries were inflicted on both sides.

At Greenford trotting track a few weeks later, Sabini, who surprisingly was without either his bodyguard or his pistol, was ambushed by the Birmingham Boys who attacked him with bottles and iron bars; as he fled, an associate threw a gun to him. He fired off a round and his attackers scattered. Charged with unlawfully and maliciously endangering life, Sabini pleaded self-defence and was acquitted. A week later, Billy Kimber attempted to broker a truce with Sabini; he was later found in the street outside Sabini's flat with a bullet in his side; his only comment to the police was, 'I ain't grassing.' Alfred Solomon, a Sabini associate, was arrested and charged with attempted murder. He was acquitted following the trial, where Kimber refused to give evidence.

And if, in the wake of all this criminality the question, 'What was the Flying Squad doing about it?' was raised, the truthful answer was, 'Very little.' It must be remembered that the various gang bosses had thousands of men at their disposal from all over the country. One very small section of the Metropolitan Police had scarcely more than a dozen men to hand. It did not mean, however, that they were doing nothing at all.

On the first day of the Derby in 1921, the Birmingham Boys decided to teach the Italian Mob a lesson, once and for all. It started before the meeting, with David Levy, one of Sabini's associates, being sentenced to three months' imprisonment for possession of a pistol and ammunition; how he came to be fingered is not entirely clear. Waiting only to see Steve Donoghue complete the third of his six Derby wins, on Humourist, the Birmingham Boys left the racetrack early in their hired charabanc. Hiding their vehicle behind some bushes in Ewell, Surrey, and with a car in a side-turning opposite, they waited for their adversaries to arrive on their way back to London. As two cars approached from the direction of Epsom, the Birmingham Boys' vehicle pulled out in front of them; they squealed to a halt, and the Boys poured out of their coach and attacked the occupants of the cars with guns, axes, hammers and housebricks. The horrified residents of Ewell screamed in sheer terror at the frenzied assault, but the attackers discovered far too late that the men who were being bludgeoned and hacked were not the Italian Mob at all – they were the Leeds Crowd, their own allies.

Kicking them into unconsciousness, the Birmingham Boys ran back to their charabanc and headed off towards London. A description of the attackers and their vehicle was quickly circulated by the police on a rather garbled 'All Stations' message; it had initially been thought at Epsom police station that this had been a Sinn Féin riot.

Detective Inspector Stevens of the Flying Squad made his way through the home-going Derby crowds to Ewell, where he admitted that even he was sickened at the state of the bookmakers' injuries. He joined forces with 'W' Division's famous 'bearded detective', Divisional Detective Inspector James Berrett and the hunt for the attackers got underway.

It was a little later that a Police Constable Shoesmith spotted the charabanc parked outside the George and Dragon public house on Kingston Hill, close to Richmond Park. He contacted his station and Police Sergeant 68'V' Merritt lost no time getting there, where he lifted the coach's bonnet and, to prevent the gang's escape, ripped the leads off the sparking plugs. At the same time, Police Sergeant 110'V' Dawson, whose superintendent had taken the highly unusual step of arming him, walked into the pub's garden where twenty-eight members of the Birmingham Boys were refreshing themselves after their exertions. Sergeant Dawson politely asked the driver of the charabanc to identify himself. The driver did so and having learnt that all of the passengers had travelled down from Birmingham, Sergeant Dawson courteously requested that all those present should consider themselves under arrest. All twenty-eight of the gang rose as one and started to rush Dawson, who with considerable style drew his revolver and said, 'I shall shoot the first man who tries to escape!'

It was sufficient for the entire gang to submit to their arrest; all but two of them were positively identified by the witnesses. The gang were remanded in custody and on their subsequent appearances at Epsom Police Court, they were handcuffed and chained together. The police who escorted the convoy were armed and used cars and motor cycles as back-up; outside the court were more armed police officers. Berrett was threatened and all those in the courtroom were verbally abused by the gang. Appearing at the Guildford Assizes, the dock had to be enlarged to contain all the men, the indictment ran to twelve pages and they stood trial for conspiring and committing grievous bodily harm and possessing firearms. Twenty-three of the gang were convicted and were sentenced to terms of incarceration varying between nine months and three years. The trial judge, Mr. Justice Rowlatt commended the plucky and resourceful Sergeant Dawson, as did the jury, and in highly commending him, (as he did both Stevens and Berrett) the commissioner also awarded Dawson the princely sum of five pounds.

Yet still the violence continued; in August, at the Bath racetrack, Alfie Solomon and some of his associates were beaten up by the Birmingham Boys but the following year, the shoe was on the other foot. In February 1922, two of the Birmingham Boys were attacked and slashed by members of Sabini's gang, which included Alfie Solomon. Two months later, Fred Gilbert, another of the Birmingham Boys, was attacked by the Italian Mob, led once again by Alfie Solomon, and Gilbert refused to prosecute. But when two months later the Sabinis shot at Gilbert whilst he was out walking with his wife, this time Gilbert did complain. Although the vast majority of those who were accused were acquitted, Joseph Sabini was not and he was sentenced to three years' penal servitude.

Six weeks after his brother's conviction, Darby and his brother, Harryboy were attacked on their home territory, in the Fratalanza Club in Great Bath Street by a rival Italian faction, the Cortesi brothers. Harryboy was shot in the stomach and Darby Sabini proved that he could be a grass and give evidence for the prosecution when the circumstances suited him. It did on this occasion: in January 1923, Augustus and Enrico Cortesi were each sentenced to three years' penal servitude.

Six months later, Harryboy had recovered sufficiently to allegedly attack a bookmaker at Epsom Racetrack, together with his brother Darby and another man. The knuckledusters supposedly used upon the victim were not recovered and the three men were acquitted.

During 1924, there was a spate of gang attacks; two murders, two serious woundings and a pitched battle on a train from Doncaster to London. A gang fight on the streets of Brixton terrorized the inhabitants and at Victoria Station a racing mob attacked PC William Gatford and threw his unconscious body on the railway lines. It did not seem that matters could get any worse, but the following year they did. Razor-slashings became an almost weekly occurrence and shots were fired in the street when a rival gang went looking for the Sabinis. In August 1925, an argument between a pickpocket and a bookmaker at Lewes racetrack resulted in the bookmaker being followed home by members of the Bethnal Green Mob, where he was mercilessly slashed with razors. And in addition, there were ten further pitched battles between opposing factions throughout England. By now, no bookmaker could work without paying an absolute minimum of £25 per day to the gangs and there was public outrage at this complete breakdown in law and order.

It prompted the Home Secretary of the day, Sir William Joynston Hicks, to call for reports from all the police forces whose areas included the affected racetracks. He appointed the Flying Squad to stamp out the gangs, telling Parliament, 'It may be difficult to get rid of the gangs all at once, but give me time. The responsibility is mine; I mean to discharge it.'

This tough bunch of detectives were tailor-made for the job but they were few in number; it would not be until four years later that the Secretary of State would authorize their strength to be increased to forty. Fortunately, amongst their insubstantial numbers were detectives who were very tough indeed.

Ted Greeno had developed a taste for adventure whilst serving as a radio operator on board an ammunition ship during the First World War. His lifelong passion for racing would stand him in good stead – that, plus his expert knowledge of gangsters, thieves and pickpockets which brought him smartly into the CID in record time and almost immediately into the Flying Squad where he would remain for seventeen years.

Billy Hill, the self-proclaimed 'Boss of Britain's Underworld' described Greeno as 'one of the best murder investigators the Yard ever had. He was also one of the best thief catchers.' Hill was quite right. The reason for Greeno's success was threefold. First, he was a natural leader of men. Second, in the days when detectives would slip five or ten shillings to a snout, in the hope that some productive information would materialize, Greeno, following a big win at the racetrack, would lavish twenty-five or fifty pounds on an informant; as a result, he would get the best, most up to date intelligence in respect of the biggest and most important cases. And lastly, Greeno was fearless. He justifiably possessed a reputation as a tough guy and as such, reckless individuals would sometimes challenge his authority. Whether this occurred in a pub, a racetrack or the street, the matter would be resolved there and then. Off would come Greeno's jacket, a makeshift ring would be hastily formed and the challenger would be taken on and thrashed. At the conclusion, Greeno and his adversary would shake hands and that would be the end of the matter. There was, of course, no question of the challenger being arrested. It was this type of behaviour which guaranteed admiration for Greeno, not only amongst his colleagues but also within the underworld.

Bob Higgins (who would later rise to be deputy head of the Squad) was posted to the Squad as a detective sergeant (second class) in January 1934 and had the good fortune to be attached to Detective Inspector 'Chesty' Corbett's team. With Daniel Frank Gooch as the Squad chief (described by Higgins as 'one of the finest policemen ever to serve at the Yard') – Higgins was in good company. As the coaches or 'race specials' containing the gangsters, tearaways and pickpockets arrived at Ascot, Goodwood, Doncaster or Aintree, so the Squad officers were waiting for them. Before they could even alight, they were told, 'Clear off', and they did.

'Nutty' Sharpe who has already been mentioned, was the terror of the racetrack gangs. It required only his presence on the racetracks to ensure instant flight by the gangs who infested them; similarly he would visit the trains known as 'race specials' prior to their departure at the station. Every door in every carriage would be opened; if Sharpe identified any of the occupants as pickpockets or cardsharps, they would be told to make themselves scarce. None demurred. On one occasion, it appeared that Sharpe was late boarding a 'race special' which was destined for the Grand National. Cardsharps were already plying their trade, so when the train arrived in Liverpool, Sharpe followed the men who boarded a coach going to the racetrack. Sharpe had a quiet word with the driver; the coach made a detour to the police station, where all the surprised fraudsters were arrested and charged. An example of the kind of thing that ensured Sharpe's reputation occurred in 1930, after the Chief Constable of Portsmouth asked the Yard for assistance, fearing a repeat of the attentions of gangs of pickpockets who had enjoyed themselves during a previous match against West Ham United. This was a situation tailor-made for Sharpe, who quickly discovered the hotel where the dips were staying; he deployed his men around the premises and then ostentatiously strolled towards the front entrance. He was immediately recognized by the pickpockets, who fled out of the back of the hotel, straight into the arms of Sharpe's men. Before the game commenced, twelve London pickpockets were commencing prison sentences of three months each, though it is not entirely clear what they had done to justify their arrest, conviction or incarceration.

By the mid-1930s, the Squad had acquired a well-justified, no-nonsense reputation amongst the gangsters and riff-raff and their knowledge of pickpockets caused them to be much in demand. In 1936, the chief constable of Luton followed the example of his

contemporary at Portsmouth because he, too, feared an
infestation of pickpockets, at the replay of the Luton vs West Ham
football match. Detective Inspector Alf Dance, who was quite
properly regarded by the gangs as 'a terror', together with two
other Squad officers was sent.

A little London pickpocket was about to enter the stadium
when he was confronted by a surge of stampeding fellow
pickpockets, fleeing from the ground. Instinctively, he joined
their ranks and demanded to know from one of them what was
wrong. 'Guy [run] for your life, Jack!' gasped the pickpocket.
'The Squad's here and they're nicking *everybody!*'

Well, perhaps not everybody – just seven persistent pickpockets
who were awarded sentences of three months' imprisonment at
Luton Borough Police Court and earned Dance and his officers
commendations from the commissioner and the Luton Justices.

Following a member of the Hoxton Gang's throat being cut by
members of Sabini's gang, a punitive raiding party composed of
factions of both the Hoxton Gang and the Bethnal Green Mob
set off for Lewes Racecourse. When Ted Greeno received
information that there was 'going to be trouble' there on 8 June
1936, it was he, Sharpe and seven other Squad officers who
rushed to the track. Before the first race at two o'clock could even
start, in the corner of the three-shilling ring, thirty of the gang
members spotted the bookmaker, Alfred Solomon. There had
been bad blood between the Birmingham Boys, their associates
the Hoxton Gang, and Solomon, ever since he had been
acquitted for the attempted murder of their leader, Billy Kimber
in 1921. A year later, Solomon had been part of Sabini's gang
who had razor-slashed two of the Birmingham Boys. But
undoubtedly the main cause of their fury was that in 1924,
Solomon had stood trial for murder once again and this time the
victim had been Barnett Blitz (also known as Buck Emden), an
associate of the Birmingham Boys. With his defence paid for by
Darby Sabini, Solomon was acquitted of murder and sentenced
to three years' penal servitude for manslaughter.

Now the gang produced their weapons – hatchets, hammers,
knuckledusters and crowbars and rushed at Solomon, who with
three or four minor injuries took to his heels. His clerk, Mark
Frater, was not so lucky and received terrible injuries which
might well have proved fatal had the police not intervened.
Arrested, the gang were astonishingly granted bail in the sum of

£50 each and the two victims were threatened with further violence if they dared to give evidence. But if they didn't, the police did; sixteen of the gang were later convicted of inflicting grievous bodily harm with intent and riotous assembly at Lewes Assizes and Mr Justice Hilbery told them:

> You had armed yourselves with weapons which have been aptly described as villainous instruments to use upon any fellow human being. You showed no mercy to your victim, and you intended to show no mercy. Crimes of gang violence in this country will meet with no mercy. Gang violence is not only a brutal breach of our law, but it also exercises terror on its victims. You men hoped to escape, and I have not the least doubt that in this case you thought that because Frater would not dare, for fear of you, to identify one of you, that you might escape. There is no case here for leniency. You will receive sentences which I hope will teach you once and for all that crimes of this sort do not pay in this country, and which will teach others who are listening here or who may read what happened in this case afterwards.

He then imposed swingeing sentences: two of the gang's ringleaders each received sentences of five years' penal servitude – one of them was Jimmy Spinks who had wielded a hatchet. Albert Blitz, who denied not only any kinship with Barnett Blitz who had been killed by Solomon, but (rather improbably) also any knowledge of the man and his demise whatsoever, received four years. Thomas Mack was one of five of the gang members sentenced to three years, five more received two years and three with no previous convictions were each given eighteen months' imprisonment.

Such salutary sentencing was the first reason that the widespread power of the racetrack gangs broke down. The effect can best be judged from the records; in 1923, 110 arrests had been carried out at Epsom Racetrack for offences including blackmail, welshing and pickpocketing. On Derby Day, 1937, the year following the attack by the Hoxton Gang, the number of arrests amounted to just eight.

Sabini could now have really consolidated his position as triumphant gang leader with the demise of his main adversaries but instead, in the second of the reasons for the break up of the racetrack gangs, he threw it all away in a rare act of stupidity. Because of the interest generated by the 'Battle of Lewes', a Sunday newspaper stated that Darby Sabini had some involvement in the fracas; Sabini sued for libel, but failed to attend the proceedings and judgement, plus £775 costs, was awarded against him. Instead of paying up, Sabini filed for bankruptcy, stating that he had no assets and debts of £800; but as a result of the searching cross-examinations into the funding of his annual £20–30,000 per year lifestyle, this brought him even more unwelcome publicity. His authority crumbled and he disappeared to Brighton. During the war years, Harryboy received nine months' imprisonment for perjury and Darby was interned as 'an enemy alien' (almost certainly a matter of convenience for the authorities, since Darby, who had an English mother had been born in the United Kingdom). Following his release he was sentenced to three years' imprisonment for receiving stolen property and that, together with the death of his son who was serving with the wartime RAF, broke his spirit, leading to his death in 1951.

And Nutty Sharpe? He became head of the Flying Squad and retired in 1937; he lived until the ripe old age of eight-four. He was one of the first Flying Squad senior officers to openly state that Squad men should mix with criminals. 'The more crooks a Squad man knows intimately,' he once said, 'the more he knows about the underworld and what it is thinking and doing, and the more likely he is to be of use.' Sharpe was quite right; perhaps he was thinking of Billy Kimber when he made those remarks. Kimber recovered sufficiently from his gunshot wound to rather surprisingly become one of the managerial staff of the Wimbledon Greyhound Association.

The Squad – 1930s

The Flying Squad was now in the process of obtaining a fleet of vehicles of really excellent quality but still there were problems. Tenders were still in use and to highlight the difficulties that they were experiencing, one cannot do better than refer to a report from 1931, submitted by Detective Inspector Young and reproduced here word-for-word:

I beg to report that at 3am, 22nd. January 1931, Inspector Allan, C.O.C.1, received a wireless message, whilst patrolling in Police Tender, of a smash and grab raid at 178, Kings Street, Hammersmith, an opticians. He at once proceeded there, and scoured the district. About 3-15am., whilst proceeding through Kensington High Street, he saw a Morris Saloon motor car, maroon colour, similar to the one described in the message, standing near some shops. The tender was slowed down to enable him and his officers to investigate, when they saw that the Morris car contained four men who upon seeing the tender waved their hands and drove rapidly away through the High Street, Kensington, and Earls Court Road, being chased by the police tender, which however, was unable to overtake the suspect's car, which made good its escape. Shortly before 4am., the door of 119, Knightsbridge, a Costumiers shop, was found forced, a car similar to the one chased by Inspector Allan being seen in the vicinity. The number of the car which was undoubtedly the one used in these three instances could not be seen owing to it being either very dirty or obscured by something.

There is very little doubt that had the police tender been capable of great speed, the Morris car would have been overtaken, the men in it interrogated and in all probability, the proceeds of the raid at 178 Kings Street, Hammersmith, would have been found in it, and the men arrested, thus preventing a further crime at 119 Knightsbridge.

Similar instances as above of the inefficiency of the Police
Tenders have occurred before. In December last, whilst on
night-duty, Inspector Ockey in response to a wireless message,
picked up a stolen Bentley car, but could not effect the arrests
of the persons in same, or the recovery of the car, although it
was chased through Wandsworth and Putney, where it was lost.

During October last Inspector Bushnell, whilst proceeding
through Kingston-on-Thames, at night, saw some men with a
Morris car acting suspiciously near some shops, a description
of a similar car having been previously wirelessed out to
patrolling Squad cars. The Inspector chased the Morris which
was driven away on approach of police tender but was unable
to catch it as the tender could not develop sufficient speed, and
the suspects got away.

It was very disheartening to Flying Squad officers patrolling
in police tenders to detect and apprehend offenders in these
cases to see them escape owing to the fact that our tenders are
not speedy enough for the purpose for which they are supplied.

The unintentionally comic properties of this report are apparent,
not that Chief Inspector Hambrook, to whom the report was
submitted, found anything remotely amusing about it, as shown
in his minute:

Submitted. The question regarding the utility of the tenders for
patrolling purposes was gone into a short time ago. Since then
one of the tenders has been speeded up and another has gone
to the works for the same purpose. The tender which has been
speeded up hardly attains a speed of 40 miles per hour which
is not fast enough to overtake any ordinary motor car.

From the conduct of the thieves when Inspector Allan saw
them in Kensington, it would appear to be common knowledge
among the criminal classes as to the chance the officers in the
tenders have of catching them. This knowledge must encourage
the motor bandit, although there are fast cars patrolling at the
same time, but the chances are so great in favour of the motor
bandit, that it appears imperative, when the officers who are
patrolling at night especially to deal with them, and have the
good fortune to drop across them whether in the tenders or fast
cars, that they should be equipped with vehicles which are able
to contend with the cars used by the thieves.

I therefore beg to bring this matter again under consideration in order that the efficiency of the Flying Squad may be maintained.

The report was dealt with sympathetically and supportively by Superintendent Nicholls and, in response to his remarks, the Assistant Commissioner (Crime) informed the Receiver that he had instructed Chief Inspector Hambrook to 'place this in your hands and discuss it informally.'

And this, it appears, is what Hambrook did. When the Receiver wished to acquire a 4½ litre Bentley, negotiations were initially carried out with Bentley Motors Ltd in 1931. But when, twelve days later, the company was in grave difficulties and in the hands of the official receiver, a Bentley was purchased second-hand for £700. This suited the Receiver down to the ground; due to the cost limitations imposed on him by the Home Secretary, this was a considerable saving over the brand new price of £1,575. This was considered to be good practice, as it was when an Invicta was discovered under a tarpaulin in a garage in Forest Hill, south London, following a Flying Squad raid in 1931. A check revealed that this streamlined 29.1hp tourer had been stolen from the eminent plastic surgeon Sir Harold Gillies some months previously. Since Sir Harold had been paid out by his insurance company, the Squad seized the car and put the matter to the Receiver by means of a pungent report – and he promptly purchased it for the knock-down price of £298.

When Ford produced the V8 saloon, the Squad acquired one in August 1932 and within a year they obtained four more. Although the top speed was 5 mph slower than the Bentley's, the Ford could out-accelerate the Bentley and at just £246 17s 3d brand-new, the Squad could have acquired six of these cars at the same price that it would have cost to obtain a new Bentley.

* * *

Dan Gooch had taken over as the Squad's new chief inspector in March 1932 and with a detective inspector (first class) as his deputy, Gooch controlled five squads, each led by a detective inspector (second class). All of the Squad's fleet were fitted with wireless sets capable of receiving Morse transmissions; three tenders and a Bentley saloon were fitted with both receiving and transmitting equipment. In 1933, under Gooch's leadership, the Squad carried out 668 arrests, mainly for larceny and receiving stolen goods. It was not surprising: the Flying Squad personnel was increased to fifty and now possessed some of its finest officers, some of whom would stay for years, with others who would leave on promotion but who returned to the Squad time and again.

One such man was Detective Inspector William Cain – one of five police officers awarded the King's Police Medal for gallantry in 1933, after he leapt from a Flying Squad car on to the running board of a car being used by three thieves and which had been blocked in – unfortunately, not well enough. Cain was knocked off as the thieves managed to accelerate away, but he chased after the car on foot, jumped on the running board again and wrestled with the driver until the car was brought to a standstill and all three men were arrested.

There was also Peter Beveridge, who took over one of Gooch's teams; he and another detective inspector in a second Squad car carried out 'leap-frog' tailing on a gang of housebreakers, before finding them in possession of housebreaking instruments on the driveway of a country house in Guildford and arresting them. The thieves went to prison, the officers received commendations and Beveridge, a tough, red-haired Scot, would later return to head the Squad during the war years.

Bob Higgins, a detective sergeant (second class), was posted to the Squad, where he became Ted Greeno's right-hand man and, together with Detective Sergeant (First Class) Ted Renson, disarmed a gunman in the act of raiding a jeweller's shop. After Billy Hill, the self-styled 'King of Britain's Underworld' had carried out a smash and grab in Berwick Street, Soho, in 1936 and was about to enter a house in Sussex Gardens with an associate, he received a sharp push between his shoulder blades and found himself propelled into the hallway of the premises. Turning, he discovered that the provider of the shove was Higgins. Inside the house were a large quantity of furs, the proceeds of the raid – though of Hill's companion, there was, mysteriously, no trace at all. In 1953, Higgins was promoted to the rank of detective superintendent and returned to the Squad as its deputy head.

Jack 'Charley Artful' Capstick arrived on the Squad having been promoted to first-class sergeant with under ten years' service; he stormed through the underworld, arresting international gangs of pickpockets, breakers of every description and receivers of stolen goods. Short and rotund, Capstick's idea of negotiating the surrender of half-a-dozen toughs who rushed him, was to draw his truncheon and 'stick' each and every one of them in the face. And Capstick, Greeno, Renson and Higgins were collectively commended by the commissioner on 14 February 1936 for displaying 'determination and detective ability in a case of burglary.'

The following story succinctly describes the fear and respect that the Squad engendered amongst the criminal fraternity.

The Flying Squad officer who was patrolling a Soho back-street on 14 May 1934 spotted a waiter named Lawrence Dennigen in the act of attempting to sell an expensive looking camera to a man whom the officer recognized as a convict on licence. Dennigen was unable to supply a satisfactory answer as to the provenance of this item and was arrested – enquiries revealed that the camera was part-proceeds of a recent robbery at a house in Cricklewood, where a maid who had disturbed the raiders had been beaten unconscious.

Dennigen admitted his part in the robbery but refused to name his accomplices. The Squad swarmed into Soho, demanding to know with whom Dennison had recently been associating and in an effort to get the detectives off their backs, the gangsters and racketeers of the area swiftly put up the name of William Stucky. His whereabouts were brusquely demanded, and the Squad car which was dispatched from the Yard arrived in Hastings fifty minutes later and collared a very surprised Mr Stucky as he was sunning himself on the pier.

The pressure which was now applied to identify and trace the other members of the gang, proved so intense that the remaining two robbers, Louis Tyfield and Louis Vaughan-Harrison, gave themselves up to the Flying Squad.

Dennigen was sentenced to three years' penal servitude and twelve strokes of the cat. Tyfield received five years' penal servitude and Vaughan-Harrison and Stucky, nine and six months' imprisonment respectively, and twelve strokes each of the birch. And if at first sight, it might be thought that three or five years' incarceration for an offence of robbery, aggravated by a woman being beaten senseless, was rather soft, nothing could be further from the truth. There was nothing easy then about penal servitude, still less with flogging or birching. The judiciary believed in giving the Flying Squad firm backing.

★   ★   ★

As the Metropolitan Police's fleet grew in size, so did the number of accidents to pedestrians and other road users. It was undoubtedly pleasing for the Squad to read the fulsome plaudits of the *Daily Mail's* 'Special Correspondent' on 28 August 1931 with the headlines: 'Lives risked in pursuits' followed by 'Terror of the car criminals'. The journalist in this case was referring to Squad officers' lives being put at risk, and the terror was being experienced by the car criminals themselves. Describing a car chase in which the reporter was allegedly a passenger in a Flying Squad vehicle and which was almost certainly the product of an over-active journalistic imagination, the correspondent enthused:

> The men of the Metropolitan Police Flying Squad have become a daredevil organization which stops at nothing. They have been given orders to catch the bandits at all costs – and they catch them.

However, in the first few months of 1934, the accident:mileage ratio in which police vehicles were involved rose to one accident per 8,000 miles. The press rightly levelled grave criticism at the police and the Commissioner, Marshall of the RAF, the Lord Trenchard, GCB, OM, GCVO, DSO, having asked the racing driver, the Earl of Cottenham, to devise a course of instruction, now asked Sir Malcolm Campbell (holder of the land speed record during the 1920s and 30s) to test a number of police drivers. Having done so, in a notice issued to the press, Sir Malcolm said:

> Recently, I was asked by the commissioner to test a number of police drivers, to give my general impressions of their efficiency as drivers ... and to make suggestions relative to the system of instruction of men destined to serve in the Flying Squad ... The drivers selected for test were drawn from all sections of the Force. Several were sent out in types of car they had never driven before. The cars ranged from fast vehicles used by the Flying Squad, to one of the radio vans used for intercommunication

between headquarters and other mobile cars. The general ability of the drivers, I found to be high ... I made many notes during the test, and found that the officers showed courtesy and care for other road users.

Not to be outdone, Chief Inspector Dan Gooch added his own comments, saying:

Many people think that Squad work is all speed and reckless driving but this is far from being the case. Speed is only employed as a means towards catching the criminal and police drivers abusing the capacity of their cars are liable to the severest penalties. It is this which accounts for the Squad hardly ever being in any serious accident involving the public. In fact, it is the crews of the police cars who daily face a risk of death by an accident.

However, it was clear that inadequate training facilities were responsible for there not being a higher standard of driving overall and in January 1935, the Metropolitan Police driving school opened at Hendon; it would become a worldwide model for the instruction of driving for police officers. And with the Yard's Information Room which had opened in 1933, messages for the Flying Squad vehicles (as well as their divisional counterparts) flashed across the capital's airwaves.

In a memo dated 3 May 1933, the Assistant Commissioner (Crime) stated that drivers and wireless operators, who, until then had formed part of the Yard's A3 Branch (and were receiving five shillings per week – twenty-five pence – in lieu of overtime) should henceforth be under the sole control of the chief inspector in charge of the Flying Squad. A year later, the ACC mentioned that the head of the Squad combined this post with other duties; the memo was passed to the commissioner, who decreed that the chief inspector in charge of the Squad should devote his full time to running the Squad and supervising its staff. It was a worthy thought and a justifiable one, but with the lack of senior officers to carry out other important duties (especially during the intervening war years) this course of action would have to be put on hold until the Squad became a separate entity in 1948.

★   ★   ★

By July 1933, the fast cars of the Flying Squad were as follows: a Talbot, an Alvis, two Lagondas, two Bentleys, three Invictas and four Ford V8 saloons, plus three tourers, namely a Bentley and two Invictas.

However, it had become clear that only cars with part-fabric bodies were really suitable for transmitting messages; the Invictas were ideal, as was the Talbot 105, but not the Lagondas. In August 1934, a trial was carried out on a Lagonda, where the aerial was constructed from a length of copper gauze, lashed to wooden blocks underneath the car's running boards and this initially proved successful. However, when the same tests were carried out on a Ford saloon, it was discovered that the signal strengths dropped considerably when the vehicle was more than two miles distant from the Yard. Matters began to improve after a receiver, in a modified form, from the Philco Radio and Television Corporation was used in conjunction with the running board aerial.

The driving skills of George 'Jack' Frost have already been mentioned, but he was far from being alone in his expertise at driving the fast Squad cars. Police Constable Charlie Dye road-tested a Lagonda, a green open tourer nick-named 'The Green Hornet' along the Eastern Avenue, a long stretch of road linking east London with the boundaries of the Essex Constabulary. After the speed of the Lagonda reached 100mph, the passenger and newcomer to the Squad, Bob Higgins, shakily informed Dye that the car's performance appeared satisfactory and that it would now be acceptable to return to a more prudent speed.

Police Constable Morrie Wells had other attributes in addition to driving; thought to be one of the strongest men in the Force, he never once had to resort to using his truncheon and his abilities in a rough-house with his iron-hard fists were much sought after in times of trouble. He was Detective Sergeant Arthur 'Squeaker' Veasey's driver – and Veasey was not considered to be a slouch in the fisticuffs department, either. When dealing with recalcitrant prisoners, it was said to be a pleasure to see the workmanlike way in which he dealt with them.

Police Constable Bob Edney was another legendary Squad driver, albeit a short-lived one. Immaculately dressed, he was known as 'The Duke of Bermondsey' (from whence he caught the 8.34 train every morning to Charing Cross), and had received a string of commendations for his driving skills. One such was from the commissioner on 28 February 1933 for, 'courage and determination for driving a police motor car in pursuit of men in possession of a stolen motor car and housebreaking implements and effecting an arrest'– for which he was also granted a monetary award as well as being commended by the magistrate at West London police court. He also received a more unofficial monetary award of £10, after Ted Greeno, who was following a gang of counterfeiters on board a train from Harwich to Liverpool Street, had bet against Edney racing the train in his Squad Lagonda the seventy-one miles to its destination.

A story that went into Squad folklore was when a Squad Lagonda was being driven, very quickly, through the City of London by a man in immaculate attire and in attempting to slip through the gap between the kerb line and a taxi, the Lagonda clipped the taxi's fender and ripped it right off. The Squad driver stopped and got out to exchange particulars, but the cab driver was in a fury over the accident. He screamed and raved until, wearied by this tirade, the Squad driver picked up the fender, drawled, 'Yours, I believe?' and with that rammed the fender right through the taxi's windscreen. Coincidentally, Edney was returned to divisional duties shortly thereafter; not that he should necessarily be held to have been the culprit – after all, there was another Lagonda on the Squad fleet at the time.

One of the finest Squad vehicles ever, arrived in July 1935. The Railton Special had been built by Messrs Thompson and Taylor of Brooklands at a cost of £521 14s 0d. The road tests which were carried out by the Yard's D1 (Transport) Branch during 1–7 July 1935 revealed 'with regard to the Railton's speed there was no opportunity to test its maximum performance but on the Great North Road amongst traffic and a strong headwind, it reached 95 mph with excellent acceleration in all gears.' The powerful 4168cc engine gave acceleration of 0–60 mph in 8.5 seconds, and it could stop in 25 feet from a speed of 30 mph. The cars were extensively tested by Flying Squad drivers and in a report to the commissioner, the head of Engineering declared, 'the car is unequalled at present in rapid acceleration,' adding, 'in my opinion, there is no car in the country that could pass it on the London streets.' A fleet of these superlative cars were acquired and they remained with the Squad for many years.

★ ★ ★

Dan Gooch retired as head of the Squad in 1935. The former gamekeeper from Norfolk was greatly admired and had been awarded a staggering 109 commissioner's commendations, but it was a short-lived retirement; sadly, five months later he was killed in a car accident on the Guildford by-pass. He was succeeded by Chief Inspector Alec Duncan (later to be appointed Assistant Commissioner of Police in Victoria, Australia), before Fred Sharpe took the reins in 1936 for a disappointingly short nine months before his retirement. And the following year saw the retirement of Walter Hambrook. He had risen to the rank of superintendent and was affectionately referred to as 'The Father of the Squad'. Sharpe's successor was Chief Inspector Donaldson and in January 1938 he requested a 'better class of officer' should be recruited for the Squad, rather than selecting officers who were already part of the C1 establishment and who might be quite unsuited for Squad work. Superintendent Askew broadly supported this initiative but instead of simply asking for volunteers, suggested to the ACC that divisional detective inspectors should put up the names of suitable applicants. The ACC agreed in principal but did add that he could foresee difficulties with wanting to pluck the best men from divisional stations, sentiments with which the commissioner concurred.

In addition, a matter that was causing Donaldson serious unease was the number of sophisticated breaking offences that were taking place, particularly where they involved explosives. He was right to be concerned. From that time, right up to the commencement of the war, explosives would figure prominently in the Flying Squad's workload.

Between March and November of 1938, no fewer than thirty-six safes were blown open and their contents plundered. The responsibility for the majority of these offences was the work of a gang led by Edward Chapman.

Chapman was an army deserter, petty thief and blackmailer who had drifted into safebreaking after he had taken a chisel and ripped the back off a dilapidated safe in the Fyffes Banana Factory offices. Later, with the assistance of his colleagues George Darry and Hugh Anson, he turned to explosives and became more and more sophisticated in their use. Chapman discovered that when a safe's lock was blown with explosives, the whole mechanism momentarily bulged outwards. Therefore, the method that he used was to insert a small amount of gelignite into a condom, which he carefully inserted into the lock and then tamped into place with chewing gum. He then hung the office typewriter (they were heavy manual machines) on a piece of string from the safe's handle. As the gelignite blew and the lock's mechanism fleetingly expanded, so the weight of the typewriter caused the handle to drop, thereby opening the safe. Not only did this method save on the quantity of gelignite being used, it also stopped undue damage being caused to the safe's contents and of course, caused far less noise.

So whilst Chapman & Co. were enjoying a lucrative crime wave, the press informed their readers that Scotland Yard had formed a 'Gelignite Squad' who were convinced that they were hunting an American gang, because of the chewing gum being inserted in the locks of the safes. Not a bit of it. The tough and resourceful Ted Greeno of the Squad knew precisely who was responsible, thanks to his racetrack informants and he was hot on Chapman's tail.

But in November 1938, Greeno had received some excellent information regarding another gang of safeblowers who intended to raid a department store in Cranbrook Road, Ilford. Greeno and a sergeant positioned themselves in the store, the gang duly arrived and, believing Greeno to be the night-watchman, launched an attack on him. It was a huge mistake. Greeno drew his truncheon and went into action, and later admitted that when the lights were switched on he'd been 'appalled' – the white walls of the office and the floor were splattered with so much of the offenders' blood that it resembled the interior of a jam sandwich. He was even more horrified when he discovered that one of the gang had eight-and-a-half sticks of 'Polar Ammon' gelignite in his pockets and another had a quantity of detonators in his; it was somewhat amazing that his thrashing of these men had not caused him and the gang to be blown up. James Robertson was sentenced to three years' penal servitude, John Fairley to five years' penal servitude and James Painter was bound over to keep the peace. Greeno was congratulated by the Justices at Stratford Petty Sessions, awarded £10 from the Bow Street Reward Fund and notched up his seventy-fourth commendation from the commissioner.

Back now, to the exploits of Chapman and his gang of safeblowers. Greeno's net was tightening around them and after they had blown a safe in Bournemouth in February 1939 and fled to the Channel Island of Jersey, Greeno discovered their whereabouts. A message to the island's police resulted in the arrest of Anson and Darry who were returned to the United Kingdom, Greeno and imprisonment. Chapman, however, escaped, broke into a safe, was arrested and under Jersey law was sentenced to two years' in jail.

Following the German occupation of the island in 1940, Chapman offered his services to the invaders as a spy. Accepted, he was parachuted into England where he offered to become a double agent, providing that all of his outstanding crimes were expunged from the record. This offer too, was taken up; Chapman ended the war with a clean sheet, the German Iron Cross and the knowledge that, very unusually, Greeno's plans for awarding him at least ten years' penal servitude had been thwarted.

But explosives used in the furtherance of opening safes were not the only combustible devices causing great concern to the police. On 12 January 1939, an IRA offensive commenced on the mainland. There came a rash of fifty-nine incendiary incidents, in which damage was caused to power stations, Hammersmith Bridge, an aqueduct on the North Circular Road, and main and Underground rail stations. On 24 June, a bomb exploded in Piccadilly Circus; it would be one of six such explosions that night, where twenty people sustained injuries. Running to the scene from his office in Vine Street police station, Detective Inspector Bob Fabian spotted a second device. He pulled a detonator from one of the ten sweating (and therefore, very unstable) sticks of gelignite and then, to ensure no more detonators were concealed in any of the other four ounce sticks of 'Polar Ammon', Fabian took out his pocket knife and cut them all to pieces before taking them back to the police station, where he deposited them in fire buckets. Highly commended by the commissioner, Fabian was awarded £15 from the Bow Street Reward Fund and a well-deserved King's Police Medal for gallantry – and later became chief of the Flying Squad.

Special Branch were responsible for detecting and arresting many of the IRA terrorists; in July 1939 twelve SB officers were commended by the commissioner in a case of conspiracy to cause explosions, including two, unnamed women police officers, obviously undercover, who were highly commended. Two months later, a further dozen Special Branch officers were commended in a similar case, plus six more in the following month.

Not that the Squad themselves were idle during this difficult and testing time. Tall, thin Detective Constable Matthew Brinnand had arrived on the Flying Squad in 1938, having served seven years in London's 'C' Division, where he had established a reputation for being a very tough customer and one not to be crossed. A year later, he met up with newly promoted Detective Sergeant (Second Class) John Neville Gosling. He, too was tall, but massively built. The men shared an impressive array of informants, Brinnand's from the West End, Gosling's from the East End and North London, who queued up to provide both men with information – Gosling, because the informants liked the big man who often turned a blind eye to their lesser transgressions, Brinnand, because they were too frightened of him to do anything else. It was one of Brinnand's informants, a prostitute, who would provide an impressive input against the IRA's mainland offensive.

One week before the outbreak of the Second World War, Brinnand received information that an IRA gang were planning to plant three large bombs at New Scotland Yard, Westminster Abbey and the Bank of England, to explode simultaneously on 25 August. That morning, Brinnand, Gosling and Special Branch officers raided 32 Leinster Gardens, Bayswater, where they discovered three bombs, each containing 28lb of potassium chlorate, as well as sticks of gelignite and detonators, hidden in a ladies' hat-box. All the devices were fitted with clockwork alarm clocks, timed to explode the bombs simultaneously at 2.30 that afternoon; in addition, two box tricycles and a carrier bicycle had been obtained for transporting the devices to their respective destinations. John Evans, Daniel Jordan, James O'Regan and John Gibson, all Irishmen in their early twenties, were arrested at the house.

At precisely 2.30, as the four men were being locked-up, a massive explosion rocked Coventry; a bomb left in the basket of a tradesman's bicycle, which had been left in Broadgate, exploded, leaving five people dead and fifty others injured. Shortly afterwards, Brinnand's informant, urgently requested a further meeting. Brinnand was told that one of the persons responsible for the outrage was Peter Barnes and at 8.45 that evening Barnes was arrested by Brinnand and Gosling at 176 Westbourne Terrace, Paddington, where a search revealed more explosives.

The four young Irishmen were each sentenced to twenty years' penal servitude. Early the following year at Warwick Assizes, Peter Barnes was found guilty of the murders in Coventry, as was his associate, James Richards. Before sentencing, Barnes said, 'My Lord, as a member of the Irish Republican Army, I am not afraid to die as I am doing it for a just cause. God bless Ireland and the men who have fought and died for her.' Both men were hanged at Winson Green Prison in February 1940.

Brinnand lost a valuable informant in the prostitute, whose handbag bulged with the unprecedented £1,000 reward as she took a last look at England from the deck of the liner bound for a new life in Australia, but Brinnand and his contemporaries had other matters to contend with. Although the threat from the IRA had largely abated after another ninety conspirators were convicted, receiving prison sentences of between ten and twenty years, Britain was now at war with Germany and the Flying Squad would have its own battles to fight on the streets of London.

The War Years

For the second time in the space of a few years, England was plunged into world war. *Police Orders* dated 31 August 1939 stated that former Inspector Hedges, warrant No. 91782 had rejoined the Force and was posted to 'A' Division; three days later, war was declared. Hedges was the first of 27,000 police pensioners and special constables recruited to form a War Reserve for the duration. To start with, a block was put on regular police officers from joining the armed services, although by the end of 1939, reservists were allowed to rejoin their units. In 1941 this rule was relaxed and police officers were permitted to volunteer for the Royal Air Force and in the following year, officers were allowed to join the Royal Navy and the Army. Over 4,000 Metropolitan Police officers were called up.

In September 1939, believing that air attacks from Germany were imminent, evacuation of schoolchildren and 'priority classes' commenced. For the first time since 1918, ration books were issued and in addition, identity cards were introduced. In November, butter and bacon were rationed, the price of petrol rose and during the following month, sugar and meat were also rationed. It was the beginning of years of austerity. The traders passed on to the Food Office a list of supplies that they expected to sell, based on the regulations and these lists were passed on to the Ministry of Supply.

A chill wind heralded the arrival of 1940 and for the first time in fifty years, the Thames froze over. On 1 January, two million men and women were called up to join the armed forces and another 1,700,000 men and women joined the Home Guard. Londoners carried their gas masks everywhere and when the expected air attacks failed to materialize, they declared that it was a 'phoney war'; though in just a few months their attitude would change. The structure of the Government had already changed. Neville Chamberlain had been a brilliant Chancellor of the Exchequer during the 1930s; as Prime Minister he was weak and vacillating and he resigned. On 10 May 1940, Winston Churchill formed a coalition government and Hitler's push against the west commenced.

With the commencement of the war, Chief Inspector Donaldson's tenure as the Squad's chief was coming to a close; but not before he and Ted Greeno had carried out a rather unusual investigation. Greeno borrowed his former right-hand man, Bob Higgins (then a detective sergeant (first class) on 'G' Division) to accompany a Squad team to Aldershot. It was there that Cove Camp was being built to house Canadian troops, with an intended completion date of 1 January 1940 – obviously a rush-job. However, serious discrepancies had been revealed in the payroll; it was discovered that East End thieves and pickpockets were drawing three sets of wages at three different pay desks, every Friday evening. Twenty young layabouts who were supposedly employed as cable-layers and who were playing cards around the back of the sheds at the camp site got the shock of their lives as the Squad officers strolled in, just before pay-time. However, a governmental decision was made not to prosecute the organizers of the scam, as it was thought that completing the camp took precedence over everything else – plus, of course, such revelations would have 'added to the public disquiet'. Instead, some of the small fry were charged with larceny and miscellaneous offences and, as Bob Higgins told me, 'we cleared out the riff-raff.'

But as far as the Flying Squad was concerned, 1940 had got off to a rousing start, with Peter Henderson Beveridge appointed as the new detective chief inspector. The son of a police constable, Beveridge had been born in Largo, Fife. During the First World War, he saw active service with the Seaforth Highlanders, and after being wounded and demobilized, he joined the Metropolitan Police in December 1919. In common with many young officers at that time, Beveridge was impressed and indeed, inspired by Wensley and after joining the CID, he teamed up with Ted Greeno in the early 1920s and they waged their own private war on the East End pickpockets. Serving a short tour on the Flying Squad as a detective inspector in 1934, he met and worked with men like Henry 'Chesty' Corbett, whom he described as being, 'tough, clever and unorthodox, with a terrier-like ability to shake a case until every prisoner was arrested.' Beveridge had a tremendous array of talent to work with on the Squad – the detective inspectors under his command were Greeno, Dance, Black, Capstick and Ball – and his debut as the head of the Squad was about to be put to the test.

On 10 February 1939, a notorious criminal named Charles 'Ruby' Sparks had been sentenced to a very well-deserved five years' penal servitude at Kingston Assizes for burglary. Exactly eleven months later, Sparks decided that he was due for a little unofficial parole and escaping from Dartmoor Prison, he sought the companionship of his lover, Lillian Goldstein, who was otherwise known as 'the Bobbed-haired Bandit' and who, at a time when few women possessed driving licences, was an expert driver of getaway cars. They teamed up with Billy Hill, then at his peak for carrying out smash and grab raids, and achieved some spectacular successes until Hill got himself arrested. He had attempted a smash and grab at a jeweller's shop in Conduit Street, in company with Georgie Ball and Harry Bryan (Sparks and Goldstein were not involved), and all three men were taken into custody. That occurred on 26 June.

Several Flying Squad officers have stated that it was by continually following Goldstein, that five months and sixteen days after his escape from Dartmoor (a record at the time) Sparks, with an impressive sun tan and wearing dark glasses, was spotted near the Ritz Cinema, Neasden. No doubt they had carried out the tailing of Goldstein. But coincidentally, the day after Hill's arrest, with Bob Higgins using his private Hillman saloon, and with the services of Woman Police Sergeant (Second Class) Stratton and Woman Police Constable 72'C' Gilchrist, as well as just about every serving Flying Squad officer on duty, there was an explosion of police as Sparks was pounced upon outside the cinema.

However, Sparks was not only in possession of an identity card in the name of Johnson, he was also a rubber-faced master of disguise and he commenced an elaborate attempt to bluff his way out of the situation, by claiming that he had been the victim of a case of mistaken identity. With Beveridge and Greeno looking on, the embarrassment and confusion spread, though some of the Flying Squad officers later claimed that they had identified Sparks or that he had blurted out his true identity to them. In fact, the discomfiture went further – when Sparks had been taken into Willesden Green police station various Squad officers bickered amongst themselves in front of Sparks, the majority of them saying that they had arrested the wrong man and that he should be released forthwith.

This must have been sweet music to Sparks' ears. Fortunately, the problem was solved after the hawk-faced (and very junior) Detective Constable Matthew Brinnand, who had been present at Kingston Assizes when Sparks had been sent down, marched over to the arguing officers and snapped, 'Let him go if you want to, but if you do, I'll arrest him on the pavement outside, because I am telling you, that man is Sparks!' Realizing the game was up, Sparks grudgingly admitted his identity.

Later at the Old Bailey, Sir Gerald Dodson, the Recorder of London, perhaps somewhat surprisingly sentenced Sparks to twelve months' hard labour, to run concurrently with his interrupted sentence and Goldstein, to six months' hard labour. Even more surprising was the fact that the Recorder later called Goldstein back and altered her sentence so that she was bound over for three years, 'a leniency she does not deserve,' irritably intoned Detective Superintendent Alec Bell of C1 Department. Ten of the army of police officers who took part in Sparks' arrest – including, quite possibly, some who were taken in by him – were commended by the commissioner. It was a time of highs and lows. Three days after receiving his commendation, Matthew Brinnand was promoted to detective sergeant (second class). It was to Bob Higgins' considerable embarrassment that he discovered that Sparks' sun-tan had been acquired over a period of weeks at Kingsbury's Swimming Pool – situated less than a mile from Higgins' home address.

So perhaps this débâcle was a matter best forgotten – or was it? Sparks was caught on the day following Hill's arrest – Sparks, who had been participating pretty-well full-time with Hill in his series of smash and grab raids. Hill, it is known, was a drinking companion of Messrs Beveridge, Greeno and Higgins and it is a fact that following his arrest, there was a meeting between Beveridge and Hill. Did Beveridge make Hill an offer he felt he couldn't refuse? Perhaps. But if Hill did prop up Sparks to Beveridge, it would explain how Hill – already sporting an imposing criminal pedigree, having been birched, sentenced to substantial terms of imprisonment and penal servitude, as well as being the undisputed leader of the gang – was subsequently sentenced to just two years' imprisonment for that offence, whilst his associates each received three years.

Matters can be pursued a little further than that. Following Sparks' arrest, he and Beveridge had a long, amicable chat. Obviously, he did not admit the offences which he had carried out with Hill (or Goldstein) but unmistakably, he would have wished to make his next step in the world of incarceration as comfortable as possible. Sparks had been just twenty-seven when he was sentenced to three years' penal servitude for burglary; it did not take him long before he sawed his way through the bars of his cell at Strangeways Prison, nor was it long before he was recaptured. But in 1930, he had been sentenced to five years' penal servitude for burglary, to be followed with five years' preventative detention. Taking an active role in the Dartford Prison mutiny of 1932, he was sentenced to an additional four years' imprisonment; and now, he had been recaptured having just commenced his sentence of five years' penal servitude. With these remarkable credentials nobody, least of all Sparks, would have been surprised to have had the book thrown at him. Instead, he had not a day added to his sentence.

Also, shortly after his arrest a Flying Squad team just happened to be keeping observation in Mayfair when a gang attempted a smash and grab and the Squad officers bagged Charlie Gibbs and Franny Daniels, a close Hill associate. All a series of coincidences? Possibly. Whatever deals were struck in those days on the Flying Squad, the details were never documented.

Whilst the Squad's personnel was still retained at fifty, the fleet had increased to seventeen, and both the men and vehicles were much needed when on 21 October that year, Detective Superintendent Thorpe dispatched a team to assist 'C' Division. In addition to dealing with the devastation caused by the Blitz which had commenced a month previously, the already overworked West End officers were tackling 4,584 cases of looting that had been reported. By the time they were returned to normal duties in April 1941, the Flying Squad had achieved great success in detecting the looters; in some cases, air-raid wardens were found to be responsible and the sentences of five years' penal servitude which were imposed on those convicted of looting served as a salutary warning to others. The Squad also helped in the six-month-long task of tracing and arresting a gang of handbag snatchers, who were taking full advantage of the blackout to ply their trade.

The German air-raids on London had now started in earnest

on a daily basis and whilst Beveridge was visiting West End Central police station at Savile Row, and had gone for a drink with some of the resident CID officers in a nearby pub, a parachute mine exploded, destroying his car, killing four police constables and causing twenty-six injuries to personnel at the Station. Eight months later the Commissioner, Sir Philip Woolcott Game GCB, GCVO, GBE, KCMG, DSO, also had a lucky escape when a high-explosive bomb scored a direct hit on the office above his at New Scotland Yard. Fortunately, he was absent from his office as tons of rubble crashed down on his desk.

Crime – in particular, sexual and violent offences, increased dramatically at this time. When spirits and cigarettes were available they carried heavy customs duty. These, and food supplies, goods and clothing, became prime targets for thieves and receivers. Normally law-abiding citizens were now tempted to break the law in order to survive and the Government imposed colossal fines and swingeing sentences of hard labour and even penal servitude, often to first-time offenders. Much of the battle against the black marketeers, the high-value thefts and the army deserters fell to the Squad to deal with, causing an exasperated Hugh Young, the Chief Constable of the CID to report to Sir Norman Kendall, the Assistant Commissioner (Crime) in a fiercely patriotic report:

> Black market offences have been the main cause of the extra work and it is pleasing to see that the *sewer rats and traitors* who impede the war effort by committing this class of offence are being brought to justice.

Greatly assisting the sewer rats and traitors on their way was Jack Capstick. At the insistence of Capstick's old friend and mentor, Alf Dance, Capstick had been summonsed from his demanding role of detective inspector (second class) at Bow Street to help the Squad smash the organized gangs. For almost exactly four years, Capstick did just that, as he and his team rampaged through the underworld, working incredibly long hours, meeting informants, carrying out observations, making arrests. When two Glaswegians were overheard by a snout discussing the price per thousand of stolen coupons in the lounge of a West End hotel, Capstick arrested them, in possession of 305,000 such coupons, stolen from the Glasgow Post office the previous week. One commendation followed another as Capstick arrested a gang of warehousebreakers and their receiver, then a gang of lorry thieves plus their receiver, who had eluded justice for some considerable time and who Capstick saw sentenced to five years' penal servitude. More commendations followed when Capstick arrested a team of shopbreakers with, naturally, their receiver and then it was the turn of a gang who attempted to break into a shop. It was perhaps after the best such coup that Alf Dance awarded Capstick the nickname by which he would be known by his colleagues and the underworld for the rest of his service.

Capstick had spent weeks working, quite literally around the clock, before he finally netted a gang who had stolen a large quantity of silk. As he sat sipping tea in the canteen at Old Street police station, in walked Beveridge and Alf Dance who strongly praised Capstick. When Dance asked him how he had achieved such an outstanding result, Capstick replied that he (Dance) only worked his men fourteen hours a day, whereas his (Capstick's) men did eighteen – on early closing days. 'Hark at him,' laughed Dance to Beveridge. 'Old Charlie Artful, himself!'

Not that Alf Dance was a slouch at arresting thieves. A former First World War soldier, after he joined the Flying Squad as a detective constable he never left, rising through the ranks until he was promoted to divisional detective inspector. Working his own squad to the limits during the war, he was commended by the commissioner in 1940 for unspecified work in connection with terrorist explosions, and four months later there was another commendation for arresting a receiver, followed by another in a case of storebreaking and receiving. An expert in disguise, he was able to get close to pickpockets to see exactly what they were doing before arresting them; not once did the pickpockets recognize him, even though he had usually arrested them many times previously.

Squad arrests climbed steadily: 663 in 1940, 767 in 1941, 862 in 1942. And when the Squad were not working an average sixteen-hour day, many could be found tearing rubble apart with their bare hands as they assisted the rescue squads, pulling survivors from bomb damaged houses. When a doctor crawled into the flooded wreckage of a house to aid an injured couple, a Flying Squad officer swam across the crater, using his body to shield them from falling debris and the threat of a collapsing wall.

Army deserters (some of them armed) and looters were wiped up by the Squad, even as the more traditional Flying Squad work was carried out. When a call was sent out regarding a suspect car in Bond Street, a Flying Squad car patrolling nearby surprised a gang just about to attach grappling hooks to a jeweller's window. A high-speed chase ensued which ended with the gang's car being forced to a standstill, followed by an inevitable punch-up. The Squad won.

One rather unusual case involved a gang of fraudsters who obtained employment for a young woman as a kennel maid at Wembley Dog Track and then attempted to persuade her to dope specified dogs. Instead, she reported the matter to Detective Sergeant John Gosling and he, and his fellow sergeant, Arthur 'Squeaker' Veasey carried out a series of observations before, on the evening of 4 July 1942, they burst into the gang's flat at Bryanston Square. Apart from seizing boxes of the drug, Corytone, which acts on the nervous system of dogs, they also apprehended two members of the gang who were too surprised to put up any resistance and were subsequently sentenced to two years and nine months' imprisonment, respectively. The third member of the gang was a prison escapee who, given both Gosling's and Veasey's ability in the fisticuffs department, unwisely put up a fierce resistance. The trial judge sentenced him to two years' imprisonment, to commence after his existing sentence expired.

It was little wonder that as early as the summer of 1943, in a report to the ACC, Beveridge was 'praised all the way through' for his leadership.

In March 1943, when Detective Sergeant Grantford of the Squad raided the flat of one Hyman Schnatz he discovered a £3,000 'float' which Schnatz was using to obtain women's stockings and underwear without clothing coupons; he was accordingly sentenced to two months' hard labour, with the promise of another two months if he failed to pay a £500 fine.

When the Ministry of Food launched an investigation into the activities of Seymour Sydney who, it was alleged, was masterminding a huge conspiracy to supply grocers, restaurateurs, and warehouses with enormous amounts of rationed foodstuffs, Detective Sergeant Henry Clark from the Flying Squad was seconded to the case. A master at the art of surveillance, Clark followed Sydney's slippery trail for weeks until there was sufficient evidence to justify a round-up of the gang. Six of the men who appeared at Bow Street police court on 18 April 1942 were committed to the Old Bailey for sentencing; Sydney, the ringleader, was given four years' penal servitude and ordered to pay a fine of £2,000; hopefully, he did so, because he was ordered to remain in prison until the fine was paid. The five other men received lesser sentences and during the week of their trial, eighty-six other prosecutions were dealt with and exactly two months after the conclusion of the trial, Clark was commended by the commissioner for 'ability and persistence in a difficult case under the Food Orders and Defence Regulations.'

In 1944, two teenagers, who had robbed a Soho wine store at gunpoint, were kept under observation by Detective Sergeant Compton and his Flying Squad team who heard them planning a further robbery outside a jeweller's shop. Arrested before they could implement the plan, a search of the home of one of the youthful robbers revealed a large quantity of ammunition, a tommy-gun, three revolvers and two masks.

Thieves broke into a showroom in Western Road, Brighton and got away with furs, valued at £1,000 on 14 March 1945; not for long, though. Information regarding their vehicle was received by the Yard and as the thieves neared the outskirts of London, so a chase by Flying Squad cars began. The gang's car headed for the East End where, throwing some of the stolen furs from their car, they turned into a Whitechapel side-street, careered across a bomb site, into the Commercial Road and came to an abrupt halt by driving straight into a building. The following day, bruised, battered but probably none the wiser, the larcenous trio made an appearance at Brighton Police Court.

★　★　★

All through the war, that indefatigable duo, John Gosling and Matthew Brinnand kept up a relentless fight against London's criminals. When Gosling was commended for arresting a receiver, so was Brinnand, as they were in many cases of conspiracy and receiving, of burglary and receiving and larceny and receiving.

By the end of 1945, John Gosling had been promoted to detective sergeant (first class) and was serving on 'C' Division and Jack Capstick was the divisional detective inspector of 'W' Division. Since his impressive work with the Ministry of Food,

Henry Clark had served on 'Z' and 'W' Divisions and, in July 1945, had been promoted to the rank of detective inspector (second class) and had been returned for his third posting to the Flying Squad. Only Matthew Brinnand had remained constantly on the Squad.

However, it would not be too long before the four men were to be reunited as a team, in a unit the like of which the Metropolitan Police had never seen before and after its demise, would never see again.

The Ghost Squad and the
Post-war Years

With six years of war at an end, Londoners sat back and licked their wounds. During the war crime had gone through the roof and, in 1945, indictable offences had reached a record level of 128,954. Whenever spirits and cigarettes were available, they carried heavy customs duty and these commodities, together with food supplies, goods and clothing (which were only legally available with the requisite ration coupons) became the targets for thieves and receivers. Men and women who had never previously considered doing anything illegal stole goods from work, obtained ration coupons using false names and purchased stolen or forged ration coupons. Companies overcharged on Government contracts, accounts were falsified and Civil Servants were bribed to secure contracts. Army deserters flooded into London where ration coupon and black market offences had become commonplace.

But with a combination of the rising crime figures, the rationing which would soon substantially increase and with the Metropolitan Police 4,000 men short, circumstances dictated that a revolutionary concept be implemented in order to deal with this predicament. Percy Worth MBE had succeeded Hugh Young as Chief Constable of the CID and, like his predecessor, he was a highly experienced detective and he provided the answer.

* * *

Worth suggested that a small group of experienced officers, preferably with a Flying Squad background and with their own proven sources of information, be detached from ordinary duties to infiltrate the organized gangs responsible for this shocking upsurge in crime. The information which was passed back by them would be acted upon by Flying Squad or divisional CID officers and the selected officers would not get involved with the arrests or be required to attend court to give evidence. Furthermore, Worth recommended doubling the funds available in the Informants Fund and never would the officers be required to divulge the names of their informants. A report was submitted to the Assistant Commissioner (Crime), Ronald Howe, who appended his own supportive, forceful remarks to it and forwarded the report to the newly appointed Commissioner, Sir Harold Scott GCVO, KCB, KBE. With a great deal of apprehension, the commissioner sent the report together with his own hesitant recommendations to the Home Office. He need not have worried, they could recognize a good thing when they saw it; it was cheap, it did not require an excess of manpower and it was possible that the scheme could curtail the growing crime wave. It would also offer reassurance that something was being done to combat the lawlessness which was so worrying for a rather shaky newly-formed Labour Government. Within one month of Howe seeing the report, the unit was up and running.

★   ★   ★

The leader of the team was Jack Capstick and no more well-informed officer could have been selected for the task; in turn, he selected Detective Inspector (Second Class) Henry Valentine Clark (he kept quiet about his middle name and was known always as Henry or 'Nobby'). Looking like a particularly benevolent bank manager, Clark's appearance belied his capabilities – he was one of the best-informed officers in South London and was regarded as a terror in a rough-house. The third and fourth members of the team were two of Capstick's Flying Squad contemporaries whom we are already familiar with: John Gosling who had been hastily retrieved from 'C' Division, and Matthew Brinnand.

On New Year's Eve, 1945, Capstick sat in one of the dark, heavy leather armchairs in the Assistant Commissioner (Crime), Sir Ronald Howe's office and puffed contentedly at his pipe, in the way his hero, Wensley used to. He glanced at the other occupants of the room; Howe was there, of course, and Worth, plus Clark, Gosling and Brinnand. He was completely satisfied with his team; what Howe referred to as 'The Special Duty

Squad' would soon be renamed by the popular press as 'The Ghost Squad'.

*   *   *

Ronald Howe surveyed the four men and gave them their terms of reference and in addition, he informed them that they would be released from their present duties and, in an unprecedented move, the room allocated to them would come with a key. A car would be provided for them, they would be able to go anywhere, at any time and they would not be required to book on or off duty.

Howe informed them that a report would be required in six months time to judge their effectiveness, telling the officers that the Special Duty Squad had got to succeed, and adding, 'I know you won't let me down.'

Their informants were pressed into service and within days the arrests started rolling in. The difficulties faced by the informants were enormous. Because the thieves and receivers were playing for such high stakes, they were very careful in whom they confided when they had committed or were contemplating committing an offence. The thieves were highly secretive concerning the location of their run-in, the place where stolen property could be stashed, prior to it being disposed of to the receiver and it was usual for no more than two members of the gang to be aware of the location of the run-in.

Capstick managed to infiltrate the gangs who worked with receivers of stolen property – men who, until now had quite properly considered themselves to be untouchable by the law – with not one, but a pair of informants. Capstick felt that two informants were more inclined to bolster each other's confidence and courage in gleaning the required information; it was good psychology and it worked. There was, of course always the informant who preferred to work alone, but Capstick believed that if they could accept his invitation to work with another informant, twice as much work would be obtained from them. This system proved to be highly successful, but Capstick realized the dangers of the same pair of informants working with two different gangs based in the same district. When it was unavoidable, Capstick ensured that either the Flying Squad or Divisional CID officers from an area quite separate from where the gang was operating made the arrests. On some occasions, informants were split up and were introduced to other informants in different districts and then continued to enjoy further successes. It was not unknown for an informant to work with an undercover police officer and Capstick, for all of his experience, never once lost sight of the fact that informants are a dangerous breed. They required (as he mentioned with masterly understatement) 'tactful handling'; otherwise, they would be running the officer instead of the officer running them. In walking an unsteady tightrope with informants, he was aware of those who would give police information as a cloak to their own criminal activities, yet the squad was obliged to encourage the informants to associate with thieves to the border-line, when the informants had to think of their own safety and communicate with the squad, as soon as possible.

The organized gangs simply did not know what had hit them; no sooner had thieves hi-jacked a lorry and taken it to the receivers' run-in, than they and the receivers were arrested. Post-office robbers would be rudely interrupted as they greedily counted out their spoils and warehousebreakers had hardly finished loading their lorry with lengths of suiting, or carpets, or canteens of cutlery before a Flying Squad Railton would screech to a halt beside them. When a deal concerning the sale of stolen jewellery was being carried out in the street in broad daylight, the look-outs that the thieves had posted disappeared, one by one, to be replaced by Flying Squad officers, wearing the look-outs' hats and raincoats. As the deal went down, the criminals would find themselves surrounded by police officers with the 'buyer' mysteriously disappearing in the confusion. Coupon forgers did not know who to trust when distributing their wares; any one of them could have betrayed them to the Ghost Squad, who were responsible for organizing raids on their centre of operations, there to seize their printing presses, dies, paper – and them.

In their first year of operations, the Ghost Squad was responsible for the arrest of 171 criminals, cleared up 204 offences and recovered stolen property valued at £24,126. In 1947, the squad made 186 arrests and recovered property to the tune of £50,231. The following year, 252 arrests were carried out and property to the value of £81,374 was recovered. In total, in the three years and ten months of its existence, the Ghost Squad was responsible for over 700 arrests, and the recovery of stolen property, valued in excess of £200,000.

When one considers that this was the work of four men – sometimes fewer – the results were nothing less (as the Home Office recorded) than phenomenal.

*   *   *

The Ghost Squad had supplied a great deal of information to the Flying Squad (as well as their divisional counterparts) which had resulted in a number of excellent arrests in the post-war period. It has been readily accepted by several authors that the Ghost Squad informants provided information for a number of other notable cases during their reign in office; the successes of the Barry Redvers Holliday investigation, 'The case of the bank manager' and 'The Battle of Heathrow' have all, at one time or another been attributed to Ghost Squad information. However, none of this is true – the Flying Squad had their own informants to provide them with top quality information.

Just prior to the end of World War Two, Peter Beveridge had been promoted and his place as head of the Squad was taken by Robert Fabian. A well-liked (and well-informed) officer, who had been awarded the King's Police Medal for gallantry in 1940, after immobilizing an IRA bomb in Piccadilly, Fabian, like his predecessor had no sooner settled at his desk when he was whisked away as part of the Murder rota to investigate a case in Warwickshire; it would be one of several. Between times, Fabian settled back into running the Squad. One of the most pressing matters which he had to address was the Flying Squad's fleet; it was in an abysmal condition which urgently needed repair or replacement. The only van used by the Squad was a V8 Ford Tender, which had first been brought into service in February 1934; it now had 97,434 miles on the clock. Fabian went out as a passenger in the van; in his subsequent report in October 1946 to the detective superintendent, he noted that the maximum speed did not exceed 30 mph, the brake drums were oval and huge pressure on the brake pedal was required to bring the vehicle to a standstill. He added that the doors, seats and windscreens rattled continuously and that rain leaked in through the roof and windows.

In addition, Fabian reported that a Flying Squad four-and-a-half litre Bentley had chased a criminal's car, of the same make, at speeds of up to 85 mph over a distance of five miles but had finally lost sight of it. When the Squad driver lifted the bonnet of his Bentley, he discovered that one of the twin carburettors was hanging off the engine and was held on only by the petrol pipe.

Fabian's report was passed to Detective Superintendent Thorpe and in his minute to the ACC, he stated that the report 'leaves one almost dumb and is nothing short of scandalous.' Warming to his theme, Thorpe continued that 'something must be done, even at the expense of other departments. I insist that everything possible should, in fact must, be done to properly equip the Flying Squad with transport adequate to its needs.'

When the report was passed to the Civilian Transport Officer for comment he claimed it was exaggerated, but in view of the post-war breakdown in law and order, the Home Secretary took up the cudgels and with his intervention, the Minister of Supply promised the commissioner that twenty of the Flying Squad fleet would be replaced within eight weeks. In fact, within one month of the Minister's pledge, four Wolseley 18hp saloons and four Humber Super Snipe saloons arrived; the rest followed in the promised time span.

*   *   *

Early in 1946, a series of clothing coupons were distributed which were so perfectly forged that they could only be detected by experts from the Board of Trade. The coupons, which were being distributed very quickly, not only in London but also on the streets of Glasgow, Derby and Brighton, were commanding a fee of over £40 per thousand. The Flying Squad was brought in to investigate this sudden upsurge of forgeries which were flooding the shops and Detective Inspector George Robinson and his team of eleven officers got to work. Suspicion fell on a woman named Burns, after she was heard to boast in a public house in Paddington, 'Coupons, my dear? I can get you thousands.' Unfortunately, it was two Flying Squad officers who overheard her injudicious comment and over a period of weeks she was followed and was seen to pass forged coupons. However, she was not arrested; it was far more important to discover the identity of her supplier.

She was observed in the company of 59-year-old William Watson (he was also known as Roberts) who, two years previously had been released from Dartmoor after serving a five year sentence for counterfeiting half-crown coins and ten shilling notes, and it took two months of shadowing Watson and Burns to lead Robinson's team to a man named Hefferman who, like Burns was a distributor of the forged coupons. Not that this was an easy task; Watson was a master of anti-surveillance techniques, but eventually simultaneous raids were carried out on the three addresses.

Watson's door was kicked in; his address at Elgin Crescent, Notting Hill was found to be the consummate forger's den, complete with camera, darkroom, printing press and a stock of paper with watermarks, showing the insignia of the Stationery Office and a crown; these, together with all of the other associated items for a top-class forgery operation took the Squad seven hours to dismantle. The forty sheets of forged coupons, which Watson admitted were his handiwork, prompted him to add, 'They aren't a bad job, are they?'

Burns was not so forthcoming and initially suggested that the twenty sheets of forged coupons found at her address had been planted, but she later admitted, 'I must be mad to get mixed up with Watson,' adding, 'I know there are thousands of these coupons in Kensington.' Ten more forged sheets were found at Hefferman's address and at the Old Bailey, Watson – alias Roberts – was sentenced to seven years' penal servitude and Burns and Hefferman to twelve months' imprisonment, each. Mrs Hefferman who, at the time of her arrest, scolded her husband, saying, 'This is what comes of mixing with those people,' was acquitted.

★   ★   ★

On 2 January 1946, a shop in Tufnell Park, North London was broken into and a quantity of dresses was stolen. There was nothing particularly remarkable about it; these offences occurred all the time. Almost two weeks later, raiders broke into Honore, a dress shop in South Audley Street, but an alarm was activated and the perpetrators fled empty-handed.

However, a week later, a stolen Humber which was later found to contain the dresses stolen from Tufnell Park, was chased by a police car – the back window of the Humber was smashed and shots were fired at the police and the raiders escaped. Then, on 6

February, there was a smash and grab at the premises of Arline Blundell in Mount Street, Mayfair in the early hours of the morning. The noise attracted the attention of a nearby resident, who looked out of her window – one of the raiders told her to mind her own business or she'd be shot. Within seconds, a stolen Norwegian army lorry appeared and the gang loaded furs valued at £3,000 into it and drove off. A police officer tried to stop the lorry and was shot at. It was high time for the Flying Squad to get involved.

The following day, Detective Inspector William Judge and his team went to a rented flat in Clerkenwell. The occupant, George Albert King was not there, but the Squad recovered two firearms, a Mauser and a Luger, a quantity of ammunition, a knuckleduster, a dagger in a sheath, a jemmy and six bunches of car keys. Their enquiries led them to another premises in St Pancras, a property belonging to a Mrs Ward; there the Squad officers discovered three black Persian Lamb coats, another eleven fur coats, all of which had been stolen from Arline Blundell's premises, plus four revolvers and twenty-one rounds of ammunition. Mrs Ward disclaimed all knowledge but nevertheless, she and her daughter were arrested for receiving stolen goods. In the meantime, Flying Squad officers were waiting at the Clerkenwell flat, where they arrested a soldier, John Papworth. The arrest of the flat's tenant, King, quickly followed. The white-faced, red-haired young tearaway who had been declared unfit for army service and who was dependent on drugs, was quite properly regarded as being highly dangerous and although six of his firearms had been seized, it was quite possible that he was still armed. So when Judge and his team discovered that King was in a West End club, they waited for him to emerge before a pugilistic detective sergeant floored him with one punch. On 8 February, William Vigars was propped up by a Ghost Squad snout and was arrested by 'D' Division officers (this was a commonly used ploy, to disassociate the Flying Squad from the arrest, if it was suspected that the informant was one used by the Squad) and all three men were charged with the Tufnell Park and the Mount Street breakings. King, who also admitted firing at the police officers, did his best to exonerate Mrs Ward and her daughter, saying they knew nothing about the compromising property found at their address, but the evidence against them was thought to be compelling and they, too, were charged. Two more of the gang – Rawson and Morgan – were implicated and three weeks later, they were also arrested. At the Old Bailey, Rawson and the two women were acquitted but the others were sentenced to terms of penal servitude; King receiving the heaviest sentence of seven years and Vigars, four.

*　*　*

Alf Dance retired on 7 July 1946 with the rank of divisional detective inspector, having served twenty-three years on the Flying Squad. Without doubt, Dance was a quintessential Squad officer, leading from the front, guiding junior officers in the ways of Squad cunning. In Jack Capstick's words, 'nobody had more influence on my career than Alf Dance, one of the greatest detectives ever to serve in the Metropolitan Police.' Dance's final commissioner's commendation – his ninety-second – for ability and intelligence in a case of false pretences, was awarded just four months prior to his last day with the Metropolitan Police. He was a colourful character; in 1937, John Horwell, the Chief Constable of the CID reduced his pay by eight shillings per week for twenty-six weeks after Alf had been found guilty on a disciplinary board for 'acting in a manner likely to bring discredit on the reputation of the Force, by behaving in a disorderly manner at a restaurant.' It was a minor set-back; a month later, the irrepressible Alf was commended by the commissioner for his ability in a case of warehousebreaking.

*　*　*

Next, the 'Case of the Bank Manager' which, for cold-blooded courage, took some beating. The Squad received information that Mr Snell, the manager of a Kentish Town bank was going to be attacked and kidnapped on his way home and relieved of his keys, so that the bank could be entered and the contents of the strongroom stolen. It had been decided that the attack would take place on a Friday when the bank held its largest amount of cash.

The bank manager was taken into the Squad's confidence and Detective Sergeant William Hosie Deans, a slim, slightly built officer with a thick moustache, who bore a marked resemblance to Mr Snell, volunteered to take his place. Wearing a topcoat similar to the manager's, Deans was also provided with identical spectacles and a heavily padded bowler hat; it would be needed. And in addition, Deans was provided with letters, addressed to Mr Snell, sets of bank keys and banknotes and coins, all of which had been marked.

On Friday, 7 February 1947, Deans left the bank and walked to the railway station where, using the bank manager's season ticket, he caught a train to Woodside Park and then walked to the manager's home in Holden Road. It was the first of three such excursions; on each occasion, members of the six-handed gang were in the vicinity, as was their van, the details of which, plus the gang's descriptions were noted by the watching Squad officers.

Two weeks later, the gang struck; Deans had seen two of the gang on the platform at Kentish Town station. They boarded the same train as him, got off at Woodside Park and walked ahead of him on his way to the bank manager's house. Suddenly, a third member of the gang hit Deans from behind with a sock, filled with wet sand and weighing three-and-a-half pounds. All protection was lost as his reinforced bowler hat was knocked from his head with the first blow; he was struck on the head four more times before being kicked into unconsciousness. Deans was thrown into the waiting van, which drove off at speed; he was blindfolded, had adhesive tape placed over his mouth and his wrists bound with rope. As the bank's keys were taken from his pocket, together with the marked coins and his wristwatch, Deans heard a concerned gang member say, 'He looks bad. You hit him too hard, Jim.'

The only member of the gang to answer to the name 'Jim' was James Cunningham, who replied, 'It doesn't matter. No one saw us do it.' He was wrong. The attack had been witnessed by Woman Detective Constable Winnie Sherwin and Detective Inspector Len Crawford, but the plan to ambush the gang had gone dramatically wrong. The Flying Squad car waiting to intercept them had failed to start; Sherwin dashed across to a telephone box and called the Yard, so that its description could be circulated.

In the meantime, Deans was thrown from the van in East Barnet; it was a freezing cold night and it had already been snowing continuously for twenty-four hours. He lay in the snow for an hour, before managing to stagger to a nearby house; Dr Charles Mervyn Scott, who was called, expressed the opinion that had Deans lain in the snow for much longer, he would have died.

Detective Inspector Crawford and his team were waiting when Leslie Beck went to open the rear door of the Midland Bank and were highly unimpressed when he told them a couple of men had told him they'd give him 'a hundred nicker' if he opened the bank door for them. Since he was also in possession of a wristwatch belonging to Deans, whose whereabouts were at that time unknown, Crawford carried out a quick interrogation of the prisoner inside a police van. As a result, three of the gang were in custody by midnight and the other two were later arrested at their hide-out in Romford. At the Old Bailey on 27 March 1947, they were sentenced to terms of penal servitude, varying from three to seven years, and totalling twenty-nine years, by Lord Goddard, the Lord Chief Justice. The sentencing completed, Lord Goddard said, 'Stand up, Detective Sergeant Deans,' and then commended the officer for his courage, with the following words:

> The country – and London in particular – are most indebted to you for the extraordinary courage and devotion to duty you have shown in this case. You have added lustre to the already great record of the Force to which you belong. I shall make it my duty to call the attention of the Secretary of State to your most commendable conduct.

Deans, who was off sick for two months and suffered from the effects of his injuries for a considerable time thereafter, was awarded £15 from the Bow Street Reward Fund and was later decorated with the King's Police Medal.

★　★　★

Barry Fieldsen first came to the notice of the police in 1924. It was a comparatively minor offence for which he was convicted – he was pointed out to Bob Lee, a young 'winter patrol' as a local thief – and then Fieldsen faded from police notice. Over twenty years passed. By now, Bob Lee was a detective chief inspector on the Flying Squad and Barry Fieldsen had become Barry Redvers Holliday, a wealthy man-about-town, whose background appeared shrouded in mystery. Obviously he was a man of means, because he attended Hunt Balls, was welcomed at lavish dinner

parties and frequented many of the better racecourses, where he
gambled heavily. Immaculately attired by Savile Row, he owned
several properties (including one in Chelsea and another in
Sunningdale) and a cabin cruiser, a Bentley and a Mercedes. He
could afford to do so, because he specialized in breaking into the
homes of the very rich; it is estimated that during his twenty-five
years of crime, he had amassed a fortune of a quarter of a million
pounds; by today's values, probably in the region of £7 million.

Some of the crimes attributed to Fieldsen included a burglary
at the Mayfair home of Lord and Lady Docker, where jewels
valued at £52,000 were stolen, two burglaries, both at the
Sunningdale home of Miss Marjory Cunliffe-Owen, who lost
precious stones, totalling £40,000 and when he broke into the
London residence of Lord Bearsted, he stole jewels valued at
£20,000.

Matters came to a head on the afternoon of 16 October 1946.
The Duke and Duchess of Windsor had been staying at Ednam
Lodge, Sunningdale, the country estate of their friends, the Earl
and Countess of Dudley. In fact, the Earl and Countess had
vacated the property and moved temporarily to Claridges Hotel,
Mayfair, so that the Duke and Duchess might enjoy the privacy
of their surroundings; either that, or to provide extra space for the
Duchess's luggage, which arrived in three army lorries.

During that afternoon, the Windsors were preparing to leave
for a trip to London. The Duchess had a jewel box which was
locked in a small trunk and this, she had been urged to deposit in
the strongroom at the Lodge. Instead, she opted for her personal
maid to move it into her bedroom. The Windsors set off for
London, the staff went to tea and two hours later the maid
returned to the Duchess's bedroom to discover that the chest had
been forced and the jewel case was missing; the balloon went up.
The furious Duke lost no time in contacting his insurance
company and lodging a claim for half-a-million pounds, although
this was possibly done during a moment's impetuosity; he later
amended the sum to £20,000.

Jack Capstick was detached from his Ghost Squad duties and
raced to the scene; and although he obviously pressed his Ghost
Squad snouts into action, none of them pointed the finger at
Fieldsen. Two suspects who were known to have operated in the
area of Cannes, near to where the Windsors lived in France were
ruled out of the investigation. Far more interesting to Capstick

r Vibart (L) and Tommy Butler (R) – 'The Terrible Twins'

Fred Wensley

Walter Hambrook

DDI Charles Cooper (l
(who headed the Squa
the 1920s) in conversat
with DC Selby, who
figured prominently in
Squad's first motorize
patrol

Bentley, circa 1930,
with Squad officers

(Top) Lea Francis tourer, (Bottom) Crossley Tender

Cars: (Top) Invicta, (Bottom) Railton Special

Officers from the Battle of
Heathrow, 1948: (L to R)
Mickey Dowse, Bob Acott,
Donald MacMillan,
Allan (Jock) Brodie,
George Draper,
John Franklyn

Barry Fieldsen

Tommy Butler and
Reg Roberts at the latter's
retirement

Guests at Reg Roberts'
retirement party: (L to R)
John Simmonds,
Reg Roberts, Dave Dilley

Sir Gordon Richards
imparting information to
Terry O'Connell QPM

A bolus, containing
Notensil for horse-doping

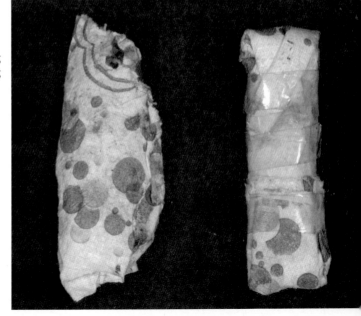

Squad drivers, circa 1959–60, in front of the Flying Squad Property store: (L to R) Bill Foster, George Lloyd, Sid Morris, Archie Stanners, Lofty Taylor, Van Hill, Glyn Powell

Tommy Butler at the end of his service

Card, showing guests at Tommy Butler's retirement

The Last of the Few ?

Flying Squad officers involved in the Glasgow murder and robbery investigation: (L to R Top) 'Nobby' Newson, Fred Snooks, Gordon Dent (Middle) Bert Barnard, Henry Poole, Jock Henderso Peter Elliott, John Batten (Front) Stuart Giblin, Ted Domachowski, Peter Jones, Jack Slipper, Peter Rimmer, Bob Robinson

Four of the Train Robbers' Team: (L to R) Steve Moore, Tommy Thorburn, Lou van Dyke, Jack Slipper

Train Robbers' Team at Tom Butler's funeral: (L to R) Lou van Dyke, Steve Moore, Jim Neville, Frank Williams, Jack Slipper, Sid Bradbury

was 28-year-old Leslie Arthur Charles Holmes who not only lived in Sunningdale but who, at the time of the burglary, was working on the Dudley estate. He was one of many people interviewed but at the time he did not have a criminal record. That changed the following year when he appeared at Surrey Quarter Sessions, pleaded guilty to charges of housebreaking and larceny and asked the court to take another twenty-six cases into consideration. He was sentenced to three years' imprisonment and since Holmes obviously thought that this was an excessive sentence for a first conviction, he appealed. This was a mistake; the Court of Appeal (Criminal Division) thought otherwise and upped his sentence to five years' imprisonment. Capstick, with some justification, felt that Holmes had committed the burglary on the Dudley estate, but this Holmes strenuously denied at the time and continued to do so during the years which followed. Capstick had Holmes's garden dug up, searched his well and continually, over the period of his incarceration, visited Holmes in prison, in the hope that he would confess all. It was not often that Capstick was wrong concerning the guilt of a suspect, but he was on this occasion.

Next, Bob Lee took charge of the investigation. Because so many of the burglaries had taken place in the Sunningdale area, he started to check out the residents of that area, without discovering a likely suspect. The years passed, and Fieldsen's larcenous activities might have remained undetected, since nobody – the police or the public – believed that there was anything remotely suspicious about him; until he made a classic mistake. Just because he was a superior housebreaker, dubbed 'a modern day Raffles' it did not necessarily mean that Fieldsen was going to relinquish petty thieving – after all, a thief is a thief. So it was the height of stupidity for Fieldsen to slip a meat pie from the counter of the Dumb Bell Hotel, Taplow, where he was a regular customer, into his pocket. The barman saw him do it and Fieldsen was aware of this – but he had got away with so much for so long, he contemptuously ignored the warning signs and swaggered out of the pub without paying for the pie. Not that the barman was about to raise a hue and cry; he liked 'The Squire' as Fieldsen was referred to, and he regarded the matter purely as the sort of eccentric behaviour for which the rich are noted. The matter was mentioned jokingly to a local police constable; and the joke reached the ears of Bob Lee at the Yard. The name 'Barry Redvers Holliday' meant nothing to Lee but when he received information that he was also known as Barry Fieldsen, a search at Criminal Records Office resulted in Lee returning to the Sunningdale area, where he kept observation on Fieldsen's house on Friary Island. Through his binoculars, he identified Barry Redvers Holliday as the local, south of the river thief, he had seen twenty-five years previously.

Lee immediately set up a surveillance team, but Fieldsen was blessed with the sixth sense given to all successful thieves. He realized from an early stage of the operation that he was being followed and during the three-month-long operation he moved to Earl's Court Square and used the most sophisticated anti-surveillance methods to shake off his pursuers. On one occasion, when Lee's men received information that Fieldsen and an associate were going to break into a premises, they kept observation only to see Fieldsen and his accomplice drive off at speed on the wrong side of the road. Perhaps, like the pie-stealing incident, he became over-confident but in December 1949, he was seen entering a bank near Sloane Square with a parcel under his arm and left the premises without it. A search warrant was granted and the safe-deposit box – it was rented in the name of Fieldsen's wife – was searched; it revealed gems to the value of £10,000, some of which were identified as being stolen. He was arrested, his house was searched and a large amount of silver and jewellery was found. Fieldsen chose to say nothing; charged with receiving stolen goods he appeared at West London Magistrates' Court on 14 December 1949 where he was granted bail.

Much of the property found in Fieldsen's house was identified as being the proceeds of burglaries and observation was again carried out in the hope that Fieldsen would lead the police to more stolen property. But on 18 December, Fieldsen once again gave his pursuers the slip. He must have known that the net was tightening around him; three days before Christmas, Fieldsen booked into a room at the Wheatsheaf Hotel in Virginia Water where he blew his brains out. Over a period of time, other safe-deposit boxes, rented by Fieldsen were discovered and jewels to a value of £100,000 were recovered. Seventeen of those items were positively identified as being the proceeds of burglaries, dating from 1932 to 1949. Although there was little doubt that Fieldsen was responsible for the burglary at Ednam Lodge, unfortunately none of the recovered jewellery belonged to the Duchess of Windsor.

★   ★   ★

Detective Chief Superintendent Bill 'The Cherub' Chapman took charge of the Flying Squad on 21 May 1948 and five weeks later, the Squad was detached from C1 Department and was given its own separate identity – 'C8 Department'. With Superintendent Bob Lee as his deputy, Chapman got off to a rousing start with 'The Battle of Heathrow' (see Prologue).

The decade came to an end with the arrest of Arthur Parkyn, a very violent character who was wanted for inflicting grievous bodily harm on a police officer. Detective Inspector Bradford and his team had received information that Parkyn was in possession of a stolen Bedford van and that he intended to collect some property at Clapham Common. A Squad nondescript van signalled Parkyn's arrival, together with his associate Berlinski and as the Bedford van moved off, it was followed at a discreet distance by the Squad vehicle. Three Flying Squad cars converged on Parkyn's vehicle in Sloane Street, forced it to a halt and surrounded the van. Parkyn and Berlinski attacked the Squad officers with a crowbar and a hammer and then Parkyn drove his van backwards and forwards, in an attempt to crush the officers against the police cars, before driving off along the pavement, scattering pedestrians as he went.

The van was abandoned on the Albert Embankment but the two men were later seen on a bus, were arrested and made one final – and unsuccessful – attempt to escape outside Gipsy Hill police station.

At the Old Bailey, both men were convicted of attempted murder and receiving stolen property. Sentencing Parkyn to twelve years' penal servitude and Berlinski to seven, Lord Goddard addressed Detective Inspector Bradford in the following terms:

Inspector, I think you and the other members of the Flying Squad are much to be commended for your action in this case. All of you showed considerable courage, and the community are much indebted to you for bringing to justice two dangerous criminals. The way in which you managed to effect the arrest within such a short time in an entirely different part of London shows what a high state of efficiency the Police Force has come to in this country, and in London especially. The thanks of the community are due to you.

Violent crime was becoming more and more common. It would escalate in the 1950s.

The Squad – 1950s

ormer Flying Squad and Ghost Squad officer, Detective Chief Inspector Percy Burgess, reporting from the East End of London in August 1950, suggested that the purchase of anything between six and twelve dilapidated cars or vans, which could be garaged at Lambeth, might be used for observation purposes in the busy London streets. They would be unobtrusive, stated Burgess, and cited a recent case involving Detective Inspector (later Detective Chief Superintendent) Steve 'The Ambush King' Glander, where such vehicles had been 'borrowed' and used to impressive effect in ambushing a gang of robbers.

The idea – which was a good one – was not adopted, but it prompted the Assistant Commissioner (Crime) Ronald Howe to suggest a shake-up in the Flying Squad fleet, which now consisted of twenty-seven cars, three taxis, one nondescript van and a tender. Of the cars, all but one was fitted with R/T apparatus; but the taxis' radio equipment permitted them only to receive messages. Arrangements were made to replace the three taxis with nondescript vans, for the Squad cars to be painted in colours other than black and that a 3.5 litre Jaguar and a Rover 75 be acquired to replace two of the rather too well-known Wolseleys. Meanwhile, 970 arrests were carried out by the Squad in 1951, 886 crimes were cleared up and property valued at £176,018 was recovered.

However, the 1950s saw a new wave of crime which was far more sophisticated than anything the police had yet to contend with.

All through the war years, there had been an organized spate of break-ins to banks and post offices, where duplicate keys had been used. As a detective chief inspector at Criminal Records Office, Bob Lee had collated these offences – 200 of them, where in excess of £50,000 had been stolen (£1,350,000 by today's values) – and was convinced that the same team was responsible.

Now, as deputy head of the Squad, Lee told Bill Chapman of his suspicions, who told him to go ahead with the investigation.

Information slowly began to filter in and a series of tailing suspects and carrying out observations commenced. Months went by and now Lee received some really compelling information from an underworld informant, and yet every job which he put up to the Squad failed to materialize. Lee came to the inescapable conclusion that there was someone at the Yard who was informing the gang of the Squad's activities. He voiced his suspicions to Assistant Commissioner Howe, who gave him a free hand to do whatever was necessary; this included the team booking off duty in the Squad's duty book and then meeting up elsewhere, briefings were held at Lee's house and when Detective Inspector Philip Periam was shown in the duty book as being assigned to 'P' Division, he was in fact keeping observation on a Post Office at Axminster, Devon.

But the secrecy, the months of observations and the information paid off. The gang were seen to reconnoitre Barclays Bank at Waterlooville, Hampshire; the following weekend, the Squad were ready for them, with some officers already inside the bank, others at various observation points in the immediate vicinity. Just before five o'clock on the evening of Saturday, 27 November 1950, three members of the gang arrived at the bank. As they opened the front door, so the Squad men, inside and out, rushed them. There was a short, sharp fight. John Saxton, who was found in possession of a skeleton key to open the front door and a key to open the bank's safe on a ring, together with fifty-two other skeleton keys, tried to escape and shouted, 'Let me get at you, you bastard!' as Inspector Periam jumped on his back and enthusiastically whacked him with his truncheon. Saxton's associate, James Howells was similarly subdued and he was found to be in possession of six keys.

With two members of the gang under lock and key, Lee now put the rest of his plan into operation. Searches of premises and arrests were carried out all over London and eight men and a woman were detained. In the woman's wardrobe, a muff had been found; inside it was a considerable amount of jewellery, bank cash bags, twenty-five numbered keys and a book with corresponding numbers to the keys, describing which premises they were for. The keys were shown to one of the male prisoners, who happened to be a locksmith. 'I haven't made all those!' he gasped and then, having committed himself, felt impelled to point out the keys he *had* made.

Mr Justice Byrne, sitting at Hampshire Assizes in April 1951 decided that Harry Bryan – he who had been convicted with Billy Hill and Georgie Ball for a smash and grab, on the day prior to Ruby Sparks' arrest – was the ringleader and sentenced him to ten years' imprisonment. Six others were convicted, with the sentences ranging down to four years' corrective training.

Strong suspicions existed in respect of other members of the gang, but there was insufficient evidence to prosecute them – and the crooked copper at the Yard was never caught.

*   *   *

In January 1951, George Albert King, who had shot at police officers during a series of burglaries in 1946 and had been arrested by the Squad, was released from prison. He carried out an armed robbery on a Post Office van on 29 February 1952 at Bruce Grove, Tottenham and escaped with mail bags containing £6,651. Two weeks later, King was one of a five-man gang who broke into 55 Honey Lane, Waltham Abbey, at two o'clock in the morning, held up Herbert and Beryl Whiten at gunpoint and demanded cash and jewellery from their safe. Mr Whiten managed to convince the robbers that the safe's keys were elsewhere and the gang left, taking just £4 in cash, driving away in a Buick. King was later arrested, refused to name his accomplices in respect of both robberies and at Essex Assizes on 18 June, he notched-up his ninth conviction when he was sentenced to twelve years' imprisonment. Never again would King threaten anybody with a firearm; less than three months later, he died in Pentonville Prison.

Meanwhile, the Buick had been traced to a thief named Cyril Burney. He stated he had sold the car to Niven Craig, who had been released from military prison in 1950, following a five-year sentence for robbery. Both had taken part in the Waltham Abbey robbery. The hunt for them continued for six months until a tip-off to a Flying Squad team led Detective Inspector Garrod and his officers to a hotel at Kensington Gardens Square. Burney was arrested as he climbed out of a window; Craig was arrested in bed and was relieved of a Luger pistol which was underneath his pillow. Asked whether or not the pistol was loaded, Craig replied, 'Yes, and there is another one up the spout.'

Craig told the Old Bailey that he had spent the night of the Waltham Abbey robbery with his younger brother at a friend's house in Norfolk and this was confirmed by both friend and brother, though not to the satisfaction of the jury who found both Craig and Burnley guilty. Both men were sentenced to twelve years' imprisonment by Mr Justice Hilbery on 30 October 1952, who told Craig, 'You are very exceptionally dangerous, quite cool and cold-blooded.'

One of the officers involved in the case was allegedly heard to say, 'At least we've put that bastard away for a few years' and it may have been these words that spurred Craig's younger brother, who had unsuccessfully attempted to alibi him, to take revenge. Three nights later, on the roof of a Croydon warehouse and in company with an older youth named Derek Bentley, young Christopher Craig shot dead Police Constable Sidney Miles. Having also wounded another officer, he shouted, 'You've just given my brother twelve years. Come on, you coppers. I am only sixteen.'

*   *   *

During the early hours of the morning of 21 May 1952, a Post Office van left Paddington Railway Station, where it had been loaded with a consignment of used bank notes from the west of England. On this occasion it contained £443,000 – over ten times the normal amount. It was destined for the East Central Post Office at St Martin's-le-Grand after which the notes would either be distributed to regional post offices or forwarded to the Bank of England for pulping – but the van never reached its destination.

At a set of traffic lights in Eastcastle Street, a Riley saloon pulled in front of the van and a Vauxhall saloon stopped behind it. Eight masked men dragged the three occupants of the Post Office van into the street and attacked them with coshes and lengths of piping. The driver of the van managed to press the button to activate the audible alarm, but this had been disconnected. Within minutes, the van and the two cars roared away, leaving the van's former occupants dazed and bleeding.

The two stolen cars were dumped at Covent Garden and the van was driven into a yard at Camden Town, where eighteen of the mailbags containing £287,000 were transferred to a fruiterer's lorry, hidden in an empty square made by apple boxes – thirteen more mailbags, containing £156,000 were left behind, because there was no more room – and the lorry was driven away. A fortnight later, some of the stolen mailbags were discovered in a flooded sandpit at Dagenham, but that was all.

Superintendent Bob Lee, the deputy head of the Squad was put on the case and in a very short space of time, he discovered who had masterminded the job – Billy Hill, the self-proclaimed 'Boss of Britain's Underworld' – how it had been carried out and the names of all of those involved. All Lee lacked was evidence. Billy Benstead, who had fortuitously escaped from the scene of carnage at 'The Battle of Heathrow' and George 'Taters' Chatham, both well respected burglars, were said to be involved but although Edward Noble and Robert King were charged with receiving some of the stolen notes, the case against them was discharged and no one was convicted.

* * *

Bob Lee took over as head of the Flying Squad on 1 July 1953 and on the same day Bob Higgins arrived as his deputy. It was not too long before their presence was requested by Mr R. L. (later Sir Richard) Jackson CBE, who had just been appointed Assistant Commissioner (Crime); his predecessor, Sir Ronald Howe had been promoted to deputy commissioner.

An extremely vicious gang had committed a series of robberies in London and the Home Counties, and the attacks had become so violent that it was feared that it would not be too long before there was a murder. The gang's capture, said Jackson, was to become the Squad's top priority.

The Squad informants were pressed into action and before long they had identified the gang, of whom the leader, William Purdey, was housed at a caravan site near Chertsey, Surrey. Observation had to be carried out to see who was meeting with the gang leader and Squad officers would have stood out like a sore thumb. Woman Detective Constable Daphne Skillern had only been a CID officer for eighteen months and at that time, there were no women officers attached to the Flying Squad. When women officers were required for observations, they were drawn from divisional duties. Miss Skillern and Edna Slack (who five years later would become one of two women officers attached to the Squad) rented an adjacent caravan. 'Our cover story, if required,' Miss Skillern told me, almost sixty years after the event, 'was that we were two private nurses taking time out between contracts. My recollection of the job was that it was long, uncomfortable, cold, muddy and miserable,' she continued, adding, 'Edna and I lived in a small, very pokey caravan ... it lasted quite a time – three months, I think – certainly over the Christmas period.' The two women took it in turns to keep observation, two hours at a time, from early morning until late at night, noting the descriptions of cars and the occupants who arrived in them. Apart from exhibiting great resolution, they also displayed considerable pluck; under cover of darkness, they crept over to the gangster's caravan, sometimes in company with a male officer, sometimes not, in order to note the registration numbers of cars which had arrived at night, peer in through the caravan's windows and overhear conversations, not withstanding that Purdey had a vicious German Shepherd guard dog. In addition, there was a great deal of criminal activity at the site; during one fight a man had his legs broken with an iron bar.

When the Squad received information that the gang were going to raid a metal smelters at New Southgate, they were ready for them – but the gang, suddenly realizing they were compromised, attacked a Squad officer and escaped. Now that they knew the Squad were on to them, they would be doubly dangerous.

The two women officers had months of waiting and watching before the gang went to work again – this time, they viciously attacked the driver of a Royal Mail van at Horley, Surrey and stole ninety-one mail sacks. The prize was nowhere near what they expected; the large consignment of cash had been taken to its destination by another van and all they had stolen was £750.

Early the following morning, 6 February 1954, one of the women detectives spotted two cars draw up outside the gangleader's caravan. After ten minutes, the cars drove off and Bob Lee mobilized officers to arrest the criminals.

Bob Higgins smashed the glass in the door of the caravan, opened it and as the German Shepherd leapt through the doorway, so police dog-handlers slipped the leads on their charges who adequately dealt with the guard dog. Purdey, his wife and child were taken away, and a search of the caravan revealed property stolen from several of the gang's raids. Leaving officers secreted at the caravan, Higgins now took his team to Box Hill,

Surrey, where he had been told another member of the gang, Ernest Robinson, was living. He, surrounded with banknotes from the Horley robbery, was also arrested and led away.

There was no information regarding the whereabouts of the third man, Geoffrey Joseph who was known to be an escapee from Brixton Prison and therefore observation was kept from the two gang member's properties. That evening, Joseph, driving a stolen Riley arrived at Chertsey but when Squad officers raced to arrest him, he jumped back into the car, evaded a Flying Squad car and as he roared past the women's caravan, Miss Skillern hurled a wooden pastry roller at his windscreen. 'By sheer luck, I scored a hit,' recalled Miss Skillern, adding ruefully, 'but the screen held.' Believing, correctly, that the man would head for Box Hill, the Squad officers there were alerted by radio. An hour later, having swapped the Riley for a stolen Bentley, the escapee arrived at Box Hill. This time, there was no mistake – there was a sharp exchange of fisticuffs before the wanted man was in custody.

Ernest Robinson was believed to have carried out a murder; he was interviewed about it in prison and then, quite inexplicably, he died. Squad detractors unkindly decided that he'd been frightened to death. The other two gang members had the misfortune to appear before Lord Chief Justice Goddard at the Old Bailey, who told them, 'I must treat you as two dangerous criminals. This is a case – and one of the most serious I have ever tried – of highway robbery of Her Majesty's mails in which you gambled for high stakes, and lost.' Both men were sentenced to fourteen years' imprisonment.

However, the last word to this story of courage and fortitude must come from Miss Skillern. During the course of the observation at the caravan site, she had been obliged to leave her caravan, in order to go and purchase provisions. Two of the gang were seated in a car and asked Miss Skillern if she would like a lift which, to the best of her recollection, she pleasantly and politely refused.

Not agreeably enough, it would appear; many months later, as she entered the witness box at the Old Bailey, one of the defendants in the box was heard to say, 'God, it's old iron face!'

'Obviously,' recalled Miss Skillern, 'they clocked my face which probably wasn't too friendly!'

★   ★   ★

'Taters' Chatham has already been mentioned for his supposed involvement in the Eastcastle Street robbery; two years later, he was once again brought to the notice of the Squad. Born in 1912, the scrawny cat burglar who, it is thought stole valuables worth £100 million during his sixty-year criminal career (which only stopped when, aged seventy-nine, he slipped and broke his ankle during an attempted burglary at an art gallery) had escaped from Brixton Prison and using a jemmy, savagely attacked a police officer who tried to arrest him.

Meanwhile, Byworth's, a jewel factory in Heddon Street, Mayfair, had been broken into; one of the gang had climbed up a knotted rope and gained entry by forcing the fanlight. The safe had been blown and jewels, gold leaf and platinum, valued at £37,000 had been stolen; it was the latest in a string of high value raids which the Squad had been investigating over a two year period.

With the four-man gang identified, Detective Superintendent Bob Higgins led the raid on a house in Kew; bursting into a bedroom, they found 'Taters' who, in spite of his previous ferocity when facing arrest, surrendered peacefully. By his bed was a two-foot long piece of rope; asked why he had it, 'Taters' cheekily replied, 'Oh, that – I use that for climbing into bed.'

Perhaps it would have been prudent to have disclaimed all knowledge of it; when the Metropolitan Police Forensic Laboratory compared it with the rope left hanging from the guttering at Byworth's, the two pieces were found to be identical. That, plus 'Taters'' comb – dust from the blown safe's ballast was found in the comb's teeth – was damning evidence. The gang were sentenced to a total of thirty-three years' imprisonment, with 'Taters' receiving ten of them.

A fortune, 'Taters' may have stolen, but he had little to show for it. Whatever profits he made, he gambled away, spending a total of thirty-five years in prison and dying, aged eighty-five, penniless in a Battersea nursing home.

*   *   *

Guy Mahon, who had smashed up the Messina Soho vice gang took over as the Squad's chief on 1 September 1954, probably for the shortest Squad posting, ever – just four months. Three weeks after his appointment, on 21 September, a lorry containing gold bullion valued at £45,500, pulled up outside the offices of KLM Dutch Airlines, at Jockeys Fields, Theobalds Road. As the crew started to unload their cargo, so a van, which had been stolen from Manor Park that morning, backed up behind it, a man leapt from the van to the lorry, threw two boxes of bullion into the van, jumped back again and the van drove off. This raid, which took place during the rush-hour displayed considerable nerve and planning. The stolen van cut across Clerkenwell and was later found abandoned a short distance away, in Queen Square.

Bob Lee, who had just taken over the Metropolitan Police's 3 District, on whose ground the job had been committed got stuck in to the investigation, as did Mahon and the rest of the Flying Squad. Once again, Lee knew who had planned the raid – Billy Hill – but the gang all had alibis and although dozens of searches were carried out and suspects and associates of suspects were pulled in and questioned, no charges were brought.

Billy Hill's alibi was the most impressive of all; at the time of the robbery, he had been dictating the closing chapters of his memoirs at the offices of *The People* Sunday newspaper. His serialized life story had commenced two weeks previously in the newspaper and when, three weeks after the robbery, Hill's memoirs revealed to the readers of *The People* precisely how the KLM robbery had been carried out, it seemed the height of foolishness to tweak Lee's nose in such an unseemly fashion. It was far more prudent for Hill to emigrate, which shortly afterwards, he did.

Nobody – especially the Flying Squad – likes to be associated with failure, even when the person who is the root cause of the breakdown is one as clever as Billy Hill. Just two raids had netted him £332,500 – £6,769,700 by today's standards. Matters were not helped when it was scoffingly alleged that fourteen, rather than thirteen mailbags were left in the abandoned Royal Mail van in the Eastcastle Street robbery, the inference being that the police had helped themselves to the other one.

★   ★   ★

But on 3 January 1955, things started to look up for the Squad; their new leader was Reginald Spooner. Although Spooner had never before served on the Flying Squad, he had a tremendous reputation as a detective, had been seconded to MI5 during the war years and was a born leader of men. With morale on the increase, past failures were quickly forgotten, as when Flying Squad officers paid a visit at two o'clock in the morning to a bungalow belonging to a 'Mr Smith'. Neighbours were shocked when they learnt of the arrest of the man 'who always smiled at children and gave them sweets,' although possibly less so, when they read their newspapers to discover that the avuncular 'Mr Smith' was no less a personage than Edward Rice, on the run from Strangeways Prison where he had been serving ten years' for safe-blowing. Following his appearance at the Old Bailey on 15 March 1955, where he was convicted of possessing explosives, he was sentenced to an additional thirteen years' imprisonment.

Another celebrated safe blower, Alfie Hinds, was serving a sentence of twelve years' preventative detention when he escaped from Nottingham Prison and remained at large for 245 days, before being found in County Wicklow, Eire. Bert Sparks of the Flying Squad had put him inside; Tommy Butler of the Flying Squad brought him back.

Peter James Sheppard lived up to his nickname of 'The Thin Man' when he squeezed through his cell window in Southampton. Having stolen a car, he managed to drive straight through a police cordon which had been set up, and vanished for a week. The Flying Squad found him at Ashwin Street, Dalston where he stoutly denied his identity. Alas, a Squad officer whipped off Sheppard's hat to reveal his tell-tale mop of black, bushy hair and he was reunited with a rather more secure cell to complete his sentence for housebreaking.

Detective Sergeant George Frampton was on night-duty patrol when he and his Flying Squad driver, Police Constable Robert Green, responded to a call in South Lambeth after shots had been fired, which had injured Police Constable Keith Burdett. The gunman, Francis Gellatly, who with two other men (who escaped) had been trying to break into an unattended car, had run off, climbed a wall into a yard and barricaded himself in an outside lavatory. When Frampton and Green, who had been joined by Police Constables Wyndham Morgan and John Lewis, forced the door, Gellatly fired the last of six shots at them. Frampton grabbed hold of the gunman and disarmed him. When Gellatly was shown PC Burdett's helmet, which had an indentation from one of the bullets, the gunman who had previously shouted, 'If you come over the wall, I'll blow your fucking head off,' now remarked, 'I shot at him to try and get away. He was a game one, I'll tell you.'

Sentencing Gellatly to seven years' imprisonment, Mr. Justice Glyn-Jones said: 'The police officers concerned acted with great gallantry, and ought to be commended for their conduct which was in the best tradition of the service to which they belong.'

PC Burdett was later awarded the George Medal and British Empire Medals for gallantry were awarded to Frampton, Green, Lewis and Morgan.

★   ★   ★

Just six weeks after the shoot-out in South Lambeth, once again the courage of the Flying Squad officers was left in no doubt. Two men walked into an Earls Court jeweller's, produced revolvers and held up the staff, one of whom was pistol-whipped when he refused to instantly comply with the demand to face the wall. The owner was forced to open the safe and whilst one of the men ransacked it, the other emptied the display counter and showcase. When two customers went to enter the shop, they saw the gunmen and ran to the sanctuary of a nearby butcher's shop. Realizing that they had been seen, the two gunmen ran from the jeweller's and got into a waiting Rover 90, which immediately sped off. But the customers had noted the registration number of the car – PXP 804 – and telephoned the police. Detective Sergeant Albert Eric Chambers was patrolling in a Squad Rover with Detective Sergeant Ernest Cooke and Police Constable Donald Cameron driving, when he received a radio message regarding the armed robbery and the registration number of the Rover 90 which was involved.

Almost immediately the Rover raced past them, PC Cameron gave chase and at Hyde Park, the robber's car was stopped in traffic. Chambers, together with Cooke leapt from the Squad car and ran towards the stolen car. Cooke grabbed hold of the steering wheel, but as the traffic started to move so the driver, John Cotten, accelerated, throwing Cooke into the road.

Running back to the Squad car, Chambers and Cameron took up the pursuit. As the robber's car swerved into Park Lane, the first of many shots was fired at the officers. The first missed, the second crazed the windscreen, just missing Cameron and Chambers who was sitting in the back. Chambers climbed into the front and smashed the windscreen to clear Cameron's view and another shot was fired at them. The stolen Rover then collided with a number of vehicles in Curzon Street and the three occupants took to their heels. Cameron chased Cotten and lost him; Chambers, meanwhile ran after the two gunmen, John Cohen and Ronald Parsons, and two uniformed officers, Police Constables David Evans Wood and George William Karn, joined in. Another shot was fired and still the officers ran on; the two gunmen split up and Parsons was lost to view. But with the officers still chasing the lone gunman, passers-by were trying to join in and a van driver had two shots fired at him. Cohen tried to escape in a taxi by holding his gun at the driver's head but the volume of traffic precluded such a course of action, as it did when he tried to get in a van travelling in the opposite direction. One of the officers, Police Constable Wood was shot at, but grabbed hold of Cohen, who then shot him in the groin at point-blank range. PC Wood fell to the pavement and the gunman ran on. Police Constable Karn threw his crash helmet at him, hitting him in the face but failing to stop him. Chambers was now running parallel to Cohen, who fired at him and missed, and Chambers dashed across the road and brought him down with a rugby tackle. Cohen fired again and Chambers was hit in the wrist, but nevertheless managed to grab the gun; with the arrival and assistance of PC Karn, Cohen was at last overpowered.

Ronald Parsons was arrested later that day in true Flying Squad tradition and John Cotten was arrested two days later, rather more peaceably. The three men learnt the error of their ways when they appeared before Lord Goddard at the Old Bailey on 8 December 1955. The Lord Chief Justice was singularly unimpressed when Cohen tried to mitigate his actions by saying, 'I panicked and did my nut' and sentenced him to twenty years' imprisonment, with Parsons receiving twelve and Cotten, ten.

As the trio were led off to the cells, Lord Goddard called the police officers before him and told them:

I have asked you men to parade in front of me to give you the thanks of the community for your gallant and devoted sense of duty on the day in question. It takes courage of no mean order to run up and tackle desperate criminals who are in possession of firearms. The Metropolitan Police Force has reason to be proud of you and, as I say again, I thank you on behalf of the community and commend you for your gallantry.

Further commendations were showered on the officers, with Chambers, Wood and Karn all being awarded the George Medal, Cameron, the British Empire Medal for gallantry and Cooke, the Queen's Commendation for brave conduct.

As well as a new chief of the Squad, there was a new commissioner, as well. Sir John Nott-Bower KCVO, KPM, was sixty-one when he was appointed commissioner and although he had been awarded the King's Police Medal for gallantry in 1931, after arresting armed criminals who had shot him in the arm, it does appear that the get-up-and-go that he had once possessed, had really got up and gone. The historian, David Ascoli was quoted as saying that Nott-Bower 'was a nice man, when what was needed was a bit of a bastard.'

Nevertheless, Sir John possessed good public relation skills with his men and the *Daily Herald*, 14 October 1955, reported that he called all the senior CID officers, together with the entire Squad personnel together and told them, 'I wish to congratulate you for all the wonderful work you have done in the past few months.' He especially praised the work of Albert Chambers and the other officers, saying, 'I, and the whole public salute you,' before visiting Chambers and PC Wood in St George's Hospital.

★   ★   ★

Within a few weeks of being demobbed from 45 Commando (Royal Marines), the late Terry O'Connell joined the Metropolitan Police and ten years later in 1956, became a member of the Flying Squad as a detective constable. At that time, only mature men of thirty were accepted into the Squad – just O'Connell's age. 'Although he did not seek popularity, Reg Spooner was well respected by everyone, uniform and CID,' he told me. 'He was one of the shrewdest men I have ever known.'

O'Connell was certainly not deficient when it came to astuteness, either. He was part of a rota who attended the racetracks – Liverpool, Ascot, Cheltenham and Goodwood, amongst others – to deal with the racetrack gangs and pickpockets who still infested the courses. Before leaving for the races, the Squad team would go down to Criminal Records Office and look at the photographs of wanted criminals who were likely to attend those meetings. It paid off. 'We were on our way to Sandown,' said O'Connell, 'and got held up in a traffic jam just outside the course. A man crossing the road leant on our Squad car. I had just seen his photo and he was a fraudsman wanted all over the country.' Arrested and lodged at Esher police station, the fraudster asked O'Connell to back a horse for him; it won, at odds of 8/1.

It was thought – unfortunately, as we noted earlier, not for the first time – that there was a mole in the Flying Squad office. Therefore, when a charity meeting was held at Sandown, which would be attended by show-business personalities (rich pickings for the dips), O'Connell and his men wrote in the Squad's duty book that they had taken annual leave. Arriving at the race course early, O'Connell and his team stood at the back, dressed casually and wearing dark glasses. After the first race, the pickpockets were at work and the Squad struck. O'Connell grabbed hold of Jimmy Kensit, aka 'Jimmy the Dip' (a friend of the Richardson brothers and the Kray twins) and told him, 'You're nicked.'

Kensit's reply was both comical and also telling. 'Lor', Guv, I thought you were a film star!' And then he added, 'You can't nick me, you're on holiday,' thereby giving credence that there was indeed a spy in the Squad office. When O'Connell repeated the first part of Kensit's reply at Kingston Magistrates' Court, its comic properties ensured that the remark became newspaper headlines.

★   ★   ★

In 1956, Charles Frend's film, *The Long Arm* was released; facilities had been granted for its filming to take place in New Scotland Yard, as well as other police premises. Starring Jack Hawkins, it told the tale of Scotland Yard's Detective Superintendent Halliday, who investigated a baffling string of break-ins to commercial premises, with the use of duplicate keys. It was more than a little reminiscent of Bob Lee's similar, real-life investigation of five years previously and it was an instant hit at the box office; it is still very popular even now.

'Now it's a record!' exclaimed the *Daily Herald* on 15 December 1956, and it was; for the first time, Flying Squad arrests had topped the thousand mark. Thirty-one of these arrests were attributed to the branch of the Squad which was concentrating on stolen vehicle enquiries – it would soon become a separate entity, 'C10' – and the knowledge which the Squad officers were acquiring in this specialized sphere of police work was passed on to their contemporaries at the Detective Training School and the Police College.

The following year, 1957, produced even better results; over 1,200 arrests were made by the Squad and stolen property valued at £194,010 was recovered. Three of those arrests in September of that year were amusingly recounted by the late Fred Lambert, then a detective sergeant with 8 squad after he was contacted by an informant, an old-time lag who had participated in the 1932 Dartmoor Mutiny. From his hovel in south London, he informed Lambert that he had been approached by two local thieves who asked if he could find a buyer for a quantity of stamps and postal orders, since they intended to break into a post office, situated in Knapmill Road, Bellingham, the following night.

Two Squad cars, an observation van and ten officers were assembled and the next night by half-past eleven they were in position as an old van drew up at the rear of the premises. Three men got out, entered the alleyway leading to the rear door of the post office and with a collection of housebreaking implements, started to try to force entry. The alleyway was sealed off and the Squadmen moved in. One of the thieves rushed straight into the arms of the officers and was arrested; the other two climbed over a wall where they were pursued into the open air swimming pool and thence into Bromley Road. As two men dashed down the road towards the junction with Southend Lane, they ran straight into the path of Squad officer Percy Lawless, who was waiting for them, truncheon drawn. The first man slipped past Lawless, but not the second who caught the full force of Lawless' truncheon on the back of his head, which flattened him. It was probably the poor standard of street lighting or the excitement of the moment which resulted in Lawless also laying out his partner, Johnnie Woodward, who was hugely unamused, but all of the miscreants were caught and convicted. As Lambert said, it proved the old saying that 'you can't get information from your local vicar'. Lambert's partner on that – and many other occasions – was Alf Durrell; and he features prominently, later in this book.

* * *

The Squad now possessed a fleet of thirty-four vehicles. The civilian staff who were responsible for supplying them had to be told (for the second time in thirty-two years) not to acquire cars bearing consecutive registration numbers, but the fleet now included three Jaguars and three Rovers. The bugbear was that four black Wolseleys were still on the strength. The worst of these had travelled 100,680 miles and during the previous seven months had been admitted to the workshops on no fewer than sixteen occasions. The other three were hardly better.

A furious acting detective chief inspector thrust a copy of form 728 into his typewriter and on 25 January 1958, acidly informed his senior officers: 'The cars are, to say the least conspicuous, and it is not unduly stretching veracity to say they constitute a hindrance to officers endeavouring to effect the arrest of any criminal possessing even a modicum of intelligence or experience.'

The author of this stern report was Thomas Marius Joseph Butler and he was a quintessential Flying Squad officer. Butler had first come to the Squad in 1941 as a detective constable, with only seven years service. He looked nothing like the public's idea of a typical Squad officer; at just over five foot nine, slim, with hair which was already starting to recede, dark eyebrows and a 'Mr Punch' nose. Butler was a bachelor who lived with his widowed mother in Barnes. Incredibly for a Flying Squad officer, he was practically teetotal, very occasionally accepting a glass of Tio Pepe sherry in the snug at the Red Lion, Derby Gate.

But if he did not fit into the accepted mould of the traditional Flying Squad officer, it mattered not. Butler was a Squad man through and through and he would eventually spend in excess of sixteen years with it. He was ruthless and cunning and the criminals were terrified of the tenacious, incorruptible little detective. Even by Flying Squad standards Butler worked incredibly long hours. The late Ernie Bond OBE, QPM, remembered seeing him in his office at two o'clock in the morning, still typing out reports. 'What, another early night?' was Butler's crusty remark to Bond.

'Tommy Butler was certainly the most dedicated police officer I've ever known,' Terry O'Connell told me. 'The job was his life. I first knew him when he was a detective inspector on 1 squad, he teamed up with Detective Sergeant (First Class) Peter Vibart. No. 1 squad was then known as the 'Inner Sanctum' because it was known they could be trusted and were given special tasks to investigate. He (Butler) was austere, non-materialistic and considerate.'

Butler and Vibart were dubbed 'The Terrible Twins' by the press and together they made the underworld tremble. A classic example of their capabilities was when the gangland boss, Jack Spot was attacked in the street by a number of thugs on 2 May 1956 near his home at Hyde Park Mansions. As a result of this savage assault, which was witnessed by Spot's wife, he required seventy-eight stitches in his face. Billy Hill, who was behind the attack was arrested but, as always, was impressively alibied and was released. However, six weeks later, two of the attackers, Bobby Warren and 'Mad Frankie' Fraser were each sentenced to seven years' imprisonment. Two other men – Bert 'Battles' Rossi and William 'Billy Boy' Blythe – were arrested in Dublin. Patrick Marrinan, the barrister who had already appeared for the defence in the trial of Warren and Fraser now rushed to Dublin in order to argue that the English warrants were flawed and judgement was deferred until after the weekend. By that time, fresh warrants had been obtained and they were in the possession of Tommy Butler and Peter Vibart, who now flew to Dublin. Since Blythe had been responsible for slashing Vibart in the face with a razor in 1945, necessitating twenty stitches, it may be imagined that the latter had a keen interest in apprehending Blythe.

According to Butler, Marrinan attempted to block his and Vibart's way, saying to Blythe, 'They are all outside and are going to nick you again. If I were you, I should make a dive for it.'

Blythe, heeding this prescient legal advice, replied, 'Too fucking right,' and attempted to do just that by struggling violently; nevertheless he and Rossi did not escape but were swiftly extradited to England. William 'Ginger' Dennis was also arrested for the attack on Spot and the three men stood trial at the Old Bailey, being represented by Marrinan. After a seven-day trial they were found guilty and Blythe, who loudly informed the court, in outraged tones, 'It's a mockery of justice,' was sentenced to five years' imprisonment, with Rossi and Dennis receiving four years, each.

Nor did the matter end there; early the following year, Marrinan was summoned before the Bar Council for improper conduct and Butler produced transcripts of intercepted telephone calls between Marrinan and Billy Hill. He was disbarred, the Benchers deciding that Marrinan's behaviour had been inconsistent with a member of the English Bar.

The following account demonstrates one of several high points in Vibart's career.

On 29 March 1958, Henry Stevens, a 'P' Division aid to CID was shot in the mouth as he went to arrest a man who had just broken into a house. Although grievously wounded Stevens hung on to his attacker, who further assaulted him before making good his escape. It was soon discovered that Stevens' assailant was Ronald Leonard Easterbrook, a south London criminal with a shocking record; at the time of the offence, he had previously been circulated as being 'wanted' for two cases of inflicting grievous bodily harm and with considerable justification, he was known as 'The Deptford Terror'. Although the investigation was being conducted by 'P' Division officers, it was not too long before information regarding Easterbrook came to the attention of the Flying Squad. They had heard that Easterbrook had acquired another gun and that of the six bullets which accompanied it, five were for any police officers who possessed sufficient impudence to try and arrest him, the sixth for himself. Having heard that much, the Squad officers pressed their sources of information harder to discover where Easterbrook was hiding and on 9 April they received the breakthrough that they were looking for.

The raid was led by Vibart. This very tough ex-soldier had joined the Metropolitan Police in 1936 and for the last twelve years, had risen through the ranks of detective constable, detective sergeant (second class) and now, detective sergeant (first class) whilst serving in the Flying Squad. He had made a speciality of arresting armed robbers and other violent criminals and at the time of the raid, he was forty-three years of age and had been commended by the commissioner on no fewer than thirty-four occasions. He was the right man to lead from the front because as he was about to demonstrate – indeed, had demonstrated in the past and would again in the future – he was simply a man without fear.

Early on the morning of 10 April, Vibart went to the Goodwood Hotel, 61–67 Queensborough Terrace, Bayswater, had the hotel surrounded, then placed officers to cover every possible exit. Obtaining the master key, Vibart, together with Detective Constable John 'Polly' Perkins and other officers crept up to the third floor. But when he inserted the key into the lock of Room 24, the door would not budge, it had been barricaded. Now Vibart charged the door, smashing it off its hinges and as he and the other officers clambered over it and into the room,

Easterbrook sat up in bed. 'We're police officers!' shouted Vibart. Easterbrook, who had a pistol under his pillow started struggling violently, collected a very heavy punch on the chin, and that, effectively, was that.

Perkins handed the .455 calibre Colt automatic pistol to Vibart – it was later identified as being one of six firearms stolen by means of a storebreaking from the artillery Museum at Woolwich, some six months previously – and upon examination, he discovered that the pistol was unloaded. Told that he would be arrested for the attempted murder of a police officer, Easterbrook replied, 'Fuck the copper. If that had been loaded, you would have got it as well.' As well as the pistol, a search of the room revealed a small canvas holster, a hatchet, a knife and a carton of pepper.

At the Old Bailey on 13 May 1958, Easterbrook pleaded not guilty to shooting Stevens with intent to murder and after the Crown offered no evidence on this charge, he pleaded guilty to shooting Stevens with intent to cause him grievous bodily harm and also, guilty to the burglary; he was also found guilty of two additional cases of inflicting grievous bodily harm, where he had attacked two men with broken glass. Mr Justice Ashworth told him,

> In my view, you are a wicked and dangerous man, and I feel it my duty to send you away for a long time. If you had been convicted of shooting with intent to murder the sentence I am about to pass would have been even longer. This was a vicious affair involving a police officer. You are a lucky man that providence intervened to save you from a charge of capital murder. If I am any judge of such matters it might well have resulted in your conviction and that might well have been the end of you. You seem to have no respect for persons, law or property.

Easterbrook was then sentenced to a total of ten years' imprisonment. 'I will bet money I will never finish it,' said Easterbrook – in fact, he was wrong. Thirty years later, again at the Old Bailey, Easterbrook received four life sentences for robbery, shooting a police officer with intent to cause grievous bodily harm and firearms offences. As he was led off to the cells in 1958, he added, 'I would like to congratulate the police on maintaining a high standard of collusion and perjury.' Since, despite his telling remarks at the time of his arrest, Easterbrook had steadfastly disclaimed any involvement in the attack on PC Stevens until he pleaded guilty, those remarks were thought by many to be a bit rich.

Police Constable Stevens' gallantry was recognized with the award of the George Cross – one of only five Metropolitan Police officers to receive it – and Vibart and Perkins were awarded the Queen's Commendation for Brave Conduct.

★   ★   ★

As Reg Spooner (described by the *Sunday Dispatch* as 'an ace detective ... a master crime-buster') was promoted to deputy commander on 19 May 1958, so his place was filled by his deputy, Bert Sparks, who was known by the nickname of 'The Iron Man.' Speaking to me in 1993, Ernie Bond stated, 'There was only one Bert Sparks; there is no doubt he *was* an iron man.' There is also no doubt that Bond (who served on the Squad for four years) knew a tough character when he met one; Bond was one of 'the Originals' with the wartime Special Air Service in the western desert.

Sparks' first contact with the Squad had been in 1927. A brand new police constable on his beat in London's West End, Sparks was called to a fight at a café in Panton Street. He was savagely attacked by the mob until his opponents were suddenly pulled from him and he heard a reassuring voice say, 'All right, son – it's the Squad!' A Flying Squad team in a passing Crossley Tender had spotted his predicament and had come to the rescue.

So when the commissioner published in *Police Orders*, 17 June 1958,

> I wish to draw the attention of all ranks to the alarming rise in crime that has taken place throughout the Metropolitan Police District during the first four months of the current year. There has been an increase of more than 15 per cent over the corresponding months of 1957 and of almost 40 per cent over the same months of 1956. The main increases have been in housebreaking, shopbreaking, stolen motor vehicles and larcenies from motor vehicles. New and improved methods for dealing with crime help to offset our serious shortage of

manpower, but improved methods are not in themselves sufficient, and our duty to prevent crime calls for sustained effort and energetic action on the part of every member of the Force, both uniform and CID.

Sparks took up the challenge. Under his leadership, the arrest figures jumped again: in 1958, 1,400 arrests were made – these included seventeen people for carrying out crimes involving the use of explosives – and property to the value of £282,538 was recovered.

'Bert Sparks was laid back, full of humour and congenial; he was imperturbable,' remembered Terry O'Connell, adding that Sparks would convulse the Squad officers with his jokes. 'He certainly contributed to the high morale that existed in those days.'

The high morale was reflected in the work rate in 1959, when over 1,500 arrests were made and stolen property to the value of £312,716 was recovered, both figures being the highest on record.

The same year, on 10 August, the Flying Squad had, for the first time, two women officers, Women Detective Constables Slack and Smith, added to their ranks and all immoderate language from their male counterparts immediately ceased – for all of ten minutes!

One of the more interesting additions to the Squad was the stocky, tough Harold Gordon Challenor who, as a member of the wartime 2 SAS, had been parachuted behind enemy lines. He had carried out demolition work, been captured, escaped and awarded the Military Medal. Joining the Metropolitan Police in 1951, Challenor displayed an aptitude for thief-taking (especially for the offence of 'suspected person') and in record time, he was appointed to the CID. Described as 'a cheerful extrovert' by many of his colleagues – less so, by the criminal fraternity, who often disputed ownership of many of the items which Challenor claimed to have found in their possession – Challenor was soon posted to the Flying Squad and enthusiastically got to work, taking on some of the Squad's toughest customers. However, one of Challenor's rather more irritating traits was his insistence of referring to everybody, irrespective of rank or status as 'me old darling'. It prompted Tommy Butler to write, with masterly understatement on one of Challenor's annual qualification reports: 'He continues to apply himself strenuously to the job in hand. Is capable and willing but is inclined to noisy tactlessness.'

For an unorthodox unit, the Squad was somewhat surprised at Challenor's increasingly eccentric behaviour, it being quite laudable to escape through enemy-occupied Italy disguised as a woman, but not to continue this cross-dressing practice when meeting an informant in a South London pub. When Challenor feared that his detective inspector, the very popular Reg Roberts (who, by then was coming to the end of his service and was about to retire) would be injured if he effected the arrest of a vicious, wanted armed robber at Liverpool Street station, he took matters into his own hands – quite literally. As the wanted man approached him, Challenor delivered a straight-arm Commando blow to the throat, then leapt on top of him; he was attacked in turn by a city gent wielding his umbrella who, with some justification, thought he had witnessed an unprovoked assault.

So as the Squad entered a new decade, it is likely that Tommy Butler breathed a sigh of relief as Challenor was promoted to detective sergeant (second class) and was later posted to West End Central. They would both have pressing problems to be addressed, which would result in each of them becoming household names; Challenor, with the disputed provenance of sections of a housebrick; Butler, with the investigation which would result in him reaching the pinnacle of his career.

The Horse Dopers

The Flying Squad had started off as an ad hoc unit and therefore it was not particularly surprising when splinter groups were formed; right from the Squad's inception, pickpockets were a menace and as the years went by 'The Dip Squad' was formed and the officers who manned the team made impressive inroads into the pickpockets' activities. The Ghost Squad had made a similarly significant incursion into post-war black marketeering and lorry thefts, and the section of the Squad who concentrated on dealing with stolen, 'ringed' cars finally set up their own, separate squad. Therefore, when during the 1960s reports of horse doping hit an all-time high, it was entirely sensible that the Flying Squad with their strong connections to racetrack crime, were called in to deal with it.

Until 1960 if a horse was tested by Jockey Club officials after a race and a stimulant was found in the horse's saliva or urine, the trainer's licence was automatically withdrawn, even when it could be shown that he was not responsible. The horse was never permitted to run again, thereby losing the owner thousands of pounds. The whole proceeding was draconian; the trainer and the owner were arraigned before the stewards and told the result of the test; legal representation was not permitted and none of the rules of evidence were observed.

So when Sir Gordon Richards, the former jockey turned trainer returned from a holiday in Switzerland in April 1960, he was horrified to discover that rumours were rife that his horses had been fed stimulants to accelerate their performance. He called in the Yard and Detective Inspector Bill Baldock and Detective Sergeant Terry O'Connell of the Flying Squad were sent to investigate the matter.

Suspicion soon fell on Sir Gordon's second stable jockey, Bert Hamlin Woodage, and during an interview with Baldock he admitted giving a number of horses stimulants in order to win and stated that he had obtained the drugs from Bertie 'Bandy' Rogers, a former horse trainer.

Rogers had lived for thirty years as a lodger in a ramshackle thatched cottage in Compton, just outside Newbury, owned by an elderly couple, 82-year-old Alan Prior and his wife, Julia. Rogers himself was 66 years of age, just five feet four, cheerful and well-liked in the community; in fact, he was the respected chairman of the local Thrift Club. But over the previous ten years, Rogers had been strongly suspected and investigated by police over allegations of horse-doping and horse 'ringing', although no charges had been brought. Six years previously, Rogers and a chemist's assistant from Yorkshire had been interviewed by West Riding Police regarding allegations of horse-doping in the Wetherby area. A few days after his initial interview, the chemist's assistant committed suicide and the enquiry also died, stillborn. Three years later, Rogers found another chemist to supply drugs to dope the horses; he, too, died.

Nevertheless, Rogers used to uncannily predict winners of forthcoming races at his local, The Red Lion, adding that 'his powders' were responsible and this news was greeted with laughter and disbelief from the locals, who considered Rogers to be an eccentric. Nevertheless, the way in which Rogers would ostentatiously produce a thick wad of fivers was at variance with his weekly wage of £12 as a lorry driver. In addition, he was occasionally seen having clandestine meetings with a glamorous couple – the woman was described as a 'beautiful blonde' – who arrived in an expensive-looking saloon car.

But a month prior to the arrival of O'Connell and Baldock, there had been a curious incident. Two men described as Londoners, one of them named Joe, pulled up in a black saloon car and Rogers drove off with them. He returned with them, late the same evening and was dumped on the front path of the cottage. 'He was in a terrible state,' commented Mr Prior, 'covered with blood, and a lump the size of an egg on his temple.' Rogers refused to see a doctor and was uncommunicative for days afterwards. 'Bandy seemed to become a completely different man,' said Errol Castle, the licensee of The Red Lion. Rogers never offered an explanation for his mistreatment, but it is possible that his 'powders' had failed to come up to scratch for his crooked associates.

Rogers had even more cause to be unhappy after Baldock's and O'Connell's arrival, and not purely because they had interrupted him tending his allotment. 'When I searched his cottage,' said O'Connell, 'I found a hypodermic syringe with traces of [what later proved to be] horse's blood on it, a quantity of caffeine and a bunch of letters received from stable lads, including Woodage. There was much reference to horses and dope.'

At Marlborough police station, Rogers confessed to sending powders to various stable lads and although he somewhat ridiculously stated that he did not know what the powders contained, he admitted obtaining his supply from Harry Tuck, a chemist's dispenser in Hednesford, Staffordshire. Released on bail, Rogers realized the game was well and truly up and the following morning he shot himself, taking the remainder of his secrets, together with the details of the crooked bookmakers behind him, to the grave. The profits from his devious game amounted to no more than £100 in a Post Office savings book. Not everybody accepted that Rogers had committed suicide, but a meticulous investigation was carried out and, as the North Berkshire Coroner, Mr N. B. Challenor, later recording a verdict of suicide, remarked, 'He found himself in a state where he felt unable to stand up to what might be ahead.'

But the discovery of the letters was sufficient for the Squadmen to bring about the arrest of five other men. It caused a sensation. On Tuesday, 5 July 1960, just as Woodage finished riding Bosphorus in the 2.30 Quidhampton Stakes at Salisbury Racecourse, he was quietly arrested by O'Connell. Robert Mason, a head lad at the East Ilsley stables of trainer R. J. Colling was similarly arrested and James Boyce, an unemployed statble lad was picked up at his home in Newmarket. Harry Tuck, the chemist's dispenser was waiting by arrangement at Hednesford police station, Staffordshire, and all of them were taken to Newbury Police station, Berkshire, where they were charged. 'Sir Gordon's jockey charged' screamed the headlines of the *Daily Sketch*, dated 6 July 1960. At the preliminary hearing at Newbury Magistrates' Court, one month later, the *Daily Herald*, for 9 August, informed their readers, 'Yes, I drugged horse, says Sir Gordon's stable lad'. In addition, Harry Tuck, who, together with the other defendants had pleaded not guilty, gave evidence saying he had supplied Rogers with quantities of caffeine in return for betting tips, telling the court that there was nothing wrong in doing so and that caffeine was not a dangerous drug. Professor James McCunn of the Royal Veterinary College told the magistrates that caffeine was a stimulant, which would make the horse more alert; however, after two hours, the effect would wear off, leaving the horse depressed. The defendants were committed for trial and although one of the stable lads was later acquitted, the remainder were convicted at Gloucester Assizes of conspiracy to cheat and defraud bookmakers by administering drugs to horses. Passing sentence on 31 October 1960, Mr Justice Barry said that all four men were of excellent character. He said:

> It is indeed a disaster that you have allowed yourselves to become involved in, what I am afraid, was obviously a quite widespread fraudulent scheme to tamper with the racehorses. It is a scheme a practice which, if it were allowed to go unchecked would undermine, as you all know quite well, the whole integrity and cleanness of the sport, which such a large number of people in this country are interested in. You know quite well that you were running a very grave risk, not only so far as yourselves were concerned, but also placing your employers in very considerable jeopardy. It is a most painful thing to impose prison sentences on men such as you, but I have to uphold my duty to the public, and I have to make it clear to all those who might be tempted to indulge in these practices that they cannot go unpunished.

The judge then sentenced Bert Woodage and Harry Tuck, each to eighteen months' imprisonment. Two stable lads, James Boyce and Robert Mason were jailed for nine months and six months, respectively.

Sir Gordon had displayed great courage in exposing the racket and it led to the relaxation of the harsh rules which had been set up by the Jockey Club. Now, trainers were encouraged to report cases of doping and complaints flooded into the Jockey Club, so many that the police refused to investigate them. The Racing Industry appointed its own research establishment at Newmarket and its own investigator: former Flying Squad officer, ex-Detective Superintendent Bob Anderson. He arranged for two dope tests to be carried out at each meeting, where the horses were chosen by lot; moreover, the security at the racecourse stables was tightened up. So now the doper's tactics changed; it was the trainer's own stables which were targeted.

* * *

Several methods were used by the dopers to affect a horse's performance; as a stimulant, a glucose solution would be injected into the horse minutes before the race was to commence, or anabolic steroids could be administered. Given the increase in racecourse security, either of these methods would present unacceptable difficulties to the dopers. But another method to accelerate the horse's performance was blood doping. Two days before a race, the dopers would drain off five to seven pints of the horse's blood; understandably, the practice was known as 'bleeding'. In a very few hours the horse would naturally make up the deficiency. Then twenty-four hours prior to the race, the blood would be re-injected into the horse, whose blood count would thus be raised by 5 per cent. The horse would now be bursting with energy and could knock seconds off its performance.

But in retarding a horse's performance, the dopers would use a depressant and the method of administering it was known as 'balling'. It was managed by two of the gang, one holding and pacifying the horse, the other administering the dope. Forcing the horse's mouth open, the doper would grasp the horse's tongue with a gloved hand, draw it down to one side and then by turning his wrist, the tongue would be held between the jaws of the horse, thereby protecting the doper's hand from injury. The ball (or bolus) of dope would then be inserted into the side of the horse's mouth as quickly, and as far back as possible, and then dropped down the horse's throat. In the event that the horse did not immediately swallow the ball, water could be offered to enable the horse to swallow or, failing that, a stick could be used to 'encourage' the animal to do so. During the operation, the gang member holding the horse's head – it was common to place a head collar on the animal – would try to prevent the horse raising its head too high. The nose could be flicked using string or a piece of rope, known as a 'twitch' to divert the horse's attention. It was an operation requiring a great deal of skill and experience.

The 'ball' containing the depressant, was a drug named Notensil. This drug had been used to sedate agitated psychiatric patients until a study, carried out in 1958 revealed that Notensil only benefited 4 per cent of patients and indeed, 44 per cent were made worse. Quantities of this drug were obtained by the gang from the West Park Mental Institute, near Epsom. In fact, Notensil can be carefully administered as an aid to controlling fractious animals, but it should never be administered to horses within four days of racing. This, of course was not the concern of the gang.

The stolen tablets were ground down, then wrapped in tissue and sticky tape, so that the outer coating of the ball would gradually dissolve in the horse's stomach. The more tissue used, the longer the dissolving process would take; the gang members were adept at ensuring that the final pieces of tissue would dissolve and the drug take effect, just prior to the commencement of the race. Therefore, the purpose of doping the favourite in these circumstances would be to prevent it from winning or being placed, thereby affecting the betting. Large sums would be placed in forecast betting, eliminating the favourite and at the same time, the gang would sell their information to dishonest bookmakers, who could then lay off the favourite.

This was the method used by a gang who used a glamorous blonde to visit over twenty stables, pretending to be a prospective owner. In this way, she was able to pass the layout of the stables on to a gang of nine men who, in October 1963, were convicted at Lewes Assizes and received prison sentences of up to four years.

One of these men was an East Ender named Joe Lowry, who was then fifty years of age and he was released just in time to get up to more mischief. On 17 September 1965, O'Connell (now a detective inspector) received information that Spare Filly, trained by Bob Read of Collingridge Stables, Lambourn, was to be entered as the favourite at odds of 6–4 in a five-horse race at Kempton Park the following day and that a gang intended doping her at the stables. Three of the other horses were regarded as 'no-hopers' – and Whisky Poker was regarded as a racing certainty if Spare Filly was stopped, in which eventuality the gang stood to collect £50,000.

An all-night observation was carried out by O'Connell, his Flying Squad team and some local officers. 'We arrived at the stables in the dark,' recounted O'Connell, 'there was little time to make an appraisal and the layout of the buildings and the surrounding neighbourhood was completely strange. The stables were surrounded by a paddock, which made the observation very difficult to keep and the weather that night could not have been worse – rain and a strong gale.'

At either end of the yard were the east and the west gates and the stables accommodated twenty-two horses, including Spare Filly. At two o'clock in the morning, after three hours patient waiting, two cars arrived, a two-tone Ford Zephyr and a blue Hillman, and they parked 100 yards from the stables. After some conversation the Hillman drove off and then three men climbed over the east gate and a light came on in Spare Filly's box. As O'Connell and his men crept forward, they saw one of the men, Leonard Lipman Steward, a former apprentice jockey and stable boy, putting a head collar on the animal and next to him was a former professional boxer named John Barnham, who was holding a stick. A third man, also holding a stick and a milk bottle of water was standing outside. O'Connell's team went into the yard where they were spotted by the gang. 'There was an almighty fight,' said O'Connell. It took four Squadmen to overpower Barnham, Steward escaped but was arrested the next day and the third man – James Cronin – got clean away. On the ground at the scene of the battle were found two packets containing dope balls, one containing the equivalent of twenty Notensil tablets, the other, sixty. All that would have been needed to slow Spare Filly's performance would have been ten tablets.

The Squad officers resumed their hiding places and soon the second car returned. Inside it, together with two pills containing Notensil, scissors and a rubber hammer, was Joe Lowry. The significance of the hammer – a similar one was found following a search of Barnham's address – was that they were used to grind up the Notensil tablets. 'Give me a bit of help if you can, Guv,' entreated Lowry to the arresting officer. 'Don't be too hard, will you?'

It appears Lowry's plea was ignored; on 8 February 1966 at Berkshire Assizes, Mr Justice Veale commented, 'This kind of offence is becoming too common. It is a serious matter and must be stopped.' Lowry's case was not helped by the fact that he had been released only thirteen months previously after serving a two-year sentence for a similar offence. He now notched up his fifteenth conviction with a five-year sentence for conspiracy to dope racehorses. Barnham and Stewart were each sentenced to four years' imprisonment.

And the fourth man, James Cronin, who escaped? He fled to Eire, where he remained for several years, but when he returned, he visited a West End club, where he was arrested. O'Connell, who had recognized him that night at the stables had not forgotten him; Cronin appeared at Oxfordshire Assizes on 19 November 1969, where he pleaded guilty to conspiring to cheat and defraud, together with Lowry, Barnham and Stewart and was sentenced to two years' imprisonment, suspended for two years.

So Spare Filly ran at Kempton Park as planned, drug-free; ironically, she was beaten into second place by Whisky Poker.

The Squad – 1960s

By the beginning of the 1960s, Bert Sparks was coming to the end of his reign. The Squad now possessed eight squads, each with a detective inspector in charge, plus two detective sergeants (first class), three detective sergeants (second class), two or three detective constables and three drivers. The drivers were all Class I, who had spent many years driving Area Cars and 'Q' cars on division, before being accepted as 'strappers' (ie drivers who would deputize for accredited Flying Squad drivers, during times of illness, leave or suspension) and then, when a vacancy arose, as a regular Squad driver. One such driver was Arthur Strain, who could drive at 100 mph without his passengers experiencing the slightest misgivings. On one occasion, he drove out of the Yard at seven o'clock in the morning when an 'all-cars call' was received, regarding a City of London police officer in Billingsgate Market who needed urgent assistance in respect of a suspect who was believed to be armed. Strain switched on the headlights, powered into top gear and headed for the City of London. He reached Billingsgate long before 'Alpha seven', the marked City police car, complete with a blue light and two-tones, did.

Some years previously someone had spiked Arthur's drink at a Squad function, which made him quite ill. He was furious. Arthur loved driving and knew that it could have led to him losing his driving licence plus, of course, his career. After that experience, he vowed never to touch another drop of alcohol and he never did.

'Dixie' Lee on the other hand, never stopped moaning about driving Squad cars, but it was all an act; he complained because he was an old soldier and therefore, it was expected of him. In fact, he loved his work and if he missed out on a job because he was on leave, he was profoundly, genuinely unhappy.

Officers worked in pairs on a day-to-day basis, spending three days in a Squad car, followed by one day 'on foot'. The Squad provided a twenty-four hours a day, seven days a week coverage across London. They utilized a system known as 'Provs' which was the abbreviated version of 'Provincials' – Early (also known as 'the Dawn Patrol'), Late and Night-duty Provs. It was the Provs who could give assistance to the provincial forces if necessary. Therefore, every eight weeks, one squad was detached for night-duty, with the Dawn Patrol taking over from them at 7.00 am. Linked into the Provs system was C9 Department (The Provincial Police Crime Branch), which was staffed by a number of Metropolitan and provincial detectives who acted as liaison for linking criminal enquiries between the Met and the Home Counties. During office hours, the provincial force would telephone their liaison officer, who would go into the Squad office, which was adjacent to theirs, and request the assistance of the Dawn Patrol, for them to carry out a search of the home of a suspected criminal, or to wait for the return home of a criminal wanted by the county officers. Out of office hours, the provincial force would telephone the Squad direct, for the matter to be dealt with by Late or Night-duty Provs. In each Metropolitan Police division, only one or two night-duty CID officers covered the whole area, which could run to hundreds of miles. Therefore, if there was a sudden, serious crime which occurred in the Met during the night and officers needed assistance, the Squad could produce eight, seasoned officers in a very short space of time.

Apart from the Squad officers and the drivers, there was the civilian staff who were a necessity for the Flying Squad's smooth running. Ernie Beer was a retired Scotland Yard radio operator who joined the Squad as a civilian telephone operator. He was known as 'Mr Voice' and was the soul of discretion. Ernie was not only trusted implicitly and revered by the Squad personnel, he was regarded as utterly dependable by the informants who telephoned to speak to their contacts. If the officer was not in the building, the informant would often give the information to Ernie, for onward transmission. Ernie, who sadly died of cancer, set the pattern for many of the highly-prized civilian telephone operators – retired Flying Squad driver Jim Moon, to mention but one – in the years to come.

'The Dip Squad' was traditionally 8 Squad and they attended most of the public gatherings where pickpockets were likely to congregate: the State opening of Parliament and the racetracks and, on a day-to-day basis, the changing of the guard at Buckingham Palace and the Underground, usually in the vicinity of Piccadilly and Leicester Square.

The Squad's main targets were lorry hi-jackings, street robberies and snatches, high-class burglaries and, always, pickpockets. To combat these crimes, the Squad relied upon information provided by the Criminal Intelligence Unit (C11) run by Detective Inspector 'Wilf' Pickles (formerly from Tommy Butler's 1 Squad), C9 Provincial Forces Liaison and the Squad's own informants.

It was a Squad informant who led Detective Inspector Len Mountford and his team to an address in Bayswater in September 1960 and the arrest of Zoe Progl, whom the press had dubbed 'the Queen of the Underworld'. Progl, a 32-year-old shoplifter, cheque fraudster, lorry thief, burglar, forger and car thief, had enjoyed five weeks of freedom after escaping from Holloway Prison with the aid of a rope ladder. She had been serving a thirty-month sentence for shopbreaking and receiving a stolen safe and had avoided arrest in the past because of the use of a variety of disguises. Not on this occasion; when Mountford burst through the door of her apartment at midnight, she was stark naked and there could be no case of mistaken identity. She was taken back to Holloway to have another eighteen months added to her sentence.

John Simmonds went to the Squad in the early sixties as a brand new detective constable – at twenty-two possibly the youngest ever – because of his ability to handle informants. Within a week, he received information from one of his established informants that tenants in a block of council flats were in possession of a large amount of electrical goods, especially television sets, but Simmonds felt that such a matter was not worthy of the Squad. He apologetically mentioned this to his detective inspector who, to his surprise was most encouraging. Remarking that, 'you can't get big jobs every day; some of the small ones are just as important,' he directed Simmonds to apply for a search warrant at Bow Street Magistrates' Court. His inspector was right; a search of the premises the following morning resulted in Simmonds filling a pantechnicon with an enormous amount of property stolen in house burglaries and shop-breakings. The arrest and conviction of three active criminals did Simmonds no harm at all; neither did the rewards from the informants fund and the insurance companies, for his informant.

This case had a knock-on effect, not unfamiliar to detectives. One of the team received an eighteen-month jail sentence and, about a month after his release, he went into an East End pub where, entirely by chance, John Simmonds was having a drink. The man became rather agitated, obviously believing that Simmonds was pursuing him. After a quarter of an hour, the man went to the lavatory and clearly indicated that Simmonds should follow him. He did so and in the doorway, the man pushed a note into his hand and vanished. The note read, 'Keep off my back' and suggested that instead, Simmonds should pay a visit to a scribbled down address. A search of this premises revealed several thousand pounds' worth of stolen property and with the resultant arrests, Simmons paid out the reward and in addition, had conscripted another worthwhile informant on to the books.

That great Squad detective, Ian Forbes, (described as being 'a small, dour Scot, tough as nails and very down to earth, a real man's man') once said, 'the CID has no place for cowards or look-before-you-leap types. They must be resolute and determined men who are ready to act on information, no matter where it comes from.' A case in question was when the Squad received information that an unknown buyer was on his way to meet three villains in a warehouse in Camden Town, to purchase a quantity of cloth which had been stolen from a factory. Only three officers and one car were available at the time; the informant had no idea when the buyer was going to arrive; indeed, he might have already arrived and there was no time to procure a search warrant.

So the Squad team raced across London and dashed into the warehouse, where the three gang members tried to run for it; they were overpowered and taken into custody, as was the suiting material valued at thousands of pounds, which had been stolen two days previously by means of a factorybreaking. Just about every officer who has served on the Flying Squad could quote making arrests in similar circumstances.

And echoing Forbes' words, that officers should be prepared to act on information, 'no matter where it comes from' was the curious case of the Flying Squad officer who executed a search warrant at a house where he had hoped to arrest the main villains who had carried out a warehousebreaking and, it was thought, would be in possession of a substantial amount of stolen property. Alas, he was to be disappointed. Upon his arrival, there was only the house occupier present and although he was in possession of some of the stolen property, it was only a very small amount. So he was arrested, went to the Magistrates' Court, pleaded guilty and was fined £40, to be paid within fourteen days or be sent to prison in default.

As he left court, he glumly remarked to the Squad officer, 'The Beak might just as well have sent me to prison straight away; there's no way I'm going to find forty quid in two weeks.' The Squad man murmured that if he wanted to earn some money, he should provide the Squad with information about the whereabouts of stolen property and the identities of the thieves responsible – obviously, he still wanted to arrest his associates and retrieve the bulk of the property – but the little thief shrugged and went on his way.

Ten days later, the Squad officer received a phone call: 'Were you serious about giving me the money to pay my fine?' The Squad man agreed, but stipulated that the job had to be worthwhile, the perpetrators had to be arrested and the amount of property recovered had to be substantial. After hesitating, the thief provided an address, saying what was found there should be sufficient to pay his fine. And before the officer could ask any more questions, such as details of the stolen property, the caller hung up.

The Squad officer was skilled in dealing with informants, and felt that this newly recruited snout was not in a position to provide any really top-notch information, so he, his partner and a driver went down to the address which had been provided.

The address was a yard, with a lock-up garage, with two men present, together with a fully-laden lorry. The officers immediately identified the lorry from tabloid headlines the previous day, 'Bogus Policemen Hijack Lorry' – an account of how two men disguised as police officers had stopped a lorry, laden with a high value load and robbed the driver of it at gunpoint. The two men at the yard, who initially decided to resist, were quickly overpowered, handcuffed and arrested. The Squad hierarchy at the Yard were delighted, as were the insurers of the load and indeed the press, coming so soon after their earlier headlines, they were able to herald the arrests with, 'Flying Squad Swoop on Hijackers'.

Rather more pressing was the matter of the thief's unpaid fine; the Squad officer quickly arranged a whip-round from the rest of his team – something which would have resulted in him being kicked-off the Flying Squad, had it been discovered – and presented the informant with the £40 he needed.

Several months later, once the case had been disposed of at court and the bogus police officers had received substantial prison sentences, the informant was taken to the underwriters. The reward he received was sufficient for him to purchase a house.

But apart from courage and daring, Squad officers required large amounts of fortitude, as demonstrated in the following account: A Flying Squad team of six officers had been sitting in an observation van, an old, unheated Bedford Dormobile, during one freezing winter's evening. They had received information that a gang were going to carry out a robbery, but the hours passed and it grew colder and colder, so that when the gang did arrive and the Squad officers got out of the van to make the arrests, their cramped limbs refused to work properly and they were unable to pursue the robbers, who escaped in their getaway car. Fortunately, the officers who were on surveillance radioed details of the car to other Squad vehicles in the vicinity, who made the arrests.

By the time they arrived home it was 2.30 in the morning, but they were immediately called back to the Yard. A reliable informant had stated that he knew the whereabouts of a lorryload of cigarettes, which had been the subject of a hijacking. The Squad officers rushed down to the farm in Essex which the informant had named and the flustered farmer agreed that he had a barn which he rented out, but had no idea what was in it. Upon searching the barn, there were the stolen cigarettes; now, it was a matter of waiting for the thieves to return.

By now, it was early morning. The Squad vehicles were concealed and one of the officers 'belly-crawled' across the farmer's fields to the nearest village shop. There, he purchased bread, cheese and milk; this sustained the team for the rest of the day. The following morning, the thieves had still not turned up, and the detective inspector in charge thought the job had been 'blown', so he radioed the Squad office and asked for two tenders to be sent from the Property Store. When they arrived, the officers spent the rest of the day loading-up the stolen cigarettes. Just as the laden tenders drove off down the lane from the farm, so the thieves drove up; upon spotting the convoy, they hurriedly reversed and roared off. By the time the Squad officers had got past the tenders, they had lost the thieves on the Southend Arterial Road.

All, however, was not lost; at the time of providing the intelligence as to the whereabouts of the stolen cigarettes, the informant also thoughtfully supplied the names of the thieves, all of whom were arrested at their home addresses. By the time the gang were charged and locked-up and the Squad officers had returned to the Yard, they had been on duty for in excess of sixty hours; and all this happened in the days when overtime was not paid to CID officers!

The Squad possessed some formidable characters who obtained information from a variety of sources and who achieved some tremendous results in clearing up serious crimes. It is debatable whether some of these characters would survive in today's modern police force. Men like Alexander Anthony Eist, who came to the Squad in the late fifties as a detective constable and stayed after promotion to sergeant. Nowadays, it is fashionable to describe Alec Eist as a corrupt officer (and this could well have been the case) but undeniably, he had first-rate sources who guided him, effortlessly, into retrieving stolen lorryloads. Eist had a profound dislike of paperwork and attending court; therefore, having obtained the information, he handed it over to other officers to carry out the arrests, the court appearances – and the subsequent correspondence. The informant's report, however, was one piece of paperwork which Eist managed to compose, type and submit, himself.

Nevertheless, Eist could prove himself to be a man of action, as when he and two other officers went to arrest David William Barnard, who five days previously had escaped from Wormwood Scrubs prison, whilst serving an eight-year sentence for assault with intent to rob, possessing a revolver with intent to endanger life and breaking and entering. Barnard threatened the officers with a loaded .22 rifle before he was overpowered and received a further five-year sentence; Detective Sergeant Laurence Scott received a George Medal; Detective Sergeant Douglas Davies and Eist were awarded British Empire Medals for gallantry.

Eist was a great racing man and every time he presented his colleagues with a good arrest, he felt compelled to take a few days unofficial leave and promptly vanished. This behaviour became rather irksome to the first class sergeant with whom he was partnered who eventually reported him and Eist was hauled over the coals. He should have displayed rather more contrition and he learnt the hard way that nobody is indispensable, because Eist was posted to 'Y' Division, on the borders of the Metropolitan Police and Hertfordshire. Not that this posting changed Eist's output of work – one stolen lorry after another was seized and the miscreants arrested; on one auspicious occasion, a stolen lorry laden with nuclear fuel arrived at the North Circular Road, at the junction with the Great Cambridge Road and the 'Y' Division 'Q' Car, who just happened to be in the vicinity, was on hand to make the arrests.

One of the division's senior officers had occasion to rebuke Eist, regarding something that he had either done or overlooked, but instead of apologizing Eist stoutly defended himself, pointing out the number of arrests in respect of stolen lorryloads which had been made, thanks to his information.

'Alec,' wearily replied the senior officer, 'before you arrived, we didn't *have* any fucking stolen lorryloads!'

James Earl Ray was arrested in England on 8 June 1968, for the murder of the peace activist, Dr Martin Luther King, Jr, two months earlier in Memphis, Tennessee; Ray's fingerprints had been found on a set of binoculars and a rifle (which was confirmed as the murder weapon) in a nearby boarding house. It was Eist who sat with him in a cell at Cannon Row police station. According to one account, Ray is supposed to have said to Eist, ''Course I shot the nigger; they're just making too much fuss about it,' but the reliability of this statement was never put to the test, because on his return to the United States, Ray pleaded guilty to the murder.

Eist rose to the rank of detective chief inspector before retiring on ill-health grounds in 1976. He had been commended on thirteen occasions and, to the shocked incredulity of many, he was presented with a Long Service and Good Conduct Medal, to accompany his BEM and his 1939–45 War Medal.

However, that was not the end of the Alec Eist story. He took a pub at Six-Mile Bottom, Hertfordshire and then in November 1978, he was asked to attend the House Assassinations Committee in the United States because Congress was re-evaluating the evidence in the Ray case. Eist told the committee a rather different account of the conversation originally attributed to him; that whilst Ray had not actually admitted the murder, he had made a number of incriminating statements. 'Ray never really told me he pulled the trigger, or anything like that,' he told the committee. 'But he said he threw the gun away.' He was supported by the testimony of Owen Summers, a veteran crime reporter for the *Daily Express*, who stated that Eist had told him some ten years previously about Ray's statements in which he had allegedly implicated himself.

Still, the house was undecided on whether or not to believe Eist; Senator Christopher Dodd (Democrat – Connecticut) stated that he was 'deeply disturbed' that Eist had not told the authorities about Ray's alleged statements when he learnt in 1977 that American Congress was reinvestigating the case. With masterly understatement, Eist replied that at the time, he had been experiencing some 'domestic problems'; this was when Eist and others were put on trial for allegedly arranging an alibi for two London thieves. The case against Eist was thrown out, with costs being awarded to him.

The controversy in the James Earl Ray case continued and it will probably never go away. Ray died in 1998, Eist some fifteen years previously and in September 2002, his three medals were auctioned at Dix, Noonan & Webb, Piccadilly. It was estimated they might fetch £300–400. Perhaps the wily spirit of Alec Eist slipped out from the grave to bring a little pressure to bear; the medals sold for four times the lower estimate.

* * *

Detective Sergeants Jimmy Smythe and Alec Marshall had a tremendous run of success, which lasted for years, thanks to a highly-placed informant who ran a second-hand premises and who pointed them in the direction of persistent housebreakers who arrived at his shop in order to dispose of their loot.

One of the great Squad characters of that era was Detective Sergeant Alf Durell. A Welshman, standing over six feet tall, he had boxed as a middleweight, under the ring name of 'Darkie' Durell and he was a formidable opponent, both in the ring and out of it. Described by the late former Detective Chief Superintendent Fred Lambert as 'a top-grade officer', Durell had one brother who worked in the docks and another, who was the licensee of a pub. He possessed an exceptionally fine knowledge of forthcoming robberies and missing lorryloads, particularly in the south London area and following the arrest of an armed robber who had previously savagely attacked a seventy-year-old night watchman with a pickaxe handle, Durell decided to redress the balance. He treated him to an exhibition of body punches and because the robber neglected to bob, weave or sway back in the way a more skilled performer might have done, he suffered accordingly and learnt a much-needed lesson.

But Durell had a compassionate side, too. The Red Lion public house in Derby Gate was a regular watering hole for the Squad officers and had been, for many years. Rosie was a barmaid in her mid-forties who looked on the Squad as 'her boys' and whenever the standard lunchtime dish of ham, pickles and new bread (costing half a crown or 2s 6d – 12 pence) was requested, Rosie always made sure that slightly more than the usual portion of ham ended up on a Squad officer's plate. Through no fault of her own, Rosie got into financial difficulties at home in Lambeth; Durell got to hear of it and organized a whip-round which made her financially solvent again. But the licensee decided that she had become too familiar with the Squad and sacked her – which, given the amount of time and money spent in the pub by the Squad officers, was an incredibly short-sighted decision. The Squad promptly boycotted the Red Lion and after a couple of days during which sales hit an all-time low, Alf Durell visited the licensee to tell him that unless Rosie was reinstated, the embargo would continue indefinitely. The licensee got the message; the following day, Rosie was back behind the bar, as were the generous portions of ham and pickle across it.

John Simmonds recounts a story of meeting the son of a villain, a few months after Durell had died. Durell had dealt with the young man's father on several occasions and as a result, he had been sentenced to terms of imprisonment. Just after his father had died, Durell visited the widow and gave her some money to tide her over. 'The son said that because of the arrests of his father, he hated Durell,' said Simmonds, 'but this single act of charity at a time of need had given him a different view and he thought Durell was "a real gent".'

Lastly, Durell had an amusing run-in, in the witness box at the Old Bailey with one of the members of the well-known Du Cann family of barristers. Durell's name was pronounced 'Doo-rell' and Du Cann was well aware of this, but in cross-examination, insisted on referring to him as Mr Durrell, as in the name of the naturalist, Gerald Durrell.

The cross-examination went on all afternoon, with Du Cann repeatedly pronouncing Durell's name as 'Durrell' until eventually, he said, 'I put it to you that your evidence is a pack of lies, Mr Durrell.'

As imperturbable as ever, Alf replied, 'No it's not, Mr Duckan.'

The detractors of the likes of Eist and Durell would comment that the jobs they received from their informants were as a result of turning a blind eye to the informant's other misdemeanours and perhaps there was some truth in those assertions. During the investigation of the great train robbery, Tommy Butler felt that Durell was 'too close' to some of the south London team and carefully excluded him from the case. Alf Durell volubly stated that he could have assisted the investigation considerably, had he been given the chance and there were those who concurred; others agreed that Tommy Butler was no fool. And when Detective Sergeant Frank Jiggins and Detective Constable James Shearon from the Squad were arrested and charged with theft – both were acquitted – part of their defence relied upon the court being told that in order to obtain search warrants, it was usual for anything but the truth to be told to the magistrate, in order to protect the informant. This caused uproar, both with the judiciary and in the Metropolitan Police. It was high time for the Flying Squad to be swept clean with a new broom.

The wind of change came with the arrival of Ernie Millen, who took charge of the Squad on 19 June 1961. Gruff and bluff, Millen had already served on the Squad as a detective sergeant (first class) and he was regarded as a strong Squad guv'nor who would back his men to the hilt – provided, of course, that they were right. Just approaching his fiftieth birthday at the time of his appointment, Millen, at just over six feet tall, was known to all as 'Hooter' – either because of his imperious nose or the fact that spurning telephones or intercoms, he bellowed his orders along the corridors of Scotland Yard. A standing joke amongst seasoned personnel to newcomers to the Squad was the comment, 'Hooter spoke to me this morning.' The goggle-eyed novice would invariably reply, 'What did he say?' The answer, amidst gales of laughter, was, 'Get out of my fucking way!' Woman Detective Constable Pat Willey described him as, 'A bit of a pain.'

Millen cracked down on two practices which were regarded as questionable; the first was the usage of 'mugs', where criminals were arrested for quite serious crimes which were way beyond their intellectual capabilities – the theft of lorryloads was a case in point – the inference being that the real perpetrators of the crime had offered them up as sacrificial lambs. The second was 'participating informants' where a Squad ambush resulted in the arrest of criminals – usually an armed robbery – where the informant, who had participated in the robbery, was allowed to escape. In Millen's words, 'It's the 1960s and this has got to stop.' A case in question was when John Simmonds took part in the arrest of a gang of armed robbers, one of whom had been seized by the first-class sergeant, and had broken away from him. Simmonds chased after him and had almost caught up when he heard a car sounding its horn. Turning, he saw the sergeant learning out of a Squad car and waving at him, to move out of the way. Simmonds was horrified to think that they intended to run the robber over but as the car drew alongside, the sergeant muttered, 'It's alright, John-boy – he's with us!' As Simmonds later told me, 'It was early days and I was learning fast.'

One case in which a participating informant was not used, was when the Squad received information that a gang intended to attack a GPO van and following a week of surveillance and enquiries, discovered that two of the men involved were Henry Edward Jeffrey and Anthony Terroni. They were using a Transit van and a Rover and it seemed likely that they would attack the van's occupants in Maple Place, a small cul-de-sac close to Tottenham Court Road. But when, on 10 May 1961, the GPO van arrived at Maple Place and left unmolested, it was thought that the robbers had left the raid for another day and the watching Squad officers stood down. Nevertheless, the GPO van was followed by two nondescript Squad vans and when it reached Duchess Street, the gang pulled out in front of it in a Ford Transit van, driven by Jeffrey.

The leading police van rammed the Transit, injuring one of the Squad officers, and as six of the gang emerged from the Transit, armed with pick-axe handles, one of them tried to open the door of the GPO van. In the meantime, one of the Squad officers was struck with a pick-axe handle and then two other officers from the second nondescript vehicle, Detective Sergeants David Burdett and George Firth, dashed forward to arrest the gang. Both were savagely attacked and had to be hospitalized with broken bones. The gang escaped in the Transit; then one of the other officers spotted the Rover nearby, which had been baulked by traffic, and the driver was arrested. Later, two other men were arrested and one had a telephone number written on a cigarette packet. The subscriber was traced and an observation was carried out on the address in Clock House Road, Beckenham. Of Terroni and Jeffrey however, there was no sign.

With no Reggie Spooner in charge of the Squad, to tell the press what they might or might not print, the newspapers had a field day, with the mighty Squad vanquished and the robbers getting away. The Squad officers were furious, both with the injuries to their comrades and the press coverage. When the Commissioner, Sir Joseph Simpson KBE, turned up at the Squad office to commiserate and inject some much-needed morale into the personnel, Alf Durell told him precisely what would happen to the gang when they caught them. Although Ernie Millen severely admonished Durell for his intemperate language afterwards, Durell was only voicing the hopes and aspirations of the rest of the Squad officers and, if the truth be known, probably those of Millen and the commissioner, as well. Nevertheless, Millen decreed that the arrest of Terroni & Co. was to become a Squad priority.

On 17 June, Terroni and two other men were seen to enter the house in Clock House Road. Fearing that the men might be listening in to police broadcasts, all Flying Squad vehicles were told to return to 'D99' – the Squad office – immediately. But as the cars slowed in Whitehall, prior to turning into the Yard, Detective Inspector Charlie Palmer was standing on the pavement and he shouted, 'Penge nick – like the clappers!'

The Squad officers, their cars parked in nearby streets, stood in the yard at Penge police station and were briefed by Detective Inspectors Charlie Palmer and George Groombridge. The wanted men were in the house, they were believed to be armed and when the Squad officers were in position, they would go in. The Squad officers were deliberately unarmed; bearing in mind the strength of feeling about the gang who had severely maltreated two of their comrades, it was thought that if the Squadmen were armed, it could lead to … misunderstandings.

Therefore, the Squad would have to rely on speed, surprise and guile and at 2.30 that afternoon, they did: the semi-detached house was hit – front, back and side. Jeffrey gave up without a struggle; Terroni and one of the other gang members, Roy Scrutton, both of whom had access to loaded Webley automatics, did not. Even after relieving Terroni of his pistol, he still continued to struggle; it required the presence of Detective Sergeant (later

Detective Chief Superintendent) Jock McFadzean, probably one of the toughest (and certainly one of the strongest) of the Squad officers to thoroughly subdue him.

The three men were led – or perhaps carried – away and then the telephone rang; it was another of the suspects, a man named Walker, who had telephoned to see if the coast was clear. Detective Inspector Charlie Palmer, posing as one of the gang, gruffly assured him that it was. It was then a race to get all of the Squad cars out of the way and the ruined front door propped up to give the impression that it was still a solid fixture. Walker discovered this was not the case, after he strolled up the garden path and was fumbling for his key, when the door fell at his feet with a crash and the waiting Squad officers inside the house, stepped out and arrested him. 'Another two seconds, and I'd have blown your head off,' said Terroni when he was arrested; it probably contributed to him and the rest of the gang receiving a total of forty-six years' imprisonment at the Old Bailey. Terroni and co probably weren't Gilbert and Sullivan fans; had they been, they might have heeded Gilbert's words in the operetta, *Patience*: 'The enemy of one, the enemy of all is.'

If the Squad worked hard, they played hard, too. The great annual dinner and dance was held at the Dorchester Hotel and it attracted celebrities, both from the underworld and show business. In 1961, one of the principal guests was Roger (now Sir Roger) Moore – his father had been a constable at Bow Street – and the impresario, Michael Black had booked an up-and-coming Irish group, The Bachelors, as part of the cabaret. In between booking them and their actual arrival, The Bachelors' career really took off and it was felt that appearing at a Squad function was rather beneath them; an attempt was made for the performance to be cancelled. Michael Black might have been a Squad officer; he resolutely waved the contract under their collective noses and the Bachelors duly appeared at the Squad dinner and dance and gave a tremendous performance.

Ian Forbes has already been mentioned. He had spent five highly successful years with the Squad in the 1950s, in the ranks of detective sergeant (both first- and second-class) and detective inspector. After a stint as an instructor at the Detective Training School, now he was back on the Squad for a further eighteen-month posting and immediately made his presence felt. His – and his team's – top-notch informants led them to thieves and receivers of lorryloads, teams of wage-snatchers and a gang of particularly vicious robbers, Ronald King, Clifford Johnson, Colin Puttock and George Stowers. The four rushed into a bookmaker's home, attacked and tied up his wife and daughter and, whilst they waited for the bookmaker to arrive home, one of the men passed the time by kicking the two women. When the bookmaker did arrive, he too was savagely attacked and bound and robbed of cash. The gang were traced and arrested and made voluble confessions which later attracted some severe cross-examination at a fiercely defended trial at Surrey Assizes, after which the four robbers were sentenced to a total of thirty-four years' imprisonment.

A Squad informant also figured prominently when Forbes and his team arrested Völker Machazek, who received a very long prison sentence at the Old Bailey. Machazek had carried out five armed robberies, using a German gas gun which he fired at his victims on two occasions.

Quite clearly, one of the reasons for Forbes' many successes was good use of informants; he gained their trust because he never went back on his word. Similarly, he was just as straight with his team members; he was loyal and supportive towards them and he expected dependability in return. If anybody crossed him or displayed 'any dodgy tendency' then that person was off the team; the same equally applied to shirkers.

Woman Detective Constables Pat Willey and Rose Tummons arrived on the Squad in 1960, replacing the two former women officers; neither was attached to one particular squad, simply moving from one squad to another where they could be of most use. For much of the time, Pat Willey worked on the Dips Squad with Detective Sergeants Peter Boorman and John Colligan, but in 1962 she and Rose Tummons were instructed by Assistant Commissioner (Crime) Sir Ranulph 'Rasher' Bacon KPM (who had succeeded Sir Richard Jackson that year, following his retirement) to carry out surveillance on Arthur Clegg, alias Green – who was suspected of carrying out housebreakings on the homes of the great and the good. Clegg would visit libraries to look at the *London Gazette*; this publication was introduced following the Great Plague and King Charles II's decision to move his court to Oxford. Since that time, it had recorded momentous occasions at home and abroad; including news about when the knights and peers of the realm had vacated their homes to travel elsewhere – hence Clegg's interest.

Over a period of six months, the women tailed Clegg all over Slough and Eton and lost him in Stoke Poges. With the assistance of Dip Squad colleagues Boorman and Colligan, Clegg was finally arrested on 8 January 1963. He accepted his arrest philosophically but requested, 'Don't tell anyone I was caught by a bleedin' tart.'

Stanley 'Steve' Moore had arrived on the Squad in September 1960 as a detective sergeant (second class) and went to work with 5 Squad; there was plenty for him to do. In 1962, he, Detective Inspector Frank Williams and Detective Sergeants Johnny Meyrick and Peter Boorman were in a nondescript van sitting outside the Midland Bank, Kingsbury Road, Kingsbury Green. An informant of Boorman's had told him that three armed men intended to rob the bank as it opened. And just as the bank opened, three men appeared outside the premises, pulled up scarves to disguise themselves and produced pistols; immediately the doors of the van burst open and two of the would-be robbers were arrested. The third man, Michael Hampshire, ran off closely pursued by Moore. Hampshire turned to threaten Moore with the gun but still Moore ran after him; then, in the middle of nearby Slough Lane, there was a getaway car, its engine revving. Hampshire scrambled into the car but Moore wrenched the door open and a fierce struggled ensued; even as the pistol was pointed directly at Moore's head, the driver suddenly let in the clutch and the car roared away. Still Moore clung on to the rapidly accelerating car, until he was at last thrown off into the roadway.

'My suit was quite ragged; my wife was upset!' Moore told me, nearly fifty years after the event, but there was a happy conclusion to the proceedings after information was received that that evening, that Hampshire would be visiting a pub in Golders Green. Even without a gun, Hampshire felt obliged to offer resistance to his arrest, which was a mistake. At the Old Bailey, he was sentenced to three-and-a-half years' imprisonment, Moore was highly commended by the commissioner and on 5 June 1963 was awarded £20 from the Bow Street Reward Fund. Moore, who served almost seven years with the Squad, later retired with the rank of detective chief superintendent at C11.

But although Millen took away 'mugs' and 'participating informants' with one hand, he gave back with the other; he increased the manpower to almost 100 officers and the returns of work for 1961 jumped accordingly. Arrests rose to 1,410 and property to the value of £484,931 was recovered; an increase of

£170,000 from the previous year. In 1962, the arrests increased to 1,684, property recovered rose to £738,094 and the commissioner, at Millen's prompting, increased the Squad personnel by another 25 per cent.

So Millen was able to address the matter of 'Spanish practices', but there were two other matters becoming more and more prevalent, as alleged by the defence counsels who defended the villains with whom the Squad came into contact. The first was the suggestion that officers had planted incriminating evidence in the criminals' possession; the other (and far more common) was that the officers had 'verballed' them; in other words, falsely attributed words of a deeply compromising nature to them. In fairness, given the strength of the evidence against the majority of the criminals, it was really all that could be alleged against the officers, in a desperate last-ditch stand to bamboozle a gullible jury into acquitting them. Sometimes it did work, but not always ...

Detective Constable (later Detective Chief Superintendent) Harry Clement BEM was a very new member of 7 squad in 1963 and the following year, he and his team were responsible for bringing half-a-dozen villains before His Honour Judge Alan King-Hamilton QC – it was his first trial as a judge – at the Old Bailey. The prosecution was led by the brilliant barrister, Michael Worsley QC; one of the defence counsels was Felix Waley QC.

'As a Flying Squad officer,' intoned Waley, during his cross-examination of Clement, 'can you tell my lord and the jury what is meant by the word "verbal"?'

'As far as I can recall, sir, it means "oral",' replied Clement, adding helpfully, 'word of mouth.'

This was clearly not the answer which Waley expected, nor was it what he wanted to hear. 'Don't bandy words with me, officer,' he snapped. 'You know perfectly well what the term means; now – tell my Lord and the members of the jury.'

Moments such as this come only seldom in the life of a police officer. Clement may have been young in service but he was already wise and well-versed in the ways of the Flying Squad. 'My Lord – members of the jury,' replied Clement. 'A verbal is a statement or admission, made by a prisoner at the time he is arrested which he immediately retracts upon receiving advice from his solicitor or counsel.'

The whole courtroom exploded with laughter. Judge King-Hamilton capitalized on it and later introduced it into after-dinner speeches; inaccurately promoting Harry Clement, he would preface the story to his fellow diners, 'A young detective sergeant on the Flying Squad said ...'

Clement's words spread like wildfire. They reached the ears of the very popular Assistant Commissioner (Crime) Sir Ranulph Bacon who sent Clement a note of appreciation, adding, 'It's about time we fought back.' Detective Chief Superintendent Ken Oxford attended a murder trial in Sussex; he telephoned to say that Clement's words had reached the court and were causing considerable amusement amongst the barristers. Detective Chief Superintendent Harry Tappin was to give evidence at a court in mid-Anglia; suspecting that an allegation of verballing would be made in cross-examination, he quickly telephoned Clement to ensure that he had the wording of the reply absolutely correct.

In the years which followed, whenever Michael Worsley encountered Clement in court corridors, he would inevitably ask with a chuckle, 'Mr Clement, what's the meaning of the word "verbal"?' Many officers have claimed to have been the originator of that classic reply, but as Harry Clement informed me, over forty-five years later, 'I claim the copyright!'

And what of Felix Waley, who prompted the answer which caused so much mirth? Later, as His Honour Judge Waley QC, he gained the reputation of being a hard-line, pro-prosecution judge.[1]

★   ★   ★

In 1963, the Squad made over 1,900 arrests but the value of property recovered slumped to £462,348 and 1964 saw the worst crime figures of the century in London. The Squad still provided 1,463 arrests, and property recovered amounted to £512,521, but it was decided to form the nationwide Regional

---

[1] The author gave evidence before Judge Waley at Maidstone Crown Court in 1987, regarding a gang of vicious armed robbers who alleged serious impropriety in respect of the Flying Squad. Judge Waley would have none of it; the night before he was due to be sentenced, the gang leader who had threatened to shoot the author, probably realized the impetuosity of his actions and hanged himself.

Crime Squad (RCS). The London-based No. 9 RCS initially had five branch offices and in 1966, it was expanded to form six sections in outer London, with four more in inner London. The RCS were tasked to deal with organized, cross-border crime and were able to liaise with each other on a nationwide basis. In 1967, those four inner offices came under the umbrella of the Flying Squad.

Meanwhile, the Flying Squad was as active as ever. In 1964, Mark Owen and Freddie Sanson had carried out bank raids south of the river, where shots had been discharged. The men had been quickly identified; armed robbers were in the minority in those days, as were racially integrated teams, so with Owen, black and Sanson, white, it was not too long before their names were circulated in *Police Gazette* as being wanted for the offences, with Owen being described as 'armed and dangerous'.

By this time, Frank Williams had moved on from the Squad and the vacancy for detective inspector which he had left on 5 squad had been filled by Jim Barnett; he and Steve Moore were keeping observation, late one night in the vicinity of The Oval, the international cricket ground in Kennington, south London. An informant of Detective Sergeant Johnny Meyrick's had told him that at ten o'clock that night, Owen would be in that vicinity. Suddenly, Moore spotted Owen and getting out of the car went to confront him; Owen turned and ran with Moore in hot pursuit. As Owen dashed into a block of flats, Moore recalled the addendum on Owen's wanted notice – 'armed and dangerous' – and for the first and only time in his career, drew his truncheon. 'I caught him right on the back of his head with it,' Moore told me. 'I remember, my 'stick' bounced when it made contact – that slowed him up!'

Sanson was picked up more peaceably, in bed; later at the Old Bailey, Owen was sentenced to ten years' imprisonment, with Sanson collecting fifteen.

The provider of that piece of information – and many others, besides – Johnny Meyrick, was held in very high esteem by his colleagues. Harry Forbes who served on the Squad from 1973 to 1978 remembered Meyrick (always known as 'Sargie'), as his detective inspector and rated him very highly. Bill Smillie stated, 'Sargie is a man for whom I had the greatest respect. I grew up in the Job with him and the two other members of that fantastic strike-force, Neesham and Slipper. He had a wonderful right hook, to which I can testify. A great detective and person but his biggest work was done in the sixties.'

★　★　★

Few Squad officers had heard of John Marson; he was serving a two-year jail sentence for vehicle offences when, on 4 November 1964, he escaped from Lewes Prison. Stealing one car after another, he acquired a 9mm Lüger automatic, a journalist and his girlfriend as companions, and a shotgun and ammunition. Marson now concentrated on the reason for his escape: to find his former girlfriend. Driving yet another stolen car he found her; only to discover she was now married. Telling her husband that he would kill both him and his wife if she refused to accompany him, Marson, the new bride and his accomplices drove off, again stealing one car after another. Threatening a motorist and firing at his car, Marson also shot and wounded the caretaker of a house. It was clear that a police hunt would now be on for the persons involved in these shootings and the journalist and his girlfriend took their leave from Marson and went to Dublin.

Marson had no real game-plan; during the two months that he had been at large, stolen cars had taken him all over the southern counties of England, then up to Shrewsbury and even farther north to York. By now, he had stolen a Mercedes sports car, belonging to the racing driver, Roy Salvatori. Another man was conscripted to join Marson and his girlfriend, and the three of them, Marson driving the stolen Mercedes with the Lüger in his lap, entered London. He was spotted by a police car but tore off, smashing into cars as he went, until he finally crashed into a car in Little Boltons, Chelsea. Detective Sergeant Peter Woodmore had been on patrol in a Flying Squad car and had picked up the radio messages from the pursuing police vehicles – so the Squad car, driven by the late Police Constable Geoffrey Bocking, joined in the chase. A police motorcyclist, Police Constable Michael Wheelhouse, ran over to the crashed Mercedes and went to open the driver's door; Marson shot him in the arm. Running from the stolen car, Marson fired three times, narrowly missing the pursuing officers. Climbing into a basement area in Collingham Road, Marson fired again, this time killing a police dog. The area had been cordoned off; Detective Inspector David Wilson of the

Squad narrowly missed being hit by a shot fired by Marson – Wilson gathered up an armful of milk bottles which he hurled at the gunman. Marson fired two more shots, one of them hitting Police Constable Roger Cross.

Peter Woodmore climbed onto the railings surrounding the basement and as Marson pointed the pistol at him, he jumped, landing on top of him and seizing his gun-arm, overpowered him. At the Old Bailey, Marson pleaded guilty to possessing a firearm with intent to endanger life, to three cases of inflicting grievous bodily harm, and to stealing cars – and asked for five other cases to be taken into consideration. He was sentenced to a total of fourteen years' imprisonment. Both Peter Woodmore and Michael Wheelhouse were awarded the George Medal, with the bravery of three other officers who pursued Marson being recognized with awards of the British Empire Medal for gallantry and commendations for many more of the officers. At the time of his arrest, Marson had shouted, 'I will kill you all!' and the fact that he did not was not through want of trying.

$$\star \quad \star \quad \star$$

Any vehicle loitering in the vicinity of a prison would rightly be regarded as being suspicious because of the possibility of its occupants aiding an escape,[2] so when the crew of 'F' Division's 'Q' Car, 'Foxtrot One-one' saw an old blue Vanguard estate aimlessly driving along Braybrook Street, which abuts Wormwood Scrubs prison, on a late summer's day, 12 August 1966, they decided to stop it and find out the reason for occupants being there. The three men in the van – Harry Maurice Roberts, John Edward Whitney and John Duddy – had no intention of helping anybody to escape; they were simply wasting time until they could carry out their intention to rob a rent collector. They had false number plates (JJJ 285D) which they intended to affix to a stolen Ford Cortina to facilitate their escape, plus a holdall containing overalls; also a Lüger automatic pistol, an Army .38 Colt and a .38 Webley.

---

[2] In fact, nine weeks later, George Blake, serving forty-two years for espionage offences, escaped from Wormwood Scrubs prison.

So when the blue Triumph 2000 'Q' Car stopped them to ask what they were doing, Roberts shot Temporary Detective Constable David Wombwell in the eye and as Detective Sergeant Christopher Head started to run back to the police car, he was chased by Duddy and Roberts, who shot him in the back. Duddy ran round to the 'Q' Car's driver, Police Constable Geoffrey Fox and shot him between the eyes. Not since the events which had triggered the siege of Sidney Street, fifty-five years before, had so many police officers been murdered at the same time.

The sixty-five-strong murder hunt which commenced conscripted a number of Flying Squad officers, including newly promoted Detective Inspector Jack Slipper. A passer-by had noted the Vanguard's registration number, PGT 726, which led Slipper to its owner – Whitney. He provided a preposterous story of selling the van to an unknown man that morning and offered an alibi; Slipper demolished the alibi, the van was found in a lock-up, containing the false number plates, three used .38 cartridges and a stocking mask and most revealing of all, the garage was rented to Whitney. Not until he was charged, did Whitney start to talk – and now the team knew who they were looking for.

Four days after the shootings, Detective Chief Inspector Bob Brown of the Glasgow CID smashed in the door of a tenement flat in Stevenson Street, Calton and with two armed officers, seized a quivering John Duddy, who gave up without a struggle. He made a full confession to Detective Chief Inspector John 'Ginger' Hensley of the Flying Squad who had flown up to Glasgow with Slipper, in order to bring Duddy back to London.

Roberts, by far the most dangerous of the trio – he had been sentenced to a seven-year jail term for almost killing a 78-year-old pensioner during a burglary – was still at large. During his National Service, he had served as a sniper in Malaya and it was thought, quite rightly, that he would utilize his guerrilla skills to avoid capture.

In mid-November 1966, the trial of Duddy and Whitney commenced at the Old Bailey, but hardly had proceedings got underway when news was received that Roberts had been arrested in Thorley Wood, Hertfordshire. From his cleverly constructed hide, which had been discovered by a young gypsy, Roberts crawled out, begging the police officers not to shoot. They recovered the .38 Colt and the Lüger; and Roberts, too, made a full confession.

The jury at the Old Bailey took barely thirty minutes to find the three men guilty of the senseless murders; on 6 December 1966, Mr Justice Glyn Jones passed sentence, saying:

> I pass on you the sentence prescribed by law for the crime of murder, on each count of which you have been convicted, that is, of imprisonment for life. You have been justly convicted of what is perhaps the most heinous crime to have been committed in this country for a generation, or more. I think it likely that no Home Secretary regarding the enormity of your crime, will ever think fit to show mercy by releasing you on licence. This is one of those crimes in which the sentence of life imprisonment may well be treated as meaning exactly what it says. Lest any Home Secretary in the future should be minded to consider your release on licence, I have to make a recommendation. My recommendation is that you should not be released on licence, any of the three of you, for a period of thirty years, to begin from today's date.

At the time of writing, only Roberts is still behind bars.

But the case was not quite closed. One of Slipper's highly placed informants fingered a north London Greek Cypriot newsagent, Costas Christos for supplying the guns to Roberts. At Christos' trial, Roberts was produced from prison but refused to identify him as being his supplier; there was, however, other compelling evidence and Christos was convicted and sentenced to six years' imprisonment.

★   ★   ★

The courage, zeal and tenacity of all those Squad officers would have brought high praise from the man who had first led the Flying Squad into action, nearly half a century previously. Walter Hambrook died peacefully, aged ninety, at his home in Sutton, Surrey, in December 1966. As *The Times* noted in his obituary, he was 'more likely to have been mistaken for a modest businessman than for the shrewd detective he was'; yet because he led by example, the man who was known as 'The Father of the Squad' was responsible for putting the Flying Squad well and truly on the map.

The Great Train Robbery

I t is the robbery that will never go away. Some of the gang are still alive but as they die, so the great train robbery will be resurrected. The anniversary of the robbery will be remembered on television programmes for the simple reason that it has great media potential and interest and therefore, when similarly eye-catching robberies are carried out in the future, the great train robbery will be held up as a template to reflect the flaws or successes in the current robbery.

There are still octogenarian Flying Squad officers around today who will wink and knowingly tap the side of their noses with a wrinkled forefinger and inform a credulous listener that they knew the great train robbery was going to come off – but little credence should be given to their wanderings.

However, the warning signs were there. On Tuesday, 27 November 1962, a group of bowler-hatted 'businessmen' wearing false moustaches attacked security guards at Comet House, the BOAC office at Heathrow Airport, stole £62,500, and jumped into two waiting Mark II Jaguars which were both expertly driven away.

The investigation was conducted by 'T' Division – the division of the Metropolitan Police covering Heathrow Airport, and the same division who, fourteen years previously had handed over the attempted bullion raid to the Flying Squad. Not, however on this occasion. But the Squad did busy themselves in the investigation because they knew that there were only two men who could drive getaway cars with such skill – Roy John James (a very promising racing driver) and Micky Ball. Therefore the two were pulled in; and since the Squad knew that they associated with Gordon Goody and Charlie Wilson, they were arrested as well. Ronald 'Buster' Edwards who exhibited exemplary violence to the custodians during the robbery was not arrested; neither was Bruce Reynolds who was alleged to have been involved in the robbery. After a series of identification parades, James was released but Ball, Goody and Wilson were charged with the robbery and rather surprisingly were released on bail. During the trial, a juror was bribed, a witness was intimidated and evidence was tampered with. Only Ball was convicted and as he commenced a five year sentence, the others walked free from court. The solicitors representing Gordon Goody had been Brian Field and John Wheater. It was this robbery which had been set up to finance the next one, in which both Field and Wheater would both feature and nobody on the Flying Squad or anywhere else had the faintest notion of when or where it was going to occur.

But now the whole world knows that it was at three o'clock in the morning of 8 August 1963, at Sears Crossing, just north of Cheddington, Buckinghamshire, that approximately fifteen determined men caused the Glasgow to London mail train to come to an unscheduled halt, due to a bogus red signal. Savagely assaulting Jack Mills, the train driver, with an iron bar – again, it was 'Buster' Edwards who was alleged to have carried out the attack – the robbers forced him to drive the train to Bridego Bridge, where the gang stormed through the train. Apart from its consignment of mail, the train was carrying a large amount of mainly untraceable bank notes and within a very short space of time, the gang helped themselves to £2,631,684 worth of them.

The cash, contained in 120 mailbags, was thrown down the embankment and on to a waiting lorry, which roared off into the night, as did the rest of the gang's vehicles, all heading to Leatherslade Farm near the village of Oakley, Buckinghamshire, which had been purchased for £5,500, ten days previously.

The ringleaders of this audacious robbery were Douglas Gordon Goody, Charlie Frederick Wilson and Bruce Reynolds. Others who played decisive roles were Ronald 'Buster' Edwards, Roy John James, Jimmy White, Jimmy Hussey, Thomas William Wisbey, Roger John Cordrey and Bob Welch. Ronnie Arthur Biggs became involved because he was a friend of Reynolds and was supposed to supply a competent train driver. In the second of these considerations, he failed miserably. Leonard Field negotiated the purchase of Leatherslade Farm, via Brian Arthur Field (no relation), who had represented Goody on the Comet House robbery, and was a totally corrupt solicitor. John Denby Wheater was also a solicitor who became involved, but in all probability he had foolishly allowed himself to be manipulated by Field.

Once the balloon had gone up, Brigadier Cheyney, the Chief Constable of Buckinghamshire, lost no time in calling in the Yard and Detective Chief Superintendent Gerald McArthur, attached to C1 Department was sent with a small team to introduce the provincial officers to the world-famous Scotland Yard major enquiry system. Loss adjusters Hart & Co. offered rewards of up to £225,000 for information leading to the arrest and conviction of the gang and the recovery of the money. Three days after the raid, Roger Cordrey and another man, William Gerald Boal were arrested in Bournemouth, having been found in possession of almost £141,000 from the robbery. Meanwhile, the gang had moved out of their hideout, which was discovered four days after the robbery.

A local herdsman, John Alfred Maris, had wandered into the farm looking for some of his cattle and noticed that the farm's windows had been blacked out, there was a lorry in one of the sheds and the garage door had a brand-new padlock. He telephoned the police, informed them of his discovery and waited patiently for them to arrive. When they did not, he telephoned them again the following day, but what with some 400 calls coming into the police station every day, his call was not given the priority it deserved. He was only stopped from telephoning for a third time by his wife telling him he was acting like a fool, shortly before the arrival of two police officers. Their discovery of mailbags containing banknote wrappings and a considerable amount of other incriminating evidence at the farm gave the investigating team the lead they had been looking for. Maurice Ray and Ian Holden from the Metropolitan Police Forensic Science Laboratory and their team of experts moved in and set to work.

But once it became clear from the witnesses that it was a London-based gang who had pulled the job, the Commander of the CID, George Hatherill, instructed the head of the Flying Squad, Ernie Millen, to get his men involved. A small team to act on information received and to make the arrests was formed; they set up an office one floor below the Flying Squad near C1 Murder Office, and the administration was carried out by Detective Chief Inspector Sid Bradbury. In charge was Frank Williams, who had seen active service as a sergeant major with an Army Commando in Italy, during World War Two. The tough, pudgy-faced detective inspector was in charge of 5 squad, and he had an outstanding record from working in south London. He was partnered by Detective Sergeant Steve Moore, now the only surviving member of the original investigating team. 'I rated Frank very highly,' he told me. 'He was very well informed.' Detective Sergeant Jack Slipper worked with Jim Neville (later to distinguish himself on the Bomb Squad), and Detective Sergeant Lou van Dyke and Detective Constable Tommy Thorburn, two East End detectives, worked together. It was a formidable team, made all the more so by the detective in overall charge – Tommy Butler.

No one better could have been chosen than Butler; the investigation of the great train robbery might have been designed for him. Fanatical in his pursuit of criminals, if Butler drove his men hard, he pushed himself even harder.

Immediately, Butler pressed his informants into action and names started appearing straight away. The Home Secretary was contacted as a matter of urgency – just as quickly, he authorized a number of intercepts on the likeliest 'faces' and these were given priority by Detective Inspector 'Wilf' Pickles, who had formally served on 1 squad with Butler and who now headed the Intercept Room at C11 Department. Pickles was nicknamed 'Deafy' and it was considered vastly humorous that someone with a hearing impediment should be in charge of the unit which undertook the task of overhearing villains' conversations. Now, Butler knew who was talking to whom; the same names started coming up, and when Maurice Ray reported finding an enormous number of fingerprints at Leatherslade Farm, Butler contacted the Yard's Fingerprint Department, handed them a list of names and said, 'Try these first.'

It paid off; identifications which normally would have taken weeks, probably months of careful scrutinizing, were achieved within hours – and then catastrophe struck. Hatherill and Millen made the incredible decision to circulate the names and photographs of some of the gang who had been identified, both in the newspapers and on television. Butler and Williams furiously opposed the decision, on the grounds that it would be their informants who would identify the whereabouts of the gang members and that if the details of the men were to be published, it would drive them underground or out of the country, perhaps for years to come. But Butler and Williams were overruled and their gloomy prophecy turned out to be only too true. Of those whose names and photographs were published, only Charlie Wilson was arrested, at his house in Clapham – because the newspaper had not arrived. When he was charged, he indignantly replied, 'I don't see how you can make it stick without the "poppy" [money] adding, 'and you will not find that.' Wilson was unaware that his fingerprints had been found on a drum of salt, some transparent wrapping and a window-sill at Leatherslade Farm.

Ronnie Biggs could have made a similar reply, because at the time of his arrest, his share of the money was buried underneath half-a-ton of coal at his home and by the time the police were informed of this the money had gone and was never recovered. All Biggs had was an alibi which did not stand close inspection; his fingerprints, found on three different items at the farm, did. He was arrested by Detective Sergeant Steve Moore, questioned by Tommy Butler, taken to Aylesbury and charged. Jimmy Hussey was shown the photograph of a lorry which had been found at Leatherslade Farm and denied going to the farm or anywhere near the lorry. Unfortunately, he had left his palm-print on the lorry's tailboard.

But on 1 October 1963, when Millen was promoted to the rank of deputy commander and Butler to detective chief superintendent of the Squad, Butler made it abundantly clear that from now on, things would be done *his* way. It was high time.

Characteristically, Butler was over-secretive and played his cards close to his chest, too close, some thought, for comfort. It was not necessarily the best way but it was Butler's way, and he and his men worked round the clock. After a sustained period of non-stop work, one of the exhausted officers asked if he might have a day off to go home. Butler was utterly dumbstruck; he simply could not comprehend that any Squad officer could want to voluntarily leave the investigation, simply to 'go home'. But Butler's tactics paid off; by the end of the enquiry, twenty-two of the twenty-four prisoners had been arrested by the Flying Squad. During the first six weeks of the enquiry, the Squad searched 419 premises and, as is so often the case, arrests were made and stolen property recovered which was nothing to do with the Great Train Robbery. In one particular case, one criminal who was strongly suspected of involvement in the robbery had his scrap metal yard at Harlesden searched. In fact, it was later established that he was unconnected with the robbery, neither was any stolen property found. However, in a locked room at the rear of the office, a printing press and plates for forging £5 notes were found. The test notes revealed a very high standard of quality and it was fortunate that this series had yet to be launched on an unsuspecting public; three people were convicted at the Old Bailey.

Some of the robbery suspects were brought in for a preliminary chat then released, so when they were told that Butler wanted another talk with them, most of them went along to the police station quite willingly, believing that Butler only wanted to clear up a few points. They were mistaken; the second interview inevitably resulted in their arrest and charging. One such was Gordon Goody; by the time his subsequent interview came around, the forensic scientists had deduced that a combination of paint and gravel, found in microscopic quantities on the soles of Goody's shoes, had originated from the farm. Tommy Wisbey was another who was arrested, then released. On his second invitation to the Yard, he was charged after providing his palm-prints, one of which matched a palm-print found on the bath rail at the farm. Bob Welch was arrested, provisionally questioned and released; then he made himself deliberately unavailable and went to north Devon.

Tommy Butler received information that £5 notes tinged with yellow (suggesting they had originally been buried) were being circulated in the north Devon area and he sent Steve Moore, together with Tom Morrison, then, a detective sergeant (first class), to try to determine their source. Although the two Squad officers spent a pleasant week in the West Country, it was all to no avail. So it was just as well that Welch, who had planned to go abroad, had with a Londoner's sentimentality returned to see the city for one last time and was grassed; the Flying Squad were waiting for him. Welch was a gang member who did wear gloves for most of the time at the farm; unfortunately for him, one of them had a small tear in it, which resulted in one of his fingerprints appearing on a can of beer. And once or twice when he neglected to wear gloves he had left his left and right palm prints on a can of beer.

One of the suspects was not even arrested, initially. Eight days after the robbery, the engine of a motorcycle overheated and its owner stopped the machine by some woods near Dorking, in Surrey. There he found some bags filled with money, amounting to £100,900; even more interesting was that also in one of the bags was a receipt in respect of the Café Pension Restaurant Sonnenbichl, Hinderlang, in the province of Allgaen, Germany. The police were already aware that Brian Field was the solicitor's clerk who had negotiated the sale of Leatherslade Farm; sadly for him the receipt was made out to a Herr and Frau Field and he was quite easily duped into admitting that he and his German-born wife, Karin, had stayed at the pension. Although he was not arrested there and then, it was the beginning of the end for Field.

The police continued searching the Surrey woods. Four miles away from where the sack of money had been found, they discovered an unoccupied caravan. Upon searching it, the police found that panelling had been disturbed. They disturbed it a little more and found £30,440 secreted there; the fingerprints inside the caravan matched those of Jimmy White.

Another of the suspects who was initially brought in for questioning, then released, was Lennie Field, who had purchased Leatherslade Farm through his namesake, Brian. When Butler received information that Field would be leaving his home at Manor House at two o'clock in the morning and intended to leave the country, John Simmonds and his team followed Field's green A35 van along Green Lanes. As it reached the junction with Brownswood Road and stopped at the traffic lights, so Simmonds ran from the Squad car to the rear of the van, slipped a metal tube over the handle on the back door, snapped it open and dived across the back of the van, pinioning the startled Field until the rest of the team came round to arrest him.

Roy James had proved to be elusive; Jack Slipper just missed him at a practice session at Goodwood racetrack and then James heard on his car radio that Wilson had been arrested and he immediately went to ground. So when information was received on 3 December 1963 that he was hiding at 14 Ryder's Terrace, St John's Wood, arrangements for his arrest were made immediately. However, at 6.30 that evening, an anonymous caller phoned the Yard to say that £50,000 of the stolen money would be left in a telephone kiosk in Great Dover Street, Newington Butts, South London. Williams was eager to go, because this fitted in with information which he had been receiving from one of his contacts, which was that 'Buster' Edwards was wishing to negotiate his surrender by returning some of the stolen money. Butler was sceptical because it was not one of his informants who had provided the information and decided it was a hoax but at Williams' insistence, he accompanied him and there, in the telephone kiosk they discovered a bag containing £47,245.

Having deposited the sack at the Yard, Butler and Williams moved straight on with their teams to Ryder's Terrace, with Butler stating quite unequivocally that if James escaped, none of the Squad officers need bother returning to the Yard, since all of them would be transferred to divisional duties. *That* put the teams on their mettle – Woman Detective Constable Pat Willey, holding a bogus parcel, knocked on the front door; that brought no results, but she heard the curtain being pulled open in the window above the front door. 'There's someone in there,' she told Butler, who was concealed in the next doorway. With that, Detective Sergeant Steve Moore climbed up to the first-floor balcony and smashed the French windows. As he entered the flat, he was in time to see James' legs disappearing through a fanlight. Moore chased him, shouting, 'Over the roof, over the roof!' to the Squad officers below and James, carrying a holdall and risking a broken leg, leapt thirty feet from the roof. He landed, quite literally in the arms of Detective Sergeant (First Class) Johnny Matthews, a former wrestler who was over six feet tall and weighed eighteen stone. An eye-witness told me that James, who was considerably smaller, and looking very much like the baby who was thrown out with the bathwater, was carried by Matthews to the Squad car, where he was gently deposited. The bag which accompanied his flight was, he stressed, nothing to do with him. It was found to contain £12,041. Asked where he had been on the night of the robbery, James replied, 'Not at that farm I read so much about.' That, and the fact that his fingerprints had been found on a plate and a magazine at the farm, delighted Butler and the threat of peremptory transfers abated.

John Daly, someone whom Frank Williams knew well from his south London days, was sought in connection with the robbery. Quite apart from being Bruce Reynolds' brother-in-law, his fingerprints had been found at the farm. However, it was not until 1964, when he and his pregnant wife were living under the aliases of 'Mr and Mrs R. J. Grant' in a basement flat at Eaton Square, Chelsea, that Tommy Butler, Frank Williams, Jack Slipper and Steve Moore, together with a number of other officers, burst into the flat. 'Daly was in a dressing gown and had just finished a breakfast of kippers,' recalled Moore. However,

Daly's appearance had changed considerably since Williams had
last seen him; now he was sporting a black beard and weighed
three stone less. According to Slipper, Williams had considerable
difficulty in recognizing Daly, although Williams' recollection of
his identification was more positive. 'Hello, Mr Williams. I'm
caught,' was the way Williams remembered Daly greeting him.

Daly later proved to be very shrewd; he denied ever going to
the farm, refused to allow his palmprints to be taken or to be
photographed. During the trial, his barrister, Wilfred Fordham
successfully argued that Daly's fingerprints, which had been
found on a Monopoly board, had got there during a game at a
friend's house in south London, several weeks before the robbery.
Because the board was a portable item and, more importantly,
because Tommy Butler with his fanatical secrecy had neglected to
inform the interviewing team of this, the Judge agreed that Daly
was entitled to be acquitted, and he was. Had the interviewing
officers known of the precise information concerning exactly
where Daly's fingerprints had been found, the questioning could
have been structured a little differently.

One by one, the train robbers were brought in, with a few
exceptions. Jimmy White, who also used the names James Bryan
and James Whitefoot, seems to have had the knack of melting into
the landscape. 'Buster' Edwards (using the name 'Jack Ryan')
and his family had rented a house in Wraysbury; from there,
Edwards went to Germany on a forged passport in the name of
'Jack Miller' and thence to Mexico City on another forged
passport, this time using his Wraysbury address alias.

Although Frank Williams had his own dedicated team,
Detective Inspector Fred Byers was in charge of 7 squad, under
instruction to be seconded to assist Williams, as and when the
need arose.

One Saturday afternoon, Tommy Butler told Byers to get his
team together and to follow him. Butler booked out a 'self-drive'
Mini Cooper and, secretive as always, led the three-car Squad
convoy to a street near Croydon market. Bruce Reynolds had
remained in England, moving from one address to another, and
now Butler had information that Reynolds was in a house nearby.
Butler briefed his men; some were to go to the rear of the
property, others were to collect a ladder from the house next door
and the rest, including Detective Constable Harry Clement, were
to go in through the front door. Butler was about to have the door

kicked-in until Clement cheekily suggested that there might be a key, hanging on the inside of the letter-box – there was, and Butler and his team were in.

As the Squad officers dashed into the different rooms in the house, so Butler and Clement ran straight ahead into the kitchen. Clement felt the stove; it was hot. So too was a nearby teapot, and a cup, waiting for the tea to be poured into it, already had milk in it. With considerable justification, Clement shouted out, 'He's in the house!' and this provoked an intensified search of the cupboards with carpets being lifted to detect loose floorboards, all to no avail; the bird had well and truly flown.

Many years later, Clement, by now retired, was on location to film a pilot of a television series involving crime and detection; so too was Bruce Reynolds. They chatted amiably about 'the old times' and then Clement mentioned the abortive search in Croydon.

Reynolds laughed and replied, 'Yes, I was there. I had just made a pot of tea when I had a sudden thought – call it intuition – that you lot were not too far away, so I decided to go, fast. I already had a bag packed with passport etcetera, also, I had taken the precaution of having another place to run to, not too far away, and I went. I reckon I went round the corner at the bottom of the road as you lot came into the street.' Reynolds chuckled again and added, 'You and I can call it "the one that got away" or "the hot teapot".'

It was a busy time for Reynolds; he and his wife moved into a flat above a cleaners in Handcroft Road, Croydon. One night, a police patrol arrived, having noticed a ladder up against the first-floor window. They believed there had been a burglary – and in fact, they were right, although Reynolds and his wife were unaware of this. Police insisted to Mrs Reynolds that for her safety they be allowed to come in and search the premises and although she protested, she knew that an outright refusal would appear highly suspicious, so she eventually let them in.

Reynolds, who had heard the conversation, acted quickly. He completely undressed and when the officers entered the lounge, Reynolds giving a convincing display of embarrassment and attempting to cover up his naked body, stammered that he was the lady of the flat's lover; something which was shame-facedly confirmed by Mrs Reynolds. By now, the officers were similarly discomfited and after Reynolds had provided a false name and address, they made their apologies and left.

The mistake was soon realized and a team of Flying Squad officers rushed to the flat. They were in possession of information that if anybody knocked on the downstairs door, no one in the flat would answer. If, however, the caller put his hand through the letter-box, a concealed bell push could be pressed and Reynolds would realize that it was a friend and open the door.

Not, however, on this occasion. The bell could have been pressed until hell froze over, because Reynolds had long gone. He would later meet up with Edwards in Mexico City.

The rest of the gang were committed for trial. The 120 police officers who had been involved in the enquiry marshalled the 1,700 exhibits and the 2,350 statements, to be ready for what was to prove one of the most closely followed trials in criminal history.

The chamber of the rural district council at Aylesbury was converted into a court to accommodate the prisoners and their small army of legal advisors and on 20 January 1964, the trial, presided over by Lord Edmund-Davies and which would last over ten weeks, commenced. It was certainly not without incident.

An approach was made to Brian Field's wife, Karin, by a man who said he could bribe three of the jurors for a consideration of £3,000. The matter was referred to the police for investigation. Detective Sergeant John Swain of the Flying Squad was severely rebuked by the judge after it appeared that he had searched the home of Gordon Goody's mother, telling her that he was in possession of a search warrant, when he was not. A witness for the prosecution, Jack Knowles, disappeared. He was supposed to give evidence against Gordon Goody, although it was later conceded that any evidence he could have provided would not have added to the case against Goody. The judge was furious when he received an anonymous letter in which the writer told him how to conduct the trial. Ronald Biggs was ordered to be retried after a police inspector was cross-examined and revealed to the jury that Biggs had stated he had served a prison term. John Daly was acquitted on the directions of the judge. Leonard Field, having given evidence on his own behalf, suddenly admitted perjury, claiming he had been the innocent dupe of the solicitors Field and Wheater. The two solicitors not unnaturally denied the accusation. A juror then reported to the judge that he had been approached with a bribe to sway the jury's verdict. Two days later, the judge directed that twenty-four-hour police protection be given to the families of the jurors when they retired to consider their verdict. Next the judge heard that a reporter had indicated he would reveal where the jury would be staying while they deliberated – the judge advised that this would not be a responsible course of action.

Lord Edmund-Davies' summing-up took six days and after deliberating for sixty-six hours and twenty-four minutes, the jury duly delivered their verdicts; Biggs had already been convicted on his re-trial. The sentencing took place on 15 April in the Assize Court and the prisoners were brought up to the dock, one by one. The judge was about to impose some of the most swingeing sentences ever to be handed out in an English courtroom. The first was Roger Cordrey and the judge addressed him in the following words:

> Roger John Cordrey, you are the first to be sentenced out of certainly eleven greedy men whom hope of gain allured. You and your co-accused have been convicted of complicity, in one way or another, of a crime which in its impudence and enormity is the first of its kind in this country. I propose to do all within my power to ensure it will also be the last of its kind; for your outrageous conduct constitutes an intolerable menace to the well-being of society.
>
> Let us clear out of the way any romantic notions of dare-devilry. This is nothing less than a sordid crime of violence inspired by vast greed. The motive of greed is obvious. As to violence, anybody who has seen that nerve-shattered engine driver can have no doubt of the terrifying effect on law-abiding citizens of a concerted assault by masked and armed robbers in lonely darkness. To deal with this case leniently would be a positively evil thing. When grave crime is committed it calls for grave punishment, not for the purpose of mere retribution but so that others similarly tempted shall be brought to the sharp realization that crime does not pay and that the crime is most certainly not worth even the most alluring candle. As the higher the price, the greater the temptation, potential criminals who may be dazzled by the enormity of the price must be taught that the punishment they risk will be proportionately greater.
>
> I therefore find myself faced with the unenviable duty of pronouncing grave sentences. You, Cordrey, and the other

accused vary widely in intelligence, strength of personality, in antecedent history, in age, and in many other ways. Some convicted on this indictment have absolutely clean characters up to the present. Some have previous convictions of a comparatively minor character and others have previous convictions of gravity which could now lead to sentences of corrective training or even of preventative detention.

To some the degradation to which you have all now sunk will bring consequences vastly more cruel than to others. I have anxiously sought to bear in mind everything that has been urged on behalf of all the accused by your learned counsel, to whom I am so greatly indebted, but whatever the past of a particular accused and whatever his position, all else pales into insignificance in the light of his present offences.

Furthermore, the evidence, or rather the lack of it, renders it impossible to determine exactly what part was played by each of the eleven accused convicted of the larger conspiracy or the eight convicted of the actual robbery.

I therefore propose, after mature deliberation, to treat you all in the same manner with but two exceptions.

You, Cordrey, are the first of the exceptions. On your own confession you stand convicted on the first count of conspiracy to rob the mail and on counts, three, four and five of receiving in all nearly £141,000 of the stolen money, but when arrested you immediately gave information to the police which enabled them to put their hands on nearly £80,000 and the remainder was eventually recovered. Furthermore, at the outset of this trial you confessed your guilt and I feel I should give recognition to that fact in determining your sentence. I do this because it is greatly in the public interest that the guilty should confess their guilt. This massive trial is the best demonstration of the truth of that proposition.

In respect of the four counts you must go to prison for concurrent terms of twenty years.

The court gasped; even the hardened newspaper crime reporters were dumb-struck – one kept repeating, 'Twenty years? On a *plea*?' It was a warning to everybody of the sentences to come. They did not have long to wait. As Cordrey was taken down, so Boal was brought into the dock. He was the first of the defendants to be convicted on both counts one and two of the indictment: conspiracy to rob and the actual robbery. Boal had just the one previous conviction, an eighteen-month prison sentence for receiving. He had vehemently denied both robbery charges and in time to come, the other members of the gang similarly disputed that Boal had been involved, either in the conspiracy or the robbery. Not, however during the trial. Since they were denying involvement themselves it would have been the height of recklessness to have supported Boal's defence.

> William Gerald Boal, you, who are substantially the oldest of the accused, have been convicted of conspiracy to rob the mail and of armed robbery itself. You have expressed no repentance for your wrong-doing, indeed, you continue to assert your innocence but you beg for mercy. I propose to extend to you some measure of mercy and I do it on two grounds. Firstly, on account of your age, you being a man of fifty and, secondly, because, having seen and heard you, I cannot believe that you were one of the originators of the conspiracy or that you played a very dynamic part in it or in the robbery itself ... In the light of these considerations the concurrent sentences you will serve are, upon the first count, twenty-one years and upon the second count, twenty-four years.

Next up was Charles Frederick Wilson; he had served prison sentences for receiving and possessing explosives and he was a committed armed robber, of that there was no doubt. The judge addressed him with the following words:

> No one has said less than you throughout this long trial. Indeed, I doubt if you have spoken half-a-dozen words. Certainly no word of repentance has been expressed by you. My duty, as I can see it, is clear. If you or any of the other accused still to be dealt with had assisted justice, that would have told strongly in your favour, but you have not. The consequence of this outrageous crime is that the vast booty of something like £2½ million still remains almost entirely unrecovered. It would be an affront to the public weal that any of you should be at liberty in anything like the near future to enjoy any of those ill-gotten gains.
>
> Accordingly, it is in no spirit of retribution that I propose to secure that such an opportunity will be denied all of you for an

extremely long time …. On the first count you will go to prison for twenty-five years and on the second count you will be sentenced to a concurrent term of thirty years.

Ronald Arthur Biggs was the next to be sentenced; having escaped from Borstal twice, he had previously served sentences of three years' imprisonment for stealing cars and another of three and a half years for robbery. In sentencing him, the judge said:

The truth is that I do not know when you entered the conspiracy or what part you played. What I do know is that you are a specious and facile liar and you have this week, in this court, perjured yourself time and again, but I add not a day to your sentence on that account. Your previous record qualifies you to be sentenced to preventative detention; that I shall not do. Instead, the sentence of the court upon you in respect of the first count is one of twenty-five years' imprisonment and in respect of the second count, thirty years' imprisonment. Those sentences to be served concurrently.

Next was Thomas William Wisbey and the judge told him:

Your previous record qualifies you for corrective training but any such sentence is plainly out of the question in the present circumstances … you have not sought to mollify the court by any admission of repentance. The sentences upon you are concurrent sentences. In respect of the first count, twenty-five years' imprisonment and in respect of the second count, thirty years' imprisonment.

As Wisbey was taken down to the cells, so his place in the dock was taken by Robert Alfred Welch who was told:

All matters urged in mitigation and your antecedents, I have sought faithfully to bear in mind. The sentence of the court upon you is that on the first count you go to prison for twenty-five years and upon the second count you go to prison for thirty years. Those sentences will be concurrent.

Keeping his composure to the end, Welch courteously replied, 'Thank you very much, Sir.'

Taking his place in the dock next was the unlikeliest of pickpockets, the massive James Hussey. He had also coshed a police inspector during a raid on a warehouse and had been sentenced to five years' imprisonment; he had been released eighteen months before the Great Train Robbery. In sentencing him, the judge told Hussey:

> You have previous convictions of gravity, including two involving substantial violence .... I balance these and all other matters to the best of my ability and having done so the concurrent sentences that you will serve are, on the first count, twenty-five years' imprisonment and on the second, thirty years.

Roy John James, who had achieved success at racing Formula III cars had been described by Graham White, the deputy clerk of Goodwood racing circuit as 'a keen young driver who took up racing seriously.' He also took criminality seriously, having been released from a three-year sentence of corrective training for shopbreaking and larceny in July 1960 and James was told by the judge:

> You are the only one out of the accused in respect of whom it has been proved that you actually received a substantial part of the stolen moneys. On your arrest you still had in your possession over £12,000 which I have no doubt was the result of exchange out of the original stolen moneys received by you. I entertain no doubt that the original sum you received substantially exceeded that figure. Your record in the past is a bad one and corrective training seems to have done you little or no good .... It may be, as you say, that you personally have never resorted to physical violence, but you nevertheless stand convicted of participating with others in armed robbery and for that you must be sentenced .... I do not find it possible to differentiate your case from that of most of the other accused. You will accordingly go to prison for concurrent terms of twenty-five years on the first count and thirty years on the second count.

Douglas Gordon Goody, who with Wilson had been acquitted of the robbery at Comet House that was used to finance the Great Train Robbery, was the last to be sentenced for both conspiracy and the robbery. However, he had convictions for shopbreaking and larceny and robbery with violence (for which he had been birched) and he was told:

> You have a bad record, notably with a conviction for grave violence at the early age of eighteen, and you qualify for preventative detention .... you have become a dangerous menace to society.

The Crown have said they do not consider this criminal enterprise was the product of any criminal master-mind. I do not know that I necessarily agree with the Crown in this respect. I strongly suspect that you played a major role, both in the conspiracy and in the actual robbery. Suspicion, however, is not good enough for me any more than it would be for a jury. It would be, therefore, quite wrong for me to cause my suspicions to lead to imposing upon you any heavier sentence than upon other accused and I shall not do so. You will go to prison for concurrent terms of twenty-five years on the first count and thirty years on the second count.

Brian Arthur Field, the crooked solicitor was acquitted of both the robbery and of receiving £100,900 where the hotel bill in his name had been found in amongst the stolen money. However, the judge told him:

> You have been convicted upon count one and count twelve of conspiracy to rob the mail and of conspiracy to obstruct the course of justice. Of the righteousness of both verdicts I personally entertain no doubt whatsoever ... whether it was simply a remarkable coincidence that two out of the four bags found in Dorking Woods containing over £100,000 were your property or whether the fact is an indication of your further complicity in the main conspiracy again I have no means of knowing, though naturally I loyally give effect to your vindication by the jury on both the robbery and the receiving charges.
>
> But that you played an essential role in the major conspiracy is clear. Out of that there naturally flowed the later conspiracy to obstruct justice ... The concurrent sentences of the court upon you are that on the first count you will go to prison for twenty-five years and on the twelfth count, you will go to prison for five years.

Similarly, Leonard Dennis Field was acquitted of the robbery, but the judge sentenced him as follows:

> You have been convicted on the first and twelfth counts in this indictment. Although you have but one previous conviction, which I ignore, you are a dangerous man. Not only have you perjured yourself repeatedly in this trial to save your own skin but on your own showing at one stage you perjured yourself in an endeavour to ruin the accused, Brian Field. I sentence you not for perjury, but I sentence you solely for conspiracy ... having done so, I can see no valid grounds for differentiating your case from Brian Field. You will accordingly be sentenced to concurrent terms of twenty-five years on the first count and five years on the twelfth count.

As the sentence was passed, Field's mother cried out from the public gallery. 'Don't worry, mother,' shouted Field. 'I'm still young.'

The last of the prisoners to be sentenced was the solicitor, John Denby Wheater. The citation for his wartime Military MBE in 1944 stated, in part, 'During the exhausting fighting in the Apennines in the winter, Captain Wheater showed great resourcefulness and imagination in most trying circumstances.' Now, with Wheater's reputation in tatters, the judge said:

> Your case is in many respects the saddest and most difficult of all. You are forty-two years old, a married man with heavy family responsibilities and of excellent character up until the present crime ... Your conviction on the twelfth count establishes, as I interpret the verdict, that at some time after the robbery that criminal purpose became clear to you, as indeed it must have done, and you could then have given the police vital information by identifying Leonard Field as your professional client. A decent citizen would have volunteered to do that very thing whatever his strictly legal obligations might be. Instead, you professed inability to do so ... I realize that the consequences of your conviction are disastrous both professionally and personally. Bearing in mind all relevant considerations I have come to the conclusion that you must go to prison for three years and you will be sentenced accordingly.

Two days later, seven other persons appeared on charges of receiving money stolen during the robbery. Four were found not guilty; William Pelham admitted receiving £545 and was conditionally discharged. Walter Albert Smith admitted receiving £2,000 and was sentenced to three years' imprisonment and Martin Harvey admitted receiving £518 and received twelve months' imprisonment.

The appeals were heard six months later. Both Brian and Lennie Field had their convictions for conspiracy to rob, quashed. However, both men had additionally been sentenced to five years' imprisonment for obstruction of justice and that sentence stood. Similarly, Boal's sentence for conspiracy to rob was quashed but a sentence of fourteen years' imprisonment was substituted for receiving stolen money and Cordrey's sentence was also reduced to fourteen years. Not so the others; the thirty-year sentences for the robbery which the appeal court judge, Mr Justice Fenton Atkinson, described as 'an act of organized banditry', stood.

As Butler and his team kept up the pressure to find the remainder of the gang, on 12 August 1964, Wilson escaped from Winson Green Prison. Butler choked with rage at all the effort which had gone into Wilson's arrest and conviction; then, eleven months later, he roared his displeasure when Biggs, too, escaped from Wandsworth Prison – they might have orchestrated the escapes purely to spite Butler. But in early 1966, Jimmy White, who was now calling himself 'Robert Lane' and living in Littlestone, Kent, was arrested. White had been a career criminal and he was in the act of relieving himself when Jack Slipper of the Squad rather kindly told him to 'put it away' and Tommy Butler later stated that White told him, 'I am only too pleased to tell you all about it. I was in on that job. I was in that coach when the money was nicked and at Leatherslade Farm, afterwards.'

This was a fairly unequivocal confession and in June, White, whose palm-print had been found on a post-robbery dated newspaper found inside a mailbag, appeared at Leicester Assizes. Initially, he pleaded not guilty but after a little mature deliberation, he changed his plea and was sentenced to eighteen years' imprisonment. Three months later, 'Buster' Edwards surrendered himself to Frank Williams; Edwards' fingerprints had been found on a bank wrapper and also on a Land Rover at the farm. Edwards had been an enthusiastic shopbreaker and robber and when he was arrested for stealing a car he was represented by Brian Field and was acquitted. However, he was convicted of driving whilst disqualified and was sentenced to fourteen days' imprisonment. That had been his only custodial sentence. That was shortly to change; at Nottinghamshire Assizes in December 1966, he was sentenced to fifteen years' imprisonment.

As Ronald Alloway drove his children to school in his Cadillac, down the hill from his home at Mountain View, Rigaud, Quebec Province, on the morning of 25 January 1968, he noticed a Dormobile van stuck in a snow drift. He stopped his car and got out to assist the three men who were pushing the van, when his arms were seized from behind. It was a classic Flying Squad ambush, aided and abetted by the Royal Canadian Mounted Police. Quickly recovering from the shock, Mr Alloway acknowledged to Tommy Butler that he was, indeed, Charlie Wilson. The arrest was symptomatic of Butler's secrecy. The wife of his aide, Ted Fuller, had no idea where her husband had gone. Fuller thought he knew where he was going, because Butler had hinted that whoever they were after was resident in Italy. But as Butler's driver dropped him and Fuller off at Heathrow Terminal Two, Butler waited until his car had disappeared from view before he and a rather bemused Fuller strolled round to Terminal Three, and thence to Canada.

Opinions vary as to what happened next, following the confrontation. The police version was that Wilson gasped, 'Oh no, it's you Mr Butler!' whereas according to a more unlikely version, Wilson is supposed to have said, off-handedly, 'Morning, Tom. Fancy seeing you out in all this cold snow. You'll catch your death!' This is hardly the type of remark that one would associate with a professional armed robber, who had escaped from a thirty-year prison sentence, having spent almost three-and-a-half years on the run and whose world was now in tatters.

But what was said matters little. Following the arrest and wasting no time, Butler seized $34,000, in American and Canadian currency, as well as Bahamian and French money from Wilson's house and whisked him straight back to resume his interrupted sentence; not at Winson Green prison but at Parkhurst, Britain's top security prison on the Isle of Wight.

Ten months later, Butler raided Villa Cap Martin, in Braddons Hill Road East, Torquay, Devon, a premises which had been rented by a Keith Miller. 'Hello, Bruce,' he said. 'It's been a long time.' Keith Miller – aka Bruce Reynolds – sighed. '*C'est la vie,*' he replied. It was. The arrest had come about after Butler had sent Detective Sergeant Bob Robinson to Torquay, having received information that Reynolds was somewhere in the area. Reynolds had used four aliases in the past; Robinson was in possession of those names and went to the local estate agencies who specialized in letting properties. On Butler's strict instructions, Robinson told the local police that he was a Fraud Squad officer, investigating a trade directory fraud. It was not too long before he discovered a letting in the name of 'Miller' and following some discreet surveillance, Robinson was able to telephone Butler with encouraging news.

At 10.30 on the evening before the arrest, Butler walked into the Squad office, selected a number of officers and cars from the night provincial team, and informed the acting detective inspector in charge he should remain in the office and maintain total radio silence. No reason was given, either to the officer in charge of the night provs, or to the men themselves. They were told to follow his car and not to communicate by radio, and when they reached the outskirts of London Butler pulled into an all-night petrol station and told them to fill their cars with petrol, still not revealing their destination. Once again, Butler was playing his cards very close to his chest and it paid off. It was also typical of Butler that he completely forgot about the existence of Bob Robinson, the man responsible for housing Reynolds, who had to make his way back to London on a train.

Tommy Butler spoke good common-sense to Reynolds, who handed back £5,000 – all that was left of his share of the proceeds. On 14 January 1969, Reynolds appeared at Aylesbury Assizes. He had eleven previous convictions, had escaped from Borstal twice, absented himself from the Army and had served sentences of three years for shopbreaking and three-and-a-half years for inflicting grievous bodily harm and assaulting the police. He had also left his prints on two Monopoly tokens and a bottle of ketchup at the farm, and now he pleaded guilty to the robbery and Mr Justice Thompson sentenced him to twenty-five years' imprisonment. Tommy Butler was asked as he left the court what he would do if he came face to face with Biggs. Butler smiled and replied, 'Well, if he is foolish enough to get close to me, I will make sure he is arrested.' However, it was not to be.

Ronnie Biggs, who left Australia in a hurry (even faster than he'd left England), settled in Rio and when his girlfriend Raimunda discovered she was pregnant, Biggs supplied her with money for an abortion. She promptly spent the money on a dress, which must have caused Biggs annoyance at the time but would later earn her his undying gratitude. When Jack Slipper went to arrest him, a local law was uncovered which revealed that the father of a Brazilian child cannot be extradited and so Slipper left and Biggs stayed; until, that is, his very poor health prompted him to return to England for proper medical treatment, combined with a prison cell.

A fictionalized (but very creditable) film of the Great Train Robbery, *Robbery*, was directed by Peter Yates in 1967 and in the years which followed, some of the train robbers returned to prison (mainly for drugs offences) and others died, as have almost all of the police officers involved in that most remembered robbery ever, including Tommy Butler.

Over the years, there have been hints (and downright accusations) that the Flying Squad fitted-up the Great Train Robbers. This, it must be said, is a bit rich, coming from the lips of some of the robbers who not only lied their heads off in court, but went on to acknowledge, in books and on television, that not only did they participate in the robbery but also in many other serious crimes for which they were not caught. In any event, the accusation of fitting-up is not true; had it been, all of the robbers – including those who were arrested and released without charge, due to lack of evidence – would have been charged and convicted. 'The suggestion that they were in any way "fitted-up" said Steve Moore, 'is ridiculous in the extreme,' although Flying Squad detractors would no doubt scornfully suggest that remarks such as those are exactly what one would expect to hear from a Flying Squad officer. However, John Simmonds had a far more insightful observation to make.

'They were really caught by Tommy Butler's cunning,' he remarked. 'His basic first question was: "Have you ever been to Leatherslade Farm?" knowing that they would naturally say 'no', but Tommy had their dabs, so on denial of being at the farm, they were nicked. Had any of them said, 'Yes, I wanted to buy the farm and looked over it', they would have walked. Tommy was in my opinion, very straight. He nailed all of those that he could by sheer hard detective work and he would not have sanctioned any malpractice that could have jeopardized the trial.'

Almost as soon as the robbery occurred, there were a series of theories regarding a 'Mr Big' who provided the information, organization and finance for it. One suggestion was that he was a miser, living in one room in Brighton from where he issued his directives and orders – that particular conjecture can be consigned to the dustbin. There was further speculation that Otto Skorzeny, the brilliant Second World War German Special Forces officer was behind the robbery and/or certain mysterious Irishmen. Maybe, maybe not. However, these and other theories were the cause of some discussion in the Squad office, and, with typical Flying Squad aplomb, the general consensus of opinion was that they were 'balls'. Leonard 'Nipper' Read QPM, the man who caught the Krays, was not a Flying Squad officer but he was part of Gerald McArthur's C1 team, who initially went to Buckinghamshire to initiate the enquiry. 'Tales of a Mister Big or some brilliant Thomas Crown have never impressed me,' he stated.

Opinions vary as to the ringleader(s). One point of view is that it was Gordon Goody, others a conglomerate of Goody, Wilson and Reynolds. It is Bruce Reynolds who comes across as the firm favourite. When this was put to Reynolds by Harry Clement, Reynolds laughed, saying the ideas came in from various sources and that he supplied the dynamo for the job, keeping on and driving the idea forward. This more or less coincides with Bob Robinson's impression that initially it was Goody and Wilson's job, but that it was Reynolds who brought it all together. Reynolds was always the favourite of Steve Moore because, 'the man with all the contacts was Bruce Reynolds.' Frank Williams had received information, weeks before the robbery that Reynolds was planning 'some crime' but observation on his flat in Putney was difficult, made more so by the fact that Reynolds often used a motorcycle on his reconnoitring excursions.

The decision by Millen and Hatherill to publish the names and photographs of the wanted men was both a bad decision and a wrong one. Hatherill, the chain-smoking, six-feet-six colossus could, to a certain extent, be excused; much of his service had been spent with Special Branch due to his ability to speak six languages fluently, but he knew little about the art of running informants. Therefore, he relied upon Millen's judgement as head of the Flying Squad. However, Millen should have heeded Butler who was a Squadman through and through, having spent his career successfully dealing with violent criminals and running informants; while Millen had not. Much of Millen's career had been spent investigating and unravelling complex frauds, which often took months and sometimes years of painstaking work. There was simply no comparison between this type of investigation and catching wily, fast-moving armed robbers, and as a man who had previously served on the Flying Squad, Millen should have known that.

Steve Moore stated that, 'the attitude of all of us on the train robbery squad was against the publication of photos for obvious reasons; but rather one of "softly, softly catchee monkey" ' – this being one of top Squadman Alf Dance's aphorisms, of many years before. 'Nipper' Read thought the decision was 'political' and John Simmonds stated bluntly, 'Hatherill and Millen were not in the same league as Tommy Butler as detectives. Both were men of repute in the past but Tommy was the "today" man, he would have weighed up the pros and cons and they should have gone with him.'

So does crime – in particular, this specific crime – pay? The robbers themselves had their shares eroded by massive payments for the services of others and the rates for laundering the stolen money were extortionate. The gang and their wives were in constant danger of betrayal, prey to 'thieves ponces' and blackmailers and just ordinary common or garden thieves; what could they do – complain to the police? Whilst they were on the run, the families of the robbers had to contend with the traumatic and often very confusing changes of identity thrust upon them, often at very short notice. Both the wives and the train robbers endured years of separation and loneliness, often coupled with mental illness; now, in old age, many of them live on state handouts, in graffiti-strewn council estates, in penury.

There was a great deal of discussion and criticism of the sentences passed on the train robbers; obviously the establishment felt that stopping the Royal Mail was sacrosanct and it demanded exemplary sentences. But it must also be remembered that the driver of the train was severely assaulted and an example had to be made so that even the most daring gang would think twice before a repeat. The proof of the pudding is that the Great Train Robbery remains a one-off; since that time, nobody has ever tried to stop and rob a mail train.

'I do think that but for Tommy Butler's commitment, tenacity and dedication, it is unlikely the result that was obtained would have happened,' unequivocally stated John Simmonds. 'It needed someone with unique skills to run this operation and I personally do not think there was anyone else available in the Job at that precise moment in time who could have matched Tommy's ability.'

These comments were pretty-well reflected on the comment made when the gang heard on the radio that firstly, their hideout had been discovered and secondly, that Tommy Butler would be leading the hunt. Roy James looked at the others and said, simply, 'We're nicked.'

They were.

Gunmen and Gallants

The 1970s got off to a cracking start. John McVicar, who had escaped from custody in May 1966 whilst serving an eight-year sentence for armed robbery and assaulting the Squad officers who arrested him, had been recaptured by Flying Squad officers, again assaulting the officer who arrested him. Three weeks previously, McVicar had fired shots from a getaway car at police officers and at the Old Bailey, in February 1967, he was sentenced to an additional fifteen years' imprisonment for using a firearm with intent to endanger life and conspiracy to rob. Five months later, McVicar again appeared at the Old Bailey and, for conspiracy to rob and assaulting a police officer, he was sentenced to a total of five years' imprisonment. McVicar, who was a keep-fit fanatic and with considerable justification was regarded as a highly violent and dangerous criminal, was sent to Durham Prison, but although it was a high security establishment, he escaped in October 1968.

Six months after his escape, McVicar sent the Home Secretary a rather plaintive letter, in which he stated he feared death or savage violence from the police, should they re-arrest him. Moreover, he continued, if he should survive his re-arrest, he had no doubt that he would be verballed and planted with fabricated and incriminating evidence. He was not in possession of a firearm, he added, and he was not engaged in criminality. Only in the presence of a solicitor of his choice, he concluded, would he assist in any investigation. The contents of the letter were released to the national press, who urged McVicar to attend any police station, anywhere in the country, in the company of a friend or solicitor. Astonishingly, this offer was not taken up.

In the meantime, the Flying Squad pursued their enquires as to McVicar's whereabouts, which paid off on 11 November 1970 when a duplicate key was obtained to Flat 1B Stratheden Parade, Blackheath, SE3, and the premises were entered at five o'clock in the morning by Detective Inspector Denis 'Dick' Barton and

Detective Sergeants Newton Scanlon and John Bates of the Flying Squad. They were prudent enough to disregard McVicar's claim that he did not possess a gun and therefore, they were all armed with .38 Smith & Wesson service revolvers.

As they moved noiselessly along the passageway, so McVicar emerged from a bedroom; with a complete lack of fuss, he was handcuffed and arrested.

So McVicar had escaped death or maiming at the hands of the Flying Squad; and he was correct in his letter to the Home Secretary when he stated he did not possess a gun; he had several. Underneath a bed in the flat was a holdall which contained two sawn-off shotguns and a number of parts, a revolver, an automatic and a quantity of ammunition. However, he had been less than frank in his assertion that he had not been involved in criminality; the holdall also contained some coshes, stocking masks and a postman's uniform.

At the Old Bailey on 17 September 1971, McVicar, unverballed, unplanted and unencumbered with fabricated evidence, meekly pleaded guilty to assorted charges related to firearms offices, two cases of conspiracy to rob, with one case taken into consideration and was sentenced to a total of three years' imprisonment, to run consecutively with his outstanding sentences; a total of twenty-six years imprisonment.

The three detectives were congratulated by the Home Secretary and commended by the Commissioner and on a lighter note, whilst McVicar had been deliberately inaccurate in his writing, John Bates' young daughter was unintentionally so when she wrote in her schoolbook, 'My daddy has caught a man called the vicar.'

In addition, the Squad played an important part in the investigation into the kidnapping and subsequent murder of Mrs Muriel McKay. This unfortunate woman had been mistaken for the wife of the newspaper magnate, Rupert Murdoch, and the Squad input assisted materially in the investigation. Flying Squad officers Detective Inspector John Bland and Detective Sergeant Jack Quarrie carried out surveillance work in freezing temperatures which helped bring about the arrest in February 1970 of two brothers, Arthur and Nizamodeen Hosein, who were found guilty of kidnapping, blackmail and – although her body has never been found – the murder of Mrs McKay.

*   *   *

Many retired police officers remember the name of Flying Squad officer Peter Jones, solely for accompanying Jack Slipper on the abortive trip to Rio in order to bring back Ronnie Biggs; however, Jones was responsible not only for arresting some very dangerous criminals but also for capturing the attention of the High Court in Glasgow, a number of newspaper reporters and the admiration of his colleagues. Jones had been posted to the Flying Squad in 1967 as a detective sergeant (second class), where he had enjoyed a run of successes working on 7, 8 and 9 squads, in the company of such luminaries as Detective Inspector John Bland and Detective Sergeant Len Buggy.

On 21 December 1973, there was a robbery early in the morning at British Rail Engineering Ltd, in Charles Street, Townhead, Glasgow. The gang had snatched £20,000 and when a security guard, John Kennedy, a married man with three young daughters confronted them, he was shot in the chest at point-blank range with a sawn-off shotgun and died, almost immediately. It was a shocking crime, although not one which would normally have attracted action from the Flying Squad; that came about after Detective Chief Superintendent Jack Slipper received a telephone call at home from Jones, to tell him that Chief Inspector Catchpole, the head of Glasgow's own Flying Squad and a team of detectives were flying down to London. The Scottish officers had the name of a London-based suspect for the murder and they wanted assistance, which the Squad was happy to provide. Slipper quickly mustered a small team of Squad officers and they headed towards the King's Cross area of London, an area much favoured by visitors from Scotland. The Glaswegian suspect's name was Robert Marley – coincidentally, he was also known as Kennedy, the same name as the murdered man – and Marley was arrested and taken to Caledonian Road Police station. Before long, he started to talk and, as is so often the case, once he had started he was unable to stop. Not only did he admit his part in the killing, he made a long written statement in which he named everybody else involved and described the part each of them had played in the crime, as well as the clothing they were wearing and how they had disposed of their clothes after the robbery.

Slipper now increased his team to fourteen officers; Marley was seated in the back of a Squad car and he took them all over London, pointing out the various addresses of his former associates. One by one, they were brought in; Stephen Doran, twenty-three, Sidney Draper, twenty-five, Alan Brown, twenty-eight.

Peter Jones and Detective Sergeant Bernie Hodgetts (later to become operational chief of the Squad) were keeping observation outside 27-year-old suspect James Aitkin's flat, when a car drew up containing both Aitkin and 35-year-old John Murphy – also a suspect. Both were arrested and Aitkin's flat was searched in the presence of his wife. The festive Christmas tree in the flat was surrounded with presents – it also held money stolen from the Townhead robbery; Mrs Elizabeth Aitkin was later sentenced to two years' imprisonment.

In the charge room at Caledonian Road, Detective Superintendent Bob Robinson noticed that amongst the property of one of the prisoners was a Scottish £20 note, which had a corner torn off. For no discernable reason, it struck him as odd. 'Make a note of that,' he told Sergeant Stuart Giblin who was processing the prisoners. In fact, it turned out to be a vital piece of evidence; the missing corner was found in an empty pay-packet, which was one of those stolen during the robbery.

Giblin dealt with half-a-dozen of the prisoners and told me, 'I was very impressed with the way the two Flying Squads – London and Glasgow – worked together.'

One of the robbery team, Billy Murray proved difficult to find and it took months of work before one of Robinson's informants found him at a boarding house in Brighton. Early in the morning, a Squad team surrounded the premises and looking through a window in the basement area, saw Murray and a girl in bed, asleep. The whole window was smashed in, Murray was told to stay exactly where he was with his hands raised and the girl was told to open the door. As she did so, officers flooded into the room and Robinson kept his service revolver levelled unwaveringly at Murray. He was wise to have done so; just a few inches away from Murray was a loaded revolver.

At the High Court, Glasgow, the case caused a sensation when Jones gave evidence of arresting Sidney Draper who, like Murray had been in bed at the time of his arrest. Jones, armed with a service revolver, was unable to see Draper's hands which were underneath the bedsheets, and he told Draper to show his hands or he would shoot.

'What would have happened, officer,' asked the judge, Lord Kissen, 'if the accused had not shown his hands?'

'I'd have shot him, my Lord,' replied Jones, simply. 'One man had already been murdered and I wasn't planning on being the next.'

There was a gasp in the crowded courtroom; followed by a mad dash as the newspaper reporters thundered towards the exit, to be the first to use the one solitary telephone in order to file their copy. 'I think,' said Lord Kissen, with a thin smile, 'we'll pause until the elephants have left the court!'

The following day, 26 March 1974, Jones' remarks were newspaper headlines. The *Scottish Daily Express* revealed, 'The day I drew my gun,' followed by, 'Detective tells of arrests after wages snatch.'

The court case was further enlivened by the flamboyant Sir Nicholas Fairburn, MP, QC, appearing for some of the prisoners. Sir Nicholas was seldom out of the tabloid headlines himself, one notable occasion being when a girlfriend, discovering that he intended to marry somebody else, endeavoured to hang herself from a lamppost outside his London flat.

But despite Sir Nicholas' most ardent pleadings, it did his clients no good whatsoever; the gang was found guilty and sentenced on 10 April 1974. Life imprisonment, with recommendations by the judge that they should serve between fifteen to twenty-five years for the murder, plus sentences of between twelve and ten years' imprisonment for the robbery – in all, 119 years' imprisonment, in what was the longest trial and the heaviest sentences in Scotland's history. It was not without its comic aspects; a woman gave evidence that during the course of an arrest and search, the Squad's behaviour was so abhorrent that she shrilly stated her intention to telephone the Police Complaints Department, A10. 'Not with this phone, you won't,' allegedly replied a Squad officer and ripped the appliance right off the wall. It caused considerable amusement during a trial noted for its bursts of excitement and the allegation was, of course, categorically denied.

An allegation which was immediately accepted concerned the Squad team's trip to Glasgow for the trial. Knowing that Slipper could be frugal when it came to buying drinks, they decided to put his parsimony to the test and at their hotel, they asked for all their evening's drinks to be put on Slipper's bill. The following morning, when Slipper discovered that £300 had been added to his otherwise modest bed and breakfast account, he hit the roof – the drinks bill was hastily divided by fourteen and settled.

So although Jones's remarks caused a sensation in respect of Sidney Draper's arrest, they paled into insignificance when, thirteen years later, controversy exploded and it was Draper's turn to hit the headlines. During the afternoon of 10 December 1987, a hijacked Bell 206L helicopter hovered over the exercise yard at Gartree maximum security prison, long enough to lift Draper and another inmate, John Kendall, serving an eight-year sentence, to freedom. Never before had such an audacious escape been executed, nor has one like it ever happened since. Although Kendall was recaptured ten days later, Draper was on the run for thirteen months. It led to the prison authorities reporting, with masterly understatement, that 'security has been tightened.'

* * *

In the fifty years since 'the bright young things' frequented 'Ma Meyrick's' club in Soho's Gerrard Street, both the clientele and the inhabitants of that thoroughfare had changed. By 1974, practically all of the premises – restaurants, shops, travel agents and clubs – were owned and occupied by Chinese. The majority of the businesses were well-run and law abiding and because it was a tightly knit community, if there was trouble, it would inevitably be sorted out by the local inhabitants, rather than involve the police.

Detective Sergeant Fred Cutts had been posted to 1 squad, the previous year and had immersed himself in the thick of the action, including infiltrating a gang of forgers whilst posing as a Latvian seaman, and recovering a quarter of a million US dollars, plus the printing equipment. Now, unexpectedly, he and his partner, the late Michael 'Taff' Howells, had been summoned to see the operational head of the Squad, Detective Chief Superintendent Jack Slipper.

What 'Uncle Jack' (as Slipper was affectionately known) had to tell them was this: several years previously, he, Slipper, had had dealings with a criminal, whom he had dealt with fairly. Now the man was part-owner of one of the basement clubs in Gerrard Street which had been 'taxed' by Triads – secret societies, renowned for heroin smuggling, people trafficking and prostitution, as well as extortion. The worst of the gangs were the 14K, the Tsui Fong and the Wo Shin Wo. Slipper committed the matter to paper. It was a highly sensitive issue and he came up with a proposal to deal with the matter secretly and diplomatically; he presented his proposition to the Squad chief, Commander John Lock QPM. Lock was a well respected officer who had served on the Squad twenty years previously as a detective sergeant (first class) and had been commended for his part in bringing to book a gang of safe-blowers; he forwarded the papers to the Assistant Commissioner (Crime) and both men agreed with Slipper's recommendations.

Cutts and Howells' brief was to concentrate on the extortion issues. Any other intelligence they acquired in respect of immigration offences, drugs or gaming was to be passed back, so that it could be disseminated to the relevant departments to be acted upon, provided that it did not compromise the Squad officers' investigations.

The two officers got to work; first a meeting with Slipper's contact and then, during the following weeks, the main Triad members were seen and identified. Witnesses to the demands were seen and made statements; not the easiest of achievements, especially when one of the interpreters appeared less than trustworthy. But Howells had been a uniformed constable and an aid to CID in the West End and had made valuable contacts in the Chinese community; these contacts he now took into his confidence and they spoke to the victims of extortion in the area, telling them to talk to the officers, who could be trusted and as a result, more witnesses came forward.

Cutts decided to arrest one of the main players, a particularly vicious individual who specialized in extortion, poncing and 'minding' drug pushers. They discovered that he was living in a luxury flat in Marylebone which would undoubtedly contain much incriminating evidence, but the search could wait until later. The man had to be arrested publicly – in the heart of 'Chinatown' – so that the reaction of the inhabitants could be gauged. If their response was a favourable one, it would give the officers the green light to press ahead with their investigations. It happened at 2.30 in the morning; Cutts and Howells strolled into Gerrard Street, their car and driver parked up in nearby Wardour Street. They spotted the suspect about to enter a club's ground-floor entrance; one of his associates saw the officers and shouted a warning and the suspect dashed into the club with Howells in hot pursuit. Within seconds, the Triad gangster rushed up the steps from the basement of the club and dashed off along Gerrard

Street, cannoning into passers-by as he ran, with Cutts chasing him. Suddenly, the suspect rushed into a restaurant and Cutts followed; inside there was no trace of the man but two women were furiously shouting at the door of the ladies' lavatory. Guessing that the man was hiding inside Cutts shouldered the door, to discover his quarry furiously screaming, with a raised razor-sharp machete in his hand. Cutts smashed the lavatory door into the man's body, he slid to the floor and, with Howells' assistance, he was divested of the weapon and dragged outside. The Squad car was summoned and as the Triad member was shoved in the back of the car a crowd of the local inhabitants formed. They were not hostile at all; judging by their beams of pleasure, the onlookers realized that that particular threat had been removed.

With the suspect charged, then remanded in custody, more witnesses came forward and further arrests were made. The word came back to the officers that the Triads were losing face, so they felt it would not be particularly surprising if some sort of retaliatory action were planned. They were right, it was. The first intimation came when Cutts and Howells received an urgent radio message to see the Commander, immediately.

★   ★   ★

It had been a busy morning ever since seven o'clock, when the editor of a national newspaper had telephoned the Home Secretary, who in turn had telephoned the Home Office, who had contacted the Commissioner, and then the Commander. It appeared that the editor had received information from a reliable source that because of the successes enjoyed by Cutts and Howells, the Triads had initially considered attempting to buy or scare off the officers, but that a new and desperate character, who had allegedly murdered police officers in Macau and was quite prepared to do the same to Cutts and Howells, had now entered the equation.

'Any court dates next week, Fred?' asked the Commander. 'Any annual leave?' Mystified, Cutts shook his head. The Commander lifted the telephone, dialled a number and spoke to the head of a department. Replacing the phone, the Commander said, 'Right, starting next Monday, you're on a week's firearms course at Old Street. You should be able to shoot straight after that; one-to-one stuff, similar to the training on a close protection course!'

'When you're doing any work on this lot,' added Slipper, 'at least one of you is armed at all times, understood?'

Outside the Commander's office, Cutts and Howells (already a firearms officer) exchanged significant glances; it was not too long before they realized that the threat was a very real one.

⋆   ⋆   ⋆

It had become a priority to identify the Triad's assassin who, it was thought, must have had contacts with the men in custody, but although the most searching enquiries were made none were successful. The principal thugs who were in custody were believed to have had convictions for crime, particularly in Holland (where it was believed the information regarding the hit-man had emanated), but the Dutch police explained that after four years, details of offences committed in their country were sent to the prisoner's country of origin – Hong Kong. However, Hong Kong claimed they had no such records which was at variance at the information given to the officers by their sources, some of whom stated they had in fact served prison sentences with them.

The breakthrough came when Cutts and Howells were invited to a reception where, amongst others, a very high-up representative from the Hong Kong government would be present. During that afternoon he had asked repeatedly if the two officers would be attending the reception. He met them and the three chatted quite amiably; the Hong Kong representative was not to know that Cutts and Howells had just seen a C11 surveillance photograph of him, keeping some very dubious company outside a club in Gerrard Street.

In the meantime, the enquiries continued. The front door of a smart, semi-detached house in East London was kicked in and a leading Triad member, wanted for attempted murder, extortion and armed robbery in Liverpool and Manchester was seized and handcuffed. Still warm from nestling next to him in bed, was a loaded sawn-off shotgun; twenty further cartridges were found. He was found guilty of the firearms offence at the Old Bailey and sentenced to four years' imprisonment; later, he was dealt with for the other serious offences.

Two Dutch police officers arrived at the Yard, ostensibly on a
'fact-finding' mission, but also with some intelligence in respect
of the persons who had been arrested; plus some information
regarding the 'threat'. They and the Squad officers liaised and
had a meal in Gerrard Street. As they left the restaurant, the
Dutch officers suddenly stopped and ushered Cutts and Howells
behind a large van which was offloading groceries. They pointed
out a small group of men standing at the top of a flight of stairs
leading from a basement club. It was the same club featured in
the surveillance photograph. What's more, the representative
from the Hong Kong government was one of the men present.
The Squad officers said nothing but the Dutch officers then
directed their attention to another of the group – a tall, thin
Chinese man, with his hair in a pony-tail, wearing tinted glasses.
Back at the Yard, and just prior to returning to Holland, the
officers told Cutts and Howells that they should pay particular
attention to the men in the group; and that they would be in
touch, as soon as possible. They were. Within days, Jack Slipper
passed them a photograph he had just received from Holland; it
was the man with the pony-tail. 'He's the one who was sent to
deal with you two,' remarked Slipper.

They raided the club in Gerrard Street – 'Don't forget your
peashooters!' urged Slipper – and there were a number of arrests
in respect of wanted persons, immigration offences and drugs.
The word was out on the street that war had been declared. The
intelligence gleaned was shared with other police forces and
similar clubs were raided in Manchester, Liverpool and Cardiff.
It disrupted the Triads; their authority and their power bases were
shaken but above all, they suffered loss of face.

The photograph of the 'hit man' was shown to some Chinese
contacts; some of whom were considered not to be as reliable as
others – and the ploy worked. The word that the police now knew
exactly who they were looking for and who he was connected
with, reached the ears of those who had first employed him, who
now thought it best if he was 'withdrawn', as it was put to the
officers.

Through an informant, much more was found out regarding
the hit man. Originally, he was from Singapore, and had killed a
Hong Kong police officer in a shoot-out, escaped to Macau and
carried out a contract killing but although he had built up an
impressive reputation, he was not trusted by his compatriots. He

had killed a high-ranking rival gang leader and after offering to assassinate the Squad officers he had gone to Amsterdam. There was an altercation in the notorious Yau Li club, to which he was later lured back, ostensibly for a peace parley and a pay-off. It was a mistake. Returning with an associate, he and the other man were both shot and their bodies placed in a car which was pushed into one of Amsterdam's canals.

The information was later confirmed by the Dutch police; two bodies were recovered from a car in a canal; one was a man wanted for armed robbery in San Francisco; the other was the hit man.

It was the end of the threat as far as Cutts and Howells were concerned; but nevertheless they ensured that they remained armed until the conclusion of the Triad cases; all the prisoners received long prison sentences at the Old Bailey.

★   ★   ★

When Flying Squad officers tackled IRA terrorists in 1939, it was as the result of a tip-off; when it happened again, thirty-six years later, it was as a matter of chance but the cool courage displayed by them, and by a number of other officers, resulted in the same satisfactory conclusion.

During 1974–75, London suffered a sustained attack by the IRA; they had caused forty explosions, resulting in the death of eleven people and injuring many more, plus eight shootings where two people had been killed. One incident was when Ross McWhirter, the co-founder of *The Guinness Book of Records*, who had offered a reward of £50,000 to anyone providing information regarding IRA activity to the authorities, had been shot dead.

The Metropolitan Police set up 'Operation Combo' — this consisted of a ring of armed police officers circling outer central London; inside the circle were unarmed surveillance officers who would hopefully spot IRA activity, then call in the armed units to make the arrests. Several hundred officers were involved, some CID, some in uniform and some in plain clothes.

Scott's Restaurant – much frequented by celebrities, including the author, Ian Fleming – at 20 Mount Street, Mayfair, had been targeted by a six-man IRA Active Service Unit (ASU) on 12 November 1975; a bomb was thrown through the restaurant's window, resulting in one death and injuries to fifteen other diners. The ASU consisted of Brendan Dowd and Liam Quinn; the latter had shot dead off-duty Police Constable Stephen Tibble who, nine months previously had tried to stop Quinn fleeing the scene of a bomb factory while being chased by other police officers. But Dowd and Quinn were not present on the night of 6 December, when the rest of the gang – Hugh Doherty, Eddie Butler, Harry Duggan and Joe O'Connell – decided to pay a return visit to Mount Street. At 9.15, in a stolen Ford Cortina, they slowed down outside Scott's before opening fire at the restaurant.

Two unarmed uniformed officers, Inspector John Purnell and Sergeant Philip McVeigh heard the radio message from a unit in Mount Street and then, almost immediately, saw the ASU's stolen Cortina roaring towards them. With no vehicle of their own, the officers flagged down a passing taxi and set off in pursuit.

Bob Fenton had joined the Squad as a detective constable a week previously; he was to patrol the area of Kensington as part of the surveillance team in a Squad car, driven by Police Constable Peter Wilson with Detective Inspector Henry Dowswell and Detective Sergeant Phil Mansfield. As they received the radio call, the Squad Granada roared north towards Mayfair, and was soon closing on the stolen car. The Cortina screeched to a halt and the four terrorists decamped; the Squad officers heard gunfire, an armed unit of the Special Patrol Group had confronted the gunmen who now rushed towards the Squad car, firing as they did so. The Squad officers leapt from their car and chased the terrorists on foot down a flight of steps. As they did so, one of the gunmen turned and fired at them; the bullet passed between Fenton and Dowswell and into the rear of the Squad car; a second shot narrowly missed Dowswell.

Hearing the commotion, 53-year-old Mrs Sheila Matthews opened the door of her flat at 22B Balcombe Street, Marylebone; but scarcely had she stepped outside to see what was happening when she was rushed by the terrorists, who bundled her back inside and barricaded the front door. For the next six days, she and her 54-year-old husband, John, were held hostage.

The terrorists demanded a plane to fly them and their hostages to Ireland; the police refused and Detective Superintendent Peter Imbert (later Lord Imbert of New Romney and Commissioner of the Metropolitan Police) was the chief negotiator. It was only after the gang picked up a classic piece of misinformation on the radio – that the Special Air Service was about to storm the flat – that they cravenly surrendered, it being one thing to kill innocent civilians for a cause but quite a different matter to die for one.

At their trial at the Old Bailey, the four were found guilty of seven murders, conspiracy to cause explosions and falsely imprisoning John and Sheila Matthews. Three of the men – O'Connell, Butler and Duggan – were each given twelve life sentences whilst Doherty was sentenced to eleven life sentences.

In May 1998 they were transferred to Portlaoise Prison, Dublin and were welcomed back in the *An Phoblacht* Republican News as 'The Balcombe Street Volunteers' who had survived 'years of isolation and sub-human conditions in British jails'. The following year they were released, as were Brendan Dowd and Liam Quinn, as part of the Good Friday Agreement.

When the boot of the stolen Cortina was searched, it was found to contain a holdall containing two sub-machine guns, a Sten gun barrel and a clip of ammunition. The Squad car had been struck with three of the gunmen's bullets, two in the front of the car, the other in the rear. It was this last bullet which was proved by ballistic tests to have come from the same weapon which had murdered Ross McWhirter, just nine days previously.

All the officers were showered with commendations and Henry Dowswell, John Purnell and Phillip McVeigh were all awarded the George Medal; Bob Fenton, Phil Mansfield and Police Constables Barry Court, Stephen Knight and Andrew Claiden were all awarded the Queen's Gallantry Medal. The Squad driver, PC Peter Wilson was awarded the Queen's Commendation for Brave Conduct, as was the taxi driver, Mr Hackett.

Referring to their ordeal, Bob Fenton told me, 'I suppose we were lucky.' Certainly, he and the other officers were fortunate not to have stopped a bullet; all of them were luckier than poor, brave Police Constable Stephen Tibble who was awarded a posthumous Queen's Police Medal.

★   ★   ★

But despite the most studied mayhem, there are, and always have been, moments of humour and lightness in the lives of Squad officers. John Jones was a detective sergeant on 3 squad in the mid-seventies working with Detective Constable Graham

'Hymie' Stadden, who was often in demand for his capabilities as a 'buyer'. Not, however, on this occasion. The officers had spent many nights attempting to catch 'Mousey' Brown, a prolific safe-blower, together with his youthful apprentice, in the act of actually blowing a safe. Brown was suspected of safe-blowings in Post Offices on the outskirts of west London and on this particular night, he was observed blowing a safe in Thames Ditton.

Unfortunately, before the arrests could be effected, Brown and his trainee managed to get to the sanctuary of their car and a hair-raising chase ensued, around Kingston Bypass, up Kingston Hill and down towards the town. With the radio commentary from the Squad cars, the uniform branch set up a roadblock across the main road, but Mousey swerved into a side road leading to the Robin Hood Gate of Richmond Park, where the car screeched to a halt and both Mousey and his novice leapt out and dashed off. Jones ran after the apprentice who had got through a side gate into the park and it became clear that with his turn of speed, plus the darkness, Jones was in imminent danger of losing his prey. 'Stop, or I'll shoot!' he roared, and Mousey's trainee skidded to a halt, his arms high in the air, his neck hunched into his shoulders in anticipation of the expected bullet. Jones ran up, seized the suspect's arms, pulled them down and handcuffed him, before murmuring, 'Fooled you – I haven't got a gun!'

Meanwhile, Mousey had run into the back garden of a large house with Stadden in hot pursuit, and as Mousey jumped into a very large, deep Victorian goldfish pond, so Stadden followed him in. The slimy water and the morass of smelly weed slowed the speed of both pursued and pursuer and eventually they both emerged, as Jones recalls, 'looking like two creatures from the Black Lagoon and stinking like pigs.' They were put into the back of a police van and conveyed to Surbiton Police station; it was not a particularly lengthy journey, but they had generated such a stench it was necessary for both of them to be hosed down before they were permitted to enter the station.

Because Jones was the officer who lived nearest to Kingston Magistrates' Court, he was deputed to attend court on a weekly basis until such time as the safe-blowers could be committed to the Crown Court for trial. Unfortunately, after several weeks of remands, a magistrate came to the conclusion that Mousey did not represent a threat to society and bailed him. Unsurprisingly, it took another three years before Mousey was brought to justice; during the interim period, he made a lucrative living blowing safes in undertakers and crematoriums. 'Which just goes to show you,' wryly commented Jones, some thirty-five years later, 'that it's worthwhile making sure that your loved ones remove your rings, gold teeth etc., before you go to meet your maker!'

⋆ ⋆ ⋆

According to the popular press, Flying Squad officers invariably 'swoop' into situations and on suspects; ironically in Detective Sergeant Chris Bird's case (a member of 7 squad in 1973) the shoe – or rather, the claw – was on the other foot. Bird received information from a snout that a well-known south London criminal was in possession of an eagle, stolen the previous evening during a burglary near Slough, Buckinghamshire, and not unnaturally imagined the eagle to be one constructed of base, semi-precious or precious metal. However, it turned out to be a real, live bird of prey and it was being kept in the villain's flat in a tower block in Wandsworth.

It took some time for Bird to both check the accuracy of the information and establish his credentials with the highly incredulous investigating officers at Langley Police station ('Hello, this is Detective Sergeant Bird from the Flying Squad – did you have an eagle stolen last night?'), but after several attempts he discovered that the information he had been given was correct. During the burglary several birds of prey had been stolen from an aviary in a rear garden and the owner, who had raised the birds since they were chicks, was distraught. He considered the birds to be priceless and was prepared to travel anywhere, at any time to identify and recover his property.

However, raiding the flat to find and recover the eagle was not without its problems; the information was privy to only a few and if detectives marched into the flat,stating that they were looking for a stolen bird of prey, suspicion would soon fall on the informant. Therefore, when Bird and his partner, Detective Sergeant Ron Noon knocked on the door of the flat in Wandsworth – to be greeted with a torrent of abuse from the sole occupant, the suspect's wife – she was told that the officers were looking for stolen jewellery and appeared slightly mollified; she told them that her husband was out, but was expected back shortly.

A meticulous search of the flat was carried out, looking in every nook and cranny where stolen jewellery might be secreted and it became clear that the absent suspect, who came from gypsy stock, had surrounded himself with crossbows, animal traps and other associated paraphernalia which suggested an interest in wildlife. At the airing cupboard in the hallway, Bird paused. 'What's in here?' he asked, innocently.

'Fuck-all,' replied the wife, rather too hurriedly, adding by way of further explanation that all the cupboard contained was dirty washing, which was sure to come tumbling out, should the door be opened.

So Bird slowly opened the door, to discover that he was staring at a prime example of *Haliaeetus albicilla* – a white-tailed eagle. The wingspan of these creatures can be as much as ninety-six inches, although this example of the breed appeared slightly more stunted, which was fortunate given its confined surroundings. At the time of Bird's discovery, the world population of this type of eagle amounted to 9,000 so it was indeed a rare specimen. It Scandinavia it is not unknown for the trees in which these birds nest to collapse under their weight; so it was providential that the perch upon which it was sitting was a sturdy one; plus it was being kept warm by means of an infra-red lamp. As the eagle slowly turned its head and fixed Bird with a particularly malevolent eye, Bird quietly closed the cupboard door.

As an attempt at *sang-froid*, the suspect's wife casually remarked, 'Oh, that's me old man's; he's had it for ages,' adding, artfully, 'we keep it in there to keep it warm!'

'Do you know,' said Ron Noon (who had also observed the eagle) thoughtfully, 'I'm sure I read in a police message that some birds of prey were stolen during a burglary last night; I believe this one fits one of the stolen birds' description.'

This statement was immediately met with a fresh torrent of abuse from the wife, who informed the officers that not only had the eagle been in residence for several months, but that her 'old man would "do" the pair of them' once he arrived home. She was obviously unaware that seasoned Flying Squad officers are immune to such threats.

At this point, Bird stated that it was his intention to go and try to authenticate the information at the local police station; in fact, as soon as he left, he telephoned the owner of the bird and asked him to attend the flat as soon as possible. Within twenty minutes, the eagle-breeder's E-type Jaguar screeched to a halt and a quick examination of the eagle revealed to him that it was indeed one of his stolen birds. The reunion, Bird stated was like 'reuniting a fond parent with its lost child' – the eagle appeared equally pleased to see its owner and hopped on to his arm, and both made their way to the local police station where the eagle became both an exhibit and prisoner's property.

Half an hour later, the suspect appeared and joined in a lively discussion with his wife, in respect of the Squad officers' disputed parentage. Undeterred, the officers took him off to Wandsworth police station. Under questioning, the suspect denied the eagle was stolen, said he had not committed a burglary and he had purchased the bird from a man in a pub, some months before. The scene was now set to descend into farce.

Sergeant Bird from the Flying Squad determined that the eagle had been bought by the prisoner in the Raven Public House in the Goldhawk Road. Meanwhile the stolen bird was kept in the police station's cell block, the owner made daily visits to feed it mice (both live and deceased) and the station officer declared that he was 'fed up with all this eagle shit' and paroled the bird into the custody of its owner, to appear at court if necessary.

In fact, it was not necessary; the prisoner pleaded guilty to receiving the eagle and was sentenced to nine months' imprisonment. It was later revealed that the other stolen birds had quickly died following their appropriation and had rather callously been disposed of down the tower block's rubbish chute.

It was little wonder that the *Daily Mirror* wanted to photograph Chris Bird, wearing a Flying Squad tie depicting a swooping eagle, with the purloined eagle sitting on his arm; and even less surprising was the concentrated mockery of his fellow Squad officers – but as Bird said of his exploit, 'It's not everybody who can claim to have rescued an eagle from a tower block airing cupboard!'

⋆ ⋆ ⋆

And finally, still on a light note, but in keeping with the general theme of gunmen which started this chapter, Fred Cutts was asked, as an authorized shot, to make up numbers on a robbery observation, since many of the original team were attending court. He was unaware of the identities of any of the gang (as were the investigating officers) who, it was believed, were going to target a security van in south London. The robbers had been seen in the vicinity over a period of several weeks and surveillance photographs had been taken; however, they were of poor quality. Cutts' driver on that occasion, Police Constable Robin Floyd, had been present the previous week when the gang had reconnoitred the area.

Cutts was positioned in a side road close to a park, some three hundred yards away from where the security van intended to make its delivery – should any of the gang 'walk the plot' to try and detect a police presence, Cutts would be too far away to excite any interest from them.

After an hour's wait, the radio crackled into life, with a transmission from the officer manning the observation point (OP). 'Stand by all units from OP-one. Money box (security van) just approaching … stand by… Oh, sweet! A fucking great tipper's blocking my view … anybody take over eyeball?'

And with that, the tipper, driven by one of the gang smashed straight into the security van and at the same time, a smoke canister was set off. 'Attack, attack, attack!' shouted the officer in the OP and Cutts could hear the commotion across the airwaves as the arrests were carried out. But Cutts obeyed orders and stayed exactly where he was.

There came a further transmission: 'Three in the bag, one on foot, believed armed towards the park.' Other units converged on a public convenience by the park and dragged a man out; the call was sent out, 'Number four in the bag.'

And still Cutts stayed where he had been told to be and there he would remain until he received the order to 'stand down'.

Just then, he noticed a man walking towards him along the pavement by the park on the other side of the road, wearing a white, full-length dust coat; he was walking purposefully but not unduly quickly, with his hands deep in his coat pockets. The driver, PC Floyd, sat bolt upright. 'He's the one from last week!' He handed Cutts the surveillance photograph. 'Look at the smudge!'

Cutts studied the photograph, which like the others was of poor quality, and frowned. 'You sure?' But Floyd – whom Cutts described as 'a 110% copper' – was very sure. And just as the white-coated man got to where the arrests had taken place and started looking behind him, so Cutts dashed across the road, grabbed him and ran him into the park railings. As Floyd ran over to assist, the man struggled furiously and Cutts, utilizing his skills as a wrestler, applied a choke lock and got him to the ground – though he continued feverishly trying to free his hands until Floyd handcuffed him. The reason for the man's efforts to get his hands clear became obvious: stuffed down the waistband of his trousers was a fully loaded, Colt .45 service automatic.

Floyd radioed the arrest to the detective inspector in charge of the operation who crossly replied, 'You do realize that we have the four prisoners here?'

Nevertheless, Cutts requested the inspector's presence and he, upon arrival, took a careful look at the prisoner and the loaded .45 and concluded that Cutts had indeed arrested the fourth member of the gang.

It transpired that the original 'fourth man' who had been arrested in the public convenience was a completely innocent young man who had been reading the racing page of the *Daily Mirror* while he evacuated his bowels – until the door to his cubicle had been kicked in and he had been dragged, trousers round his ankles, into captivity.

The *Daily Mirror* paid him for a rather amusing story which was featured on page two and, to his credit (and certainly unlike nowadays, when his modern-day counterpart might seriously have considered suing the Metropolitan Police on a variety of counts) the young man joined the Flying Squad team in a celebratory glass.

That was the sort of hazard occasionally encountered by the Flying Squad and by innocent members of the public, becoming the source of a story with which to thrill their grandchildren.

All part of the Flying Squad legend.

The Bank of America

The robbery at the Bank of America in Davies Street, Mayfair, was sophisticated, featured top criminals and was slickly carried out. Unfortunately for the participants, it was an amalgamation of a premier Flying Squad team and the resources of C11 – Scotland Yard's Criminal Intelligence Department – who successfully investigated the robbery and brought about the gang's successful prosecution.

Prior to the actual raid, which was carried out on Thursday, 24 April 1975, there had been an attempt to break into the vaults. Oxyacetylene equipment and drills had been used but despite the liberal usage of 'Pepsi' and 'Coca-Cola' from the company's vending machines, the drills overheated and the attempt was abandoned.

Although they were unaware of the attempt to open the vaults at the Mayfair branch of the bank, it was at this time that C11 became involved. Set up in March 1960, the unit (it was then known as C5 (2) Department) was staffed by experienced detectives, many of whom had served on the Flying Squad. Their remit was to obtain, collate and disseminate intelligence on the country's top criminals, who would become known as 'Main Index' criminals. The man in charge of the operation which followed was Detective Inspector Trevor Lloyd-Hughes who, as a detective constable, had made a substantial input into the Kray enquiry and was held in high regard by the head of that investigation, Leonard 'Nipper' Read, QPM.

The information had originally come from Detective Chief Superintendent Steve Moore, who twelve years previously had been part of the small Flying Squad team investigating the Great Train Robbery. He was attached to the Home Office when he was approached by an informant who was in possession of some highly valuable information. Moore lost no time in contacting Commander Dave Dilley, the head of C11 Department, which led to Lloyd-Hughes acquiring pertinent information in respect of some underworld characters and quickly realizing that Moore's information had great value. He instructed two valued and trusted members of his team to monitor a greengrocer's premises in south London, whilst at the time covering their work with a fictitious operation in order that interest should not be aroused in the 'wrong' quarters.

It paid off. Jimmy O'Loughlin who, whilst he was well known to the police had been regarded as a third-division villain, was about to be promoted to the premier league. It was at about this time that he was seen to associate with Leonard Wilde, also known as Leonard Minchingdon but popularly known to police and underworld alike, as 'Johnny the Bosch' because it was said that he resembled a German. Wilde's speciality was safe-breaking, especially with the use of duplicate keys. A story was circulated, in which Wilde was allegedly handed a piece of cuttlefish into which the impressions of two different safe keys had been pressed and that he produced one key, which was capable of opening both safes. Whilst this story was possibly apocryphal, it does give an indication of the high esteem in which Wilde was held by the underworld. He and the Flying Squad were already known to each other. Almost twenty years previously, newly promoted Detective Sergeant Terry O'Connell, who had received a tip-off as to Wilde's whereabouts, arrested him after a violent struggle and charged him with possessing explosives and housebreaking implements by night. Wilde, who had only been released from prison the previous year, having completed a five-year sentence for officebreaking, notched-up his eleventh conviction at the Old Bailey and was sentenced to ten years' preventative detention.

So Wilde and O'Loughlin were kept under surveillance by the C11 operatives. But then they were also seen in the company of a young man named Stuart Buckley and when it was discovered that Buckley was a freelance electrician who had carried out work including installing telephones at both the City and Mayfair branches of the Bank of America, C11's interest intensified.

Because the men had been tailed to the City branch of the Bank of America on several occasions, where the layout of the vaults was identical to those in the Mayfair branch, the C11 team came to the not unreasonable conclusion that they planned to break into the City branch of the bank. As is common with this type of burglary, it seemed probable that the robbery would take place over a weekend, when they were less likely to be disturbed; especially given the City's shortage of residential premises. C11 kept observation on the bank for a couple of weekends, but nothing happened. They were right about the gang's intention to break into the Bank of America; but wrong about the time and place.

Buckley (who had supplied information to the gang in respect of the first, unsuccessful raid on the bank) discovered that the keys for the front door of the bank were regularly left on top of the switchboard, so he took an impression of them on a piece of cuttlefish and handed it to Wilde, the gang's key-man. From then on, the gang could use the duplicate keys to go in and out of the premises whenever they wanted and on one occasion, took their alarm expert, Micky 'Skinny' Gervaise in to evaluate the bank's alarm system. When their venal specialist commented, 'It's so old, I was looking for the handle to start it up,' the raid took another, substantial step forward. But what settled the matter was the second of Buckley's bright ideas, which was to provide the gang with the vault's combination. Due to his electrical and telephone work he had virtually unrestricted access to the premises and knew the entire layout of the bank, including the whereabouts of the vaults containing hundreds of safe deposit boxes. Buckley arrived at the bank early one morning, prior to the arrival of the cleaners and, using the duplicate keys to gain access to the building, eased his slim frame into the false ceiling which housed the bank's ventilation system, above the doors to the vault. There, he poked a hole in one of the polystyrene ceiling tiles with a screwdriver. With the aid of tiny telescope, he was able to determine the combinations of the locks, when dialled by the manager and his assistant.

At six o'clock on the evening of the raid, the gang – Buckley was not present – had opened the front door of the bank. They had to complete their work by 9.30, because the mobile security patrol checked the premises every four hours. Seven men entered the building, including Leonard Wilde and Peter Colson, who had planned the job at the Oasis swimming pool, Princes Circus, High Holborn. The gang went into the vaults and using a special crowbar opened seventy-eight safe deposit boxes, helping themselves to piles of gold bars and precious gems, sovereigns, Krugerrands and thick wads of currency. The total value, due to the secretive nature of many of the renters of the boxes, cannot be precisely stated, but it is fair to say that the total value of the property stolen was certainly in excess of £8 million and could well have been as much as £12 million. The gang had so far committed only an offence of burglary and the harshest penalty the law can impose for that offence is fourteen years' imprisonment. But that was about to change.

What nobody – Wilde, Colson or indeed Buckley – knew, was that the staff who managed the bank's computers were still in the building. When the gang started drilling into the boxes, the staff, attracted by the noise, went to investigate and were promptly tied up. Because force had been used, the offence now became one of robbery, for which the maximum penalty is life imprisonment.

The loot was quickly taken to a flat (known colloquially as 'a flop') in south London, where it was split into eight shares – one for each of the seven members of the gang, plus another set aside for Buckley – and, in addition, a smaller pile for 'expenses' which included recompense for the owner of the flat. The gang then each selected a number from a hat, took the pile with the corresponding number and went their separate ways.

The following day, C11 personnel walked into their office to discover the job had been pulled during the working week; however, they had a great many leads. The C11 suite of offices on the fourth floor at the Yard was just across the corridor to the Squad offices; it took a couple of quick steps by C11's Commander Dave Dilley to apprise the Squad Commander, John Lock, QPM and the operational head, Detective Chief Superintendent Jack Slipper, of the situation.

Matters were now moving very fast indeed. C11's strongest lead was Jimmy O'Loughlin; on the day following the robbery, he was seen entering Harrods and when he emerged, he was carrying a number of newly purchased suitcases. He was followed to a house and when he left, carrying one of the suitcases, he was stopped by a Flying Squad team. A search of the suitcase revealed a quarter-of-a-million pounds' worth of jewellery and gold, much of which was identified as coming from the deposit boxes – plus a substantial amount of cash. O'Loughlin was arrested and was taken to West End Central police station and the Squad soon pulled in Wilde and Buckley; it quickly became clear that Buckley was the weak link and he cracked under a little pressure and started talking. His decision to talk may have had something to do that whilst the seven members of the gang had split the loot into eight shares, his cut of £150,000 was substantially less than the others. He directed the Squad officers to where his portion of the loot was hidden – in a stove pipe, buried in a field – and started to make a very lengthy statement. Whilst Buckley had not physically taken part in the actual raid, he was nevertheless able to tell the story of the planning of the raid and the names of some of those who had participated in it. As a result, the Director of Public Prosecutions awarded him 'Supergrass' status – after he had admitted his own guilt in court, he would give evidence against his co-defendants for a lesser sentence.

This was an enormous break-through in the investigation and on the directions of Commander Lock and Deputy Assistant Commissioner Ernie Bond OBE, QPM, two officers, Detective Superintendent Bob Robinson and Detective Chief Inspector Mick O'Leary, both highly experienced in the handling of informants, were dispatched to West End Central to deal with Buckley's debriefing. It was a task which would take two years of their lives.

The enquiry moved into top gear, with the Squad searching premises and making arrests, C11 working overtime with their acquisition of information, and divisional detectives at West End Central obtaining statements and compiling reports for the Director of Public Prosecutions, in order to substantiate the charges.

Micky Gervaise was arrested and denied everything; it was only when a diagram of a circuit was found in his wife's purse that he admitted everything. He was later sentenced to eighteen months' imprisonment.

Billy Gear was caught because on the day of the robbery, his wife had insisted that he take their son to the dentists. The dental work took longer than expected, so after dropping the boy off home, Gear, worried that he would be late for the raid, used his wife's car to drive to Davies Street. Leaving the car parked on a double yellow line, a warden stuck a ticket on it; it led to Mrs Gear's arrest and the subsequent surrender of her husband. With his wife released from custody, Billy Gear made a statement, in which he confessed his own misdeeds without implicating anybody else and took the Squad officers to recover of his share of the loot. It was found safe and sound, in a safe deposit box in Hatton Garden.

Gear, like many professional criminals, was a likeable and humorous character, who won the admiration of the Squad officers after the prison van in which he was travelling clipped the kerb and overturned. He could have escaped; instead he chose to stay and assist the injured driver.

Not so Jimmy O'Loughlin. Appearing at Marlborough Street Magistrates' Court, prior to being committed to the Old Bailey for trial, O'Loughlin's solicitor handed him a bundle of committal papers for him to peruse. He did, wandering into the communal lavatory in the detention area and taking a little longer than usual before he emerged. When he did so, his first reaction was, as he later told the investigating officers, 'They've gone without me!' and so they had; the prison van was on its way to Brixton Prison, minus O'Loughlin. It might not have been as much of an accident as was initially thought; O'Loughlin, like the other prisoners, usually wore casual, designer clothing for court appearances. But not on this occasion; O'Loughlin was impressively 'booted and suited', to such an extent that it was the subject of comment amongst the accompanying officers. Now, smartly attired, he strolled over to the jailer, casually waved the bundle of committal papers, neatly tied with pink ribbon and drawled, 'Solicitor's clerk.' This was accepted, because solicitors and police officers often mingled with the prisoners in that area, and the door was opened. O'Loughlin walked out and before anyone realized that something was amiss, he was in a taxi and away.

Information was received that O'Loughlin had teamed up with someone alleged to have been a participant in the robbery, a well-known 'key-man' and that they planned to drive to Spain; however, en route, in the Pyrenees, they crashed the Jaguar they were using. This information was three days old by the time it reached the Squad, but nevertheless a call was put through to Interpol, Paris. An enquiry by the French police revealed that the car had been found, undriveable, in a garage close to the border with Spain. However, of the occupants there was no sign and a search by both the French and Spanish police failed to reveal their whereabouts. In fact, both men had returned to England.

Weeks went by and it was Detective Chief Inspector Mick O'Leary's informant who steered the Squad in the direction of O'Loughlin, who was in his girlfriend's flat, in a well-made hidey-hole under the stairs. O'Loughlin was recaptured and back in custody; his accomplice on the ill-fated trip to Spain made himself unavailable for a considerable time. When he was finally arrested, there was insufficient evidence upon which he could be prosecuted.

One member of the gang who could not be found was Peter Colson. However, it was discovered that every lunchtime he would telephone one of his two girlfriends, on each occasion from a different public telephone box. The Squad was split into areas and during the lunchtime period they checked each call box in that vicinity. Detective Constable Reg Leonard was patrolling with Detective Sergeant Guy Mills in a Squad car driven by PC Bill Parsons, when at two o'clock, the order came on the radio to 'stand-down' the search of the telephone boxes for the day. The car was travelling west along Knightsbridge when Leonard, who had previously worked the area as a divisional officer, exclaimed, 'Hang on – there's one call box we haven't checked out – it's just ahead at Trevor Square.'

Guy Mills grumbled, 'I want my lunch!' but nevertheless, Bill Parsons turned left into Trevor Street and parked. Mills and Leonard got out and strolled down towards the square, at the bottom of which was the kiosk. They were still some way away from it, when Leonard noticed that a caller was inside. He did not know exactly what Colson looked like, because a photograph of him did not exist, although a good description of him had been provided. What Leonard did know was that Colson had apparently stated that 'he wouldn't come easily' which, as far as he was concerned, meant that Colson intended to shoot his way out of trouble.

Now, Leonard and Mills were ten yards away from the kiosk and whoever the caller was, he was engrossed in his conversation. 'Guy, I'm sure that's Colson,' muttered Leonard. 'You sure?' queried Mills, and now they were five yards away. Leonard was as sure as he could be; he pulled open the kiosk door, grabbed hold of the caller round the neck and at the same time, drew his Smith & Wesson model 36 revolver and stuck it in the startled occupant's ear. The caller was indeed Peter Colson, who wasn't armed and came along peacefully. However, he was a conceited, smooth operator and was convinced that Buckley would never give evidence which would incriminate him. In fact, he was almost right.

After Buckley pleaded guilty and was sentenced to seven years' imprisonment, he was taken from the safety of the cells at West End Central, prior to giving evidence for the prosecution, to

Reading Prison. Because there was no facility for the housing of Supergrasses, he was placed in 'the nonces' wing' – that part of the prison reserved for some of the most depraved sexual offenders, murderers and child molesters, who were segregated from the other prisoners. Unsurprisingly, in such insalubrious company, Buckley stated on several occasions that he would not give evidence and it was only with the considerable, extremely valuable assistance of one of the prison warders that he was encouraged to do so.

Meanwhile, Colson had his own problems on remand. He received visits from his girlfriends on alternate days, each of them being unaware of the other's existence. In addition, he wrote them the most passionate letters which, for security reasons had to be routed through the prison staff in unsealed envelopes, prior to posting. Due to his inexperience of prison life, Colson made a complaint against one of the staff. Unfortunately, shortly afterwards, the letters got mixed up, with one of the girlfriends receiving the letter intended for the other, and vice versa. Colson then complained to the Flying Squad team that the prison staff had 'stitched-up his love life' and the Squad officers, remembering his reluctance to fully assist them with their enquiries, commiserated rather unconvincingly.

Stuart Buckley did give evidence for the prosecution and all the prisoners were convicted at the Old Bailey. Passing sentence on 16 November 1976, Judge Alan King-Hamilton said that he was determined that the gang would not enjoy the fruits of their labours, of which just half-a-million pounds had been recovered. He said:

What has been concealed will remain salted away so far as you are concerned for a great many years. Whatever has happened to it, it will not be used for your benefit.

Leonard Wilde, the master safe-cracker, received the longest sentence – twenty-three years' imprisonment, followed by Peter Colson, who was sentenced to twenty-one years. Criminal bankruptcy orders in the sums of £500,000 each were ordered in respect of both men. Others in the gang received sentences ranging from eighteen years for robbery down to three years' imprisonment for handling stolen goods.

With the last of the prisoners led away, the judge addressed the detectives in the case, commending them for their detective ability – these sentiments were echoed by the Director of Public Prosecutions and senior treasury counsel. A report of these comments were, as was the norm, recorded by the court inspector and forwarded to the commissioner, for further commendation. However, in respect of Detective Sergeant Fred Cutts, the judge had appended the following unusual remark: 'He managed to give the trial a much needed lift at a strategic stage!' and it is interesting to note how that occurred.

After Leonard Wilde – 'Johnny the Bosch' – had been charged and remanded into custody, it was Cutts' job to convey him to Brixton Prison. En route, Cutts felt that little would be lost if he injected into the conversation a little commiseration ('when you get out of this one, John, the old chap will be permanently at half-past six') followed by manipulation ('your parcel will be eroded by thieves' friends, to say nothing of inflation...') before resorting to motivation ('John, why not give your parcel back and get a good brief?')

Wilde appeared to consider the idea, before muttering, 'I can't trust you Old Bill, none of you.'

'OK John, I understand,' soothingly replied Cutts. 'You make your mind up to put the parcel back and I'll get the commissioner out to oversee it!'

Every kind of emotion, even tears, flooded over Wilde's face for minutes before he regained his power of speech. 'No, get me to Brixton!' he shouted. 'This is out of order, you cunt – you nearly got me at it, then!'

At the trial, Cutts, who had interviewed many of the defendants, was in the witness box at the Old Bailey for just over three weeks. During this time he was vigorously cross-examined, but what caused the uproar in court was when he referred to his comment to Wilde concerning 'putting his parcel back and getting a good brief'. At this, Judge King-Hamilton leaned forward and said, somewhat patronizingly, 'Well, he did, didn't he, officer?'

'What, put the parcel back, my lord?' replied Cutts, innocently. 'Oh no, he certainly didn't!'

Seeking to redress the balance, the judge replied, 'No, no, I meant he got a good brief in his eminent counsel,' and gestured towards Wilde's Queens Counsel, who smiled back at the judge and justifiably preened himself.

'Well, that remains to be seen, my lord,' replied Cutts who by now, was rather pressing his luck, because whilst the majority of the court howled with laughter, the puce-faced defence counsel glared at him and the judge – who like many judges believed that if anybody is going to crack jokes in court, it should be them – gave Cutts a piercing look. Realizing he had gone a little too far, Cutts gave every appearance of contrition and murmured, 'I do know Mr Wilde's counsel to be an excellent lawyer,' and as the light comedy ended, the battle of cross-examination recommenced.

★　★　★

As a footnote to this story, I should say that Supergrass handling was still in its infancy at that time, and one of the senior divisional officers at West End Central became alarmed at what he perceived to be the excessive lassitude permitted to Buckley after he had been granted Supergrass status. Feeling quite certain that he could smell alcohol on Buckley's breath – an allegation which was categorically denied – after one outing when he had been accompanied by Squad officers, the officer demanded that Bob Robinson take stern action to stop this kind of behaviour. So Robinson issued a written order, stating that when Buckley was allowed out of the police station, he had to be handcuffed to his escort.

A little later the same nervous officer noticed that after Buckley had returned from an outing, his hair, as well as that of his two escorts, was damp and demanded to know why; Buckley admitted that they had been swimming in the Serpentine.

Addressing one of the accompanying officers, whose name happened to be Detective Sergeant Fred Cutts, the divisional officer shrilly demanded to know if he had seen Detective Superintendent Robinson's unequivocal memo regarding the use of handcuffs. Cutts admitted that he had. And had he, Cutts, obeyed that order? He had.

'How, then,' expostulated the furious officer, 'did you manage to swim whilst wearing handcuffs?'

Ever laconic, Fred Cutts replied, 'Backstroke.'

Corruption, Supergrasses and Devolvement

Back now to 1970, when Squad arrests totalled 1,550 and stolen property valued in excess of £1 million was recovered. The following year, the results were even better – whilst arrests had dropped slightly to 1,347, the property recovered amounted to a staggering £5,750,000.

After a period of calm, the troubles had resurfaced in Northern Ireland. On 9 March 1971, three young soldiers from the Royal Highland Fusiliers, two of them brothers, who were off duty drinking in a Belfast bar, were lured to a remote road in Ligoniel, just outside the city, where they were all shot in the head at point-blank range. Officers from the Flying Squad were amongst those asked to assemble a team to investigate the killings; unfortunately the briefing of the officers was left to the commander of C1 Department, the deeply corrupt Wally Virgo. Not that Virgo's venality was the problem when he addressed the team; it was his sheer incompetence. He asked the officers to imagine that Belfast was London; that being so, he said, the trouble was centred in the City of London, the RUC station from which they would be working would be in Sydenham and that their hotel would be in Bromley. As easy as that. Virgo was asked if the officers would be insured? Certainly they would, replied Virgo. They weren't. They would be there for two weeks, said Virgo; they stayed for three months. Obviously, they would need transport; the Yard sent them ten Hillmans, all the same colour with consecutive, mainland number plates. It is hard to imagine more studied stupidity, but by the time the cars arrived the enquiry team had other problems; the RUC station from where they worked was barricaded against sniper fire and their hotel was situated at the lower part of Newtownards Road, a hot-spot for both Loyalists and Republicans.

One of the officers, working under the direction of the very popular Detective Inspector Don Brown, was Les Bell. 'Hurray for Wally Virgo!' was his embittered comment, made thirty-seven years later. That the Flying Squad team returned home unscathed was a tribute to their ingenuity – that, and a gracious dispensation of providence. The *Daily Mail*, dated 9 June 1971 declared,

> Terrorists have threatened reprisals against Scotland Yard detectives working in Ulster because they are becoming too successful in infiltrating gangs. The warning came yesterday as troops escaped death in two bomb ambushes ... The Provisional IRA in their reprisal warning claimed 'attempts are being made to convict Republicans by means of planted evidence and perjured statements'. Warned one of their spokesmen, 'In the event of members of the Republican movement being convicted on trumped-up charges and planted evidence, strong action will be taken against those responsible.

Much of the Squad's work in Ulster is still classified, although in a document marked 'Secret', Brown and seven of his officers were commended by the commissioner for 'valuable assistance leading to the arrest and conviction of two men in a dangerous and complicated case.'

*   *   *

But by 1972, something had clearly gone wrong – arrests had diminished to 1,081 and the property which the Squad recovered had dropped to an almost miserly £782,000. Why was this?

For over fifty years the Squad had been in the public eye. It had been identified as being the top crime-busting arm of the Metropolitan Police, staffed with tough, incorruptible detectives who always got their man. Their image was certainly bolstered by the press, who were prone to inflate their stories with a certain amount of hyperbole but nevertheless, the description of the Flying Squad was essentially an accurate one. And because the gangs who had been targeted and arrested by the Squad for very serious offences knew that if they were convicted they could expect commensurately lengthy sentences, many of them alleged malpractice by the officers – planting evidence, verballing and of course, accepting bribes. In the vast majority of cases these allegations were utterly malicious and they were dismissed out of hand by the magistrates and judges to whom they were made.

Sometimes the complaints were made to the Yard, but although meticulous investigations were carried out, very few of the allegations of impropriety were found to have any basis in fact.

Thus, the vast majority of honest Squad officers were quite properly vindicated; however, there were undeniably rotten apples at the bottom of the Squad barrel who escaped the net and were allowed to fester.

Peter Brodie OBE, QPM, had been appointed Assistant Commissioner (Crime) in 1966, succeeding Sir Ranulph Bacon, who had taken up the post of deputy commissioner. Brodie had joined the Metropolitan Police in 1934 and becoming a junior station inspector under Trenchard's 'Officer Scheme', he was seconded to the Ceylonese Police Force from 1943 until 1947. After a very short stay back with the Metropolitan Police, Brodie was off again in 1949, to become Chief Constable of Stirling and Clackmannanshire and then, in 1958, Chief Constable of Warwickshire. A year after his appointment as ACC, he was elected to the executive committee of Interpol. Brodie was well-liked and thoroughly supported the 3,250 CID officers under his command, whom he referred to as 'his chaps' and he was thought to be a very strong contender as a future commissioner.

The very popular commissioner, Sir Joseph Simpson had died in office on 20 March 1968. He was succeeded in a caretaker role by Deputy Commissioner Sir John Waldron KCVO and it was he whom many thought Brodie would replace, when Waldron retired two years later at the age of sixty.

However, the vacancy of deputy commissioner left by Waldron was filled by Sir Robert Mark GBE. Prior to that, he had been the Met's Assistant Commissioner 'B' Department (in charge of Traffic), before that Assistant Commissioner 'D' Department (in charge of recruitment and training) and before joining the Met, Chief Constable of Leicester. In stepping into the role of deputy commissioner, Mark was now in charge of discipline throughout the Force. It became quite clear that his appointment was not liked by many of the senior officers at the Yard and before long quite a number of more junior officers would have added their own feelings of general dislike.

Mark immediately put a stop to the practice of permitting officers who had been dismissed from the Force and who were awaiting the outcome of their appeal, to be suspended from duty on full pay. And where the Director of Public Prosecutions had declined to prosecute officers who had been accused of criminal offences, where there was insufficient evidence or no evidence at all, Mark now wished to consider the papers pertaining to the investigation, to see if there were sufficient grounds to bring disciplinary offences against the officers even if they had been acquitted at court – thereby placing them in double jeopardy.

What became known as 'The *Times* Enquiry' quite literally hit that newspaper's headlines in November 1969. Although the matter had nothing to do with the Flying Squad – the officers concerned had been attached to C9 Department (The Provincial Police Crime Branch) – it was immensely damaging for the CID in general, with allegations of corruption and extortion, and as a result three corrupt police officers were eventually sentenced to terms of imprisonment.

Mark criticized the way in which Metropolitan Police officers had investigated each other in the past and a phrase which emanated from 'The *Times* Enquiry' – 'a firm within a firm' – would become beloved of defence barristers for years afterwards. These enquiries, Mark stated, had seldom led to disciplinary proceedings, let alone a court appearance. During a meeting at the Yard where Brodie was unfortunately absent (he was attending an Interpol conference in Kyoto, Japan), Waldron grudgingly told Mark to go ahead and 'do something about it'. He did; Mark formed A10, the first official police complaints department and filled it with senior CID officers – those he believed he could trust – and senior uniform officers, who had little or no experience of investigation. It was, of course, overseen by a senior uniform officer. It appeared to be not a moment too soon; questions were starting to be raised about the activities of the Drugs Squad and the Obscene Publications Squad.

On 1 November 1971, Mark was asked by the Home Secretary, Reginald Maudling if, following Waldron's retirement, he would take up the post of commissioner. Mark agreed, with one stipulation – that he be given the authority to change assistant commissioners from one department to another – and this was agreed.

When Mark took up the reins of commissioner on 17 April 1972, he was determined to tackle corruption, break the power of the CID and ensure that the uniform branch took supremacy in the Metropolitan Police. In fact, he had been considerably helped in his objectives with the revelation in the *Sunday People* newspaper for 27 February, that the head of the Flying Squad, Ken Drury and his wife had been on holiday in Cyprus with a well-known Soho businessman, Jimmy Humphries and his ex-stripper wife, Rusty. This was bad enough given that Humphries had a chequered criminal past, including serving a six-year sentence for safe-breaking. But in addition, he had paid for the entire holiday and when Drury blustered that, firstly, he had paid his own way and that secondly, the reason for him going to Cyprus was to track down Great Train Robber Ronnie Biggs (who had escaped from prison six years previously), Humphries, realizing the dangers of being labelled a grass, swiftly repudiated the whole idea.

It was a crushing blow for Drury who, a week later was suspended from duty and, on 1 May, resigned; indeed, it was demoralizing for the whole of the Flying Squad. And matters were about to get worse. In October, three days after Rusty Humphries was released from prison for possession of a firearm, her former lover, Peter 'Pookie' Garfarth was attacked and slashed around the head, face and arms with a knife. It was rumoured that Humphries had heard that the relationship between Garfarth and his wife was about to be reignited and Garfarth had to be taught a lesson. Humphries fled the country, but when he was later arrested in Holland and extradited, he was sentenced to eight years' imprisonment, and from his prison cell he began to talk. He had a great deal to say about the corrupt dealings he had experienced with Metropolitan Police officers and as a result, Drury and eleven other officers, from the Flying Squad and the Obscene Publications Squad were arrested. Drury was a tough and well-liked Flying Squad chief. A soldier prior to, and during World War Two, Drury had joined the Metropolitan Police immediately after demobilization and was noted for his bravery, being commended on twenty-three occasions.

Les Bell had good reason to like and admire Drury, before either of them went to the Flying Squad. As a divisional detective sergeant (second class), Bell suffered a terrible tragedy when two of his young children died. Drury, his senior officer, sent him home for twelve weeks, to cope with his bereavement; and there was no question of Bell having to submit complicated and intrusive reports to explain his absence. As far as Drury was concerned, Bell was not absent; his non-attendance was suitably covered and his allowances remained intact. 'I sneaked back to work after five weeks,' recalled Bell, 'he [Drury] caught me, gave me an almighty bollocking and sent me home again. He was obviously my hero.'

Drury had taken up the post of commander of the Squad on 1 January 1971; up until then, he had been second-in-command to Frank 'Jeepers' Davies MBE, who retired to run the security at Marks & Spencer. It is fair to say that Drury was over-promoted; even Drury himself was amazed at his appointment. But the Squad officers were delighted, especially Les Bell, who had arrived to work on 5 Squad three years earlier. 'Ken Drury was an excellent man, a man's man,' he recalled. 'His copperplate writing and his ability to put together lengthy, complicated reports was unsurpassed.' Drury was noisy and sometimes tactless; at a dinner given for the American astronauts who had landed on the moon, he praised their achievements but added, 'if I told my blokes to go to the moon, they'd do it – and if, when they got up there, they couldn't find the moon, they'd fucking-well plant one there!' But although he could be appallingly rude, Drury, as has already been noted, had his compassionate side. He knew the first names of every one of his 100 officers and when he was sentenced to eight years' imprisonment for corruption (later reduced to five years, on appeal) the Squad wives wept, remembering the kindness of the Squad's chief who would make it his personal business to telephone them when their husbands were likely to be out all night, carrying out searches, arrests – or, quite possibly, mischievously inserting a moon into an otherwise barren sky.

In the same way that disgraced army officers have the epaulets ripped from their shoulders, Drury's photograph was removed from the wall outside the Flying Squad commander's office. It was an action regarded by many as being incredibly small-minded.

Drury had become a 'non-person' to the new elite of the Yard's senior CID officers. But not to the rank and file, who flocked to pay their respects at Drury's funeral a few years later. Larger than life, even in death, Drury had instructed his executors to, 'Give the boys a drink; not too much as they can be expensive and put the four London phone books in my coffin, with a phone. I might give some of them a ring.'

★   ★   ★

In fairness to Mark, in many ways he was a good commissioner. He was a forceful and very articulate speaker who could certainly hold his own in any kind of public debate. Mark was against organized gangs of criminals who manipulated juries to their own advantage and their lawyers who deliberately twisted the legal system to suit their own ends and those of their clients; and what's more, he was not afraid to say so.

The Notting Hill Carnival was a particular *bête noire* (no pun intended) to Mark, who commented 'Those who urge a kind of Black Saturnalia in the interests of good race relations either need their heads examining or have sinister motives' and he had no truck with pressure groups, especially the National Council for Civil Liberties. When that organization wrote to Mark, complaining about an officer who had been the subject of unsubstantiated complaints from members of the black population while serving at Notting Hill, and had now been posted back there, they received very short shift indeed. Terrorist groups he held in absolute contempt and made it quite clear that he would never negotiate with them.

Mark hit corruption head on; and it was needed. There was corruption in the CID – the uniform branch, as well – which needed addressing and eradicating.

What was also necessary was wise counsel. Mark could have filled the spaces left by those senior CID officers who were imprisoned or sacked by promoting suitable, honest CID officers, of whom there were many; it would have been a 'new broom' policy which would have worked. But eschewing the use of a broom, new or otherwise, Mark swept through the CID like an exterminating angel bearing a flaming sword. Within a week of his appointment, all divisional detectives were placed under the command of the uniform commanders and, two weeks after that, Mark called a meeting of senior CID officers and told them that he was going to eradicate corruption and, if necessary, he would put the whole of the CID back into uniform and start afresh. He left the meeting to the accompaniment of a thunderous silence. Brodie was out and the new Assistant Commissioner (Crime), Colin Woods, who had previously been in charge of traffic, was in. Later, Gilbert Kellend who had monitored the intricacies of the licensing laws and, like Woods had never served one day in the Met's CID, took charge of all of London's detectives.

In August 1975, Mark abolished the detective duty allowance

and for the first time in almost 100 years of the Criminal Investigation Department's existence, detectives were paid overtime for the actual work they carried out. Because of the excessive hours they worked, their salaries practically doubled. Perhaps Mark thought that this cash bonus would placate the detectives, who were getting more mutinous by the hour. And perhaps he thought that by paying them extra, it would make them disinclined to accept bribes. If so, he was wrong. If any person in a position of trust, as CID staff were, was bent, getting extra lawful money would not stop them being crooked. A thief is a thief and a bent copper is a bent copper. However, what is likely is that Mark had little idea of the tremendous workload shouldered by the CID, who until that time had been paid a miserly allowance of £38 per month. Now, with the officers working their – to them – normal seventy-plus hours per week, the Receiver's office gave a horrified gasp and realized that in no time at all, the Metropolitan Police would be bankrupt. Overtime restrictions were implemented and when these parameters were reached, the detectives simply had to stop working and go home. Of course, if it was a matter of meeting an informant and the officer met him in his off-duty hours, and this became apparent, a question of corrupt practices might well raise its ugly head. At one time, the matter could be explained away to senior officers who had been detectives all their lives; now, senior management was an entirely different kettle of fish.

Informants' names, which had been the jealously guarded secret of the detectives running them, were now to be divulged to the Deputy Assistant Commissioner 'C' Department (Operations). Many CID officers would not have particularly minded, had the DAC still been Ernie Bond OBE, QPM, a former SAS soldier and dyed-in-the-wool detective, who was worshipped by all the CID personnel. But Bond had retired after thirty years service ('to the day,' as he reminded me) and his place had been taken by David Powis, whose CID experience was no more than a dim, distant memory. From his office on the fifth floor at the Yard, Powis (whose most repeatable nickname was 'Crazy Horse' and whose way of working was greeted with derision by many detectives) decided – initially, at least – that all rewards for informants in excess of £500 would be paid personally by him. He addressed astonishing homilies to the paid-out informants which, according to their characters either bemused or convulsed them, leaving their handlers utterly humiliated. But at the same time, Powis introduced an incredibly complex system of rules to cover the eventuality of detectives meeting their informants who were on bail (ie, the vast majority of them). The new regulations demanded that the meeting take place in a police station, after prior permission had been obtained from a senior officer. This, together with details of the meeting being written in the officer's pocket book, an entry in the station's occurrence book (plus a further entry, if the officer worked elsewhere, in *his* station's or department's occurrence book) and the submission of a pro-forma, counter-signed by the senior officer authorizing the meeting, was little more than ludicrous. Quite apart from the expenditure of time, with the name of the informant being thus bandied about there was a real threat of their exposure, especially if defence lawyers got to hear of the documentation and demanded its production in court. In consequence, these strictures caused many detectives to break the rules, in order to get the job done. If one got away with it, all well and good. But if not, the alternative, which was often the case, was the return to uniform – or the sacking – of a hard-working, though injudicious officer. It was little wonder that many industrious officers hated, despised and feared the despotic DAC and his cohorts. Powis' sources of information were notoriously unreliable; their inability to glean any sensible intelligence from telephone intercepts were the source of much hilarity. However, the laughter died away when working CID officers were expected to waste time by following up the nonsense which had been fed to Powis, it having been given official authenticity and thus set in stone.

Mark had also introduced the practice of interchange – the swapping of officers between uniform and CID. Men whose careers had been devoted to the smooth-running of London's traffic, the intricacies of the licensing laws or just the matter of handing over what remained at the end of a shift to the succeeding officer, suddenly found themselves in charge of squads and teams of detectives. And vice versa.

Jack Slipper had been a career detective throughout his service. Joining the Flying Squad as a detective constable in 1962, he rose through the ranks, leaving six years later as a detective inspector for divisional duties. In 1973, he returned to the Squad for a four year posting as the operational detective chief superintendent. He had contributed to some of the most famous Squad cases and was widely admired. 'Jack Slipper was a man of few words,' Reg Leonard told me. 'He had a presence, a practical copper.'

But that admiration was not shared by the newly appointed senior officers in the CID; Slipper represented everything they hated about the old guard. He was everything they were not; a born leader of men, knowledgeable about criminals, knowing how to deal with them and if it was necessary, knowing how short-cuts could be effected, to 'get things done'. They set their pet weasels to work and as a result Slipper, admitting he was 'stunned', was returned to uniform duties; he retired two years earlier than was necessary.

The fifth floor had a mighty weapon in its armoury – Con. Memo 4. This pernicious piece of internal legislation catered for everything in a detective's life, between being born and dying. Broadly speaking, it meant if there was the slightest hint of a suspicion regarding the probity of an officer in a specialized department where actual proof fell far below the standards for disciplining, sacking or arrest, that officer could be returned to uniform duties. In Slipper's case, it was a query over a case he had dealt with some fifteen years previously. In another case, a detective superintendent was thought to be 'too close' to an informant; a source that the officer had run for years, who was responsible for providing the intelligence for some of the Squad's most sensational arrests. He too was returned to uniform. Astonishingly, for one who was thought to be so untrustworthy, he was further promoted in uniform.

Exactly the same thing happened to a detective chief inspector who was caught up in a fifth floor 'whispering campaign' and suspended from duty. After a year, the white-faced weasels reported back to their master, telling him that they could find absolutely no evidence whatsoever of wrongdoing, either from a criminal or disciplinary point of view. 'Carry on until you *do* find something!' barked Powis, but again they failed miserably; nevertheless, the officer was returned to uniform. Again, despite being regarded as not to be trusted, by the end of his career he had been promoted to the rank of commander. Many officers rapidly came to the conclusion that the Russian Revolution's OGPU of the 1920s or the depredations of Senator Joseph McCarthy during the 1950s were pretty tame stuff, compared to Con. Memo 4.

With the Squad on the fourth floor of the Yard and Powis' office on the fifth, one Squad officer commented on the curious smell emanating between the floors and came to the conclusion that it was a mixture of bullshit, spite and fear.

As a result of Mark's activities during the period 1973-76, eighty-two officers were sacked and another 301 left, following criminal or disciplinary enquiries. In his report to Parliament for 1973, Mark, referring to the Squad, stated, 'morale … is high and there is every indication that it will remain so.' Don't you believe it. Morale had crashed to an all-time low and was now all set to plumb the depths. And when much, much later, after his retirement, Mark admitted, 'On reflection, I am sorry that I did not make the point that the great majority of the CID must not only have been honest but anxious for reform,' it was too little and far too late. The CID had started sliding down a very slippery slope, from which it would never recover.

★   ★   ★

'Operation Countryman' commenced in 1978 after allegations were made that three armed robberies had been carried out, with the connivance of City of London police officers. Interestingly, the allegations were made by Don Neesham QPM, the commander of the Flying Squad. The Home Office, in conjunction with the new Commissioner, Sir David McNee QPM, appointed the Assistant Chief Constable of the Dorset Constabulary, Leonard Burt, to investigate the allegations.

According to a number of sources, it is fashionable to state that the man leading the enquiry was Leonard Burt CVO, CBE, the highly respected Metropolitan Police officer who rose to the rank of CID Commander, who was an astute murder investigator and had worked for MI5 during the war. Wrong. *That* Leonard Burt, who had been commended on thirty-nine occasions and in addition to his other decorations had also been appointed *Légion d'Honneur*, awarded the Order of Orange Nassau and the Order of the Dannebrog and had retired after almost forty-six years service, and the assistant chief constable of Dorset were two completely different people.

Because if it had been the London-based Burt, he would not have chosen a team made up of mainly uniform and traffic personnel from provincial forces, many of whom had been unwisely promoted by one rank for the enquiry, to track down some of the allegedly most corrupt cops in history.

His officers would not have been so naïve as to believe just about anything alleged by experienced, self-serving, professional criminals, who were eager to be let off the hook. His officers would have taken written statements from those making the allegations, rather than being satisfied with oral statements, many of which were later denied. It was not before long that those provincial officers were mockingly referred to as 'The Swedey'.

Their offices in Camberwell police station were broken into and attempts were made to interfere with their records and documentation and they were moved to Godalming police station in the Surrey constabulary. Their thirty-strong workforce was utterly overwhelmed with rumoured claims, as well as some undeniably factual information and they asked for, and were granted, an increase to over eighty officers.

As the allegations drifted in to the Metropolitan Police, the Chief Constable of Dorset, Arthur Hambleton, stated that the staff of 'Countryman' complained that they were being blocked at every turn by the Yard. It was something that Neesham denied but he was shifted from the Squad and resigned – his widow told me that he died broken-hearted. It appeared that the 'Countryman' team also did not trust the Yard's deputy commissioner, the assistant commissioner (crime), the Director of Public Prosecutions or the Attorney General.

Wholly innocent officers were named by wily criminals, desperate for an early release from prison, to have pending charges dropped or to settle old scores in the biggest and probably most incompetent witch hunt in police history. The Yard was furious because they wanted to know details of the allegations being made against their officers; the 'Countryman' team refused to divulge them. When Hambleton decided to resign, seventeen months after the commencement of the enquiry, the Chief Constable of Surrey, Sir Peter Matthews was asked to take over the enquiry and he did so, leaving Burt in operational charge.

The 'Countryman' team made their first arrest in early 1980. The man arrested was a detective chief inspector from the City of London police, in respect of a matter unconnected with the initial enquiry. In an astonishing sequence of events, the enquiry team completely bypassed the representative from the office of the

Director of Public Prosecutions, who had been working full-time
with the team for three months. The City officer appeared at a
court in Hertfordshire, where the 'Countryman' officers were
represented by a local, Dorset solicitor. At his application, the
magistrates remanded the officer in police custody for three days,
whereupon he was whisked away to Dorset.

A representative from the Director of Public Prosecutions office
later attended court, to ask that the charges be dropped, due to lack
of evidence. 'Countryman' were furious; and so were the police
officers who had been the subject of the enquiry. It appeared to
them, with considerable justification, that 'Countryman' was not
only out of its depth, it was also out of control.

After four long years, 'Countryman' came to a halt. In spite of
accusing a number of Flying Squad officers of corruption (and
succeeding in getting some of them suspended from duty) the
eight Metropolitan Police officers who were charged were all
found not guilty. Two City of London officers – from where the
enquiry had commenced – were convicted and imprisoned.

'Operation Countryman' was an unmitigated disaster, and an
expensive one, having cost the taxpayer almost £4 million.

★   ★   ★

But whilst all this turmoil was underway, the Flying Squad
continued making its presence felt against teams of organized
criminals. Back in 1972, a series of armed robberies culminating
at Barclays Bank, Wembley, where £138,111 was stolen, had
resulted in the formation of a robbery squad, made up of officers
who had served on the Flying Squad and Regional Crime Squad.
The gang were arrested, their number including one Derek
Creighton Smalls, popularly known as 'Bertie'. Smalls became
the first Supergrass and walked free from court, having provided
the evidence which had sent his associates to a total of 308 years'
imprisonment. But despite the success of this investigation,
allegations of corruption emerged from the enquiry; a woman
detective constable complained that her informant had not
received her proper reward money and later resigned from the
Force. In addition, the wife of one of the convicted robbers
alleged that not only was £25,000 missing from her husband's
safe deposit box, but that the police were responsible for its
disappearance.

One Supergrass followed another and the tariff decided upon to recognize their assistance was one of just five years' imprisonment. This was the sentence handed down to Maurice O'Mahoney, who named 120 people, giving information on their involvement in seventy offences. During the court case following the Wembley bank robbery investigation, one of the witnesses called by Danny Allpress (who was one of the gang's main participants) in order to discredit Bertie Smalls, was Roger Louis Denhart. It did Allpress little good; after a series of trials, appeals and a prison escape, he was sentenced to a total of eighteen years' imprisonment. Denhart, however, might have been seen to be getting a little practice in the witness box; a convicted and notorious robber, he was later to become an equally notorious Supergrass. And Charlie Lowe broke the mould for Supergrass sentences after he received eleven-and-a-half years' imprisonment. Still smarting from this unexpected shock, he received another even more painful, when Donald Walter Barratt, who was still understandably annoyed at receiving seventeen years courtesy of Bertie Smalls, decided to exact revenge for all grassed-up inmates; leaping upon the unfortunate Lowe, he took a sizeable bite out of his nose. Yet people are unpredictable. Barratt later became a Supergrass himself and not content with that, became the only person in history to be a Supergrass twice. But when 'Skinny' Gervaise (of the Bank of America robbery fame) became a Supergrass, having participated in a robbery in early 1980 of silver ingots, worth almost £3½ million, it began to signal the demise of the Supergrass system. Six men had been charged with the robbery (including Gervaise) and all had pleaded guilty, save one. Gervaise gave evidence against him, but when he was given credit for naming the robbers and providing the whereabouts of the stolen silver, it transpired that the reward had not gone to him. The trial judge wished to know if he was giving evidence in the hope of financial advantage and it was revealed in court that Gervaise had indeed enquired about a reward.

'You would not honestly hang a dog on his evidence, would you?' Judge Peter Slot rhetorically asked the jury, during his summing up. 'You would not dream of finding a man guilty on the basis of his evidence alone, would you?' Just in case the jury was in any doubt whatsoever, the judge added emphatically, 'Well, I would not.'

The jury decided they wouldn't either and returned a verdict of not guilty, so the accused man walked free from the dock.

But there is no doubt that properly managed and motivated, Supergrasses were a fabulous weapon in the battle against organized crime; and many of their co-accused pleaded guilty, due to the overwhelming evidence thus amassed against them. One Flying Squad officer who obtained tremendous results as a result of managing Supergrasses was Detective Chief Inspector Tony Lundy. In 1977, Lundy flew to Montreal, Canada, to collect a prisoner who was wanted for robbery in London. Whilst he was there, he was highly impressed with the way Montreal's Homicide and Robbery Squad collated the information on these offences and thought, with considerable justification that the same should be done at the Yard, to establish a dedicated unit for the collation, investigation and prosecution of all offences of armed robbery. Whilst Flying Squad officers had certainly arrested armed robbers in the past, it was quite often the case that the investigation had been carried out – often in a fragmented way – by their divisional counterparts. If the same gang they were investigating were linked to other robberies on other divisions and areas, they rarely had time to fully investigate these matters.

Lundy mentioned this idea on his return to the Yard and on 10 July 1978, the concept was put into action. The Flying Squad was devolved from the Yard. Four offices, at Rotherhithe, Barnes, Finchley and Walthamstow, were set up for the investigation of armed robberies to the exclusion of any other offence, taking 110 Squad personnel with them. They were given a new name: The Central Robbery Squad, which was not to the taste of the personnel. 'We're the Flying Squad,' muttered one of them, mutinously, 'and we're going to *stay* the fucking Squad!' And as the Squad was leaving the Yard, so the fourth and final television series of the very popular *The Sweeney* was also coming to an end. It had lasted almost four years and its authenticity came from the advice of a former Flying Squad officer, the late Jack Quarrie BEM.

★   ★   ★

But Central Robbery Squad or Flying Squad, they still shared the same tie. In years gone by, legend had it that the Flying Squad Social and Athletic Club wanted some form of identity. So far as the then head of the Squad, Tommy Butler, was concerned, being a member of the Squad was identity enough, so when it was suggested at a committee meeting that a Flying Squad tie might be struck, Butler snapped, 'Right, anyone who wants a Squad tie, stand up!' After considerable hesitation, just one officer hesitantly got to his feet. 'Motion rejected,' said Butler, crisply, giving the courageous officer a piercing look that suggested that his days on the Squad might be well and truly numbered. And there the matter rested.

Sometime later, Detective Chief Inspector Tom Morrison was being driven in a Squad car along Sutton High Street, towards London. Looking out to his left, something caught his eye and he told his driver to pull up. 'That's the motif I want for the Squad,' he muttered and at the next meeting of the Social Club, he put his suggestion to Butler's rather more tolerant successor, Frank 'Jeepers' Davies MBE. Morrison's proposal was eagerly accepted.

It was after the order had been placed that a telephone call was received in the Squad office from an East End crook. During the course of a 'jump-up' he and his gang had stolen a block of cloth from the back of a lorry in east London, only to discover the Squad emblem imprinted on it. Not only did they propose to return it, they also offered to further display their contrition by having the ties made up at their own expense. This undoubtedly well-meant gesture was politely declined, but a Squad car was dispatched to recover the cloth which had gone off course. On the way back to the Yard, evening newspaper billboards proclaimed both the loss and the recovery of the cloth; Tommy Morrison was never one to let a golden opportunity slip by!

And *that* was how the proud emblem of the Eagle Star Insurance Company became adopted by the Flying Squad.

But irrespective of whether they were known as the Central Robbery Squad or Flying Squad, having a dedicated team of detectives to take on the *crème de la crème* of London's villains, the armed robbers, was a brilliant concept. Wasn't it? Yes and no.

Epilogue

ighty percent of the Squad's workforce had left the Yard. Just four squads were left – 9 & 11, 10 & 12.

That the four Robbery Squad offices carried out tremendous work is not in dispute. Armed robberies were reported to them; they obtained the evidence, followed up leads and although they certainly utilized their own informants and carried out surveillance, they often solved the cases by using pure detective ability. They smashed up gangs of dedicated armed robbers, ran supergrasses and saw the gangs sentenced to substantial terms of imprisonment. It was high time that such dedicated teams were formed. Armed robberies in 1978 totalled 734; within four years they had more than doubled, to 1,778. The year following their formation (although no numbers of persons arrested were given in the commissioner's report) the Robbery Squads seized 74 shotguns and 44 handguns, and recovered cash and other valuables in excess of £2 million.

To this day they continue to make impressive inroads into criminal gangs and for my part, I hope that they always will be in the forefront of crime-busting in the Metropolitan Police.

The squads left at the Yard were told to similarly concentrate on armed robbers but in order to do so, they could not rely upon leads from reported crimes; they needed information. This they got from the people they arrested; receivers of stolen property, burglars and most important, dips, who had always been the Squad's most prolific source of information. All of them were pressed to provide information regarding serious crime; and in particular, gangs of armed robbers; it paid off.

The Dips Squad was still functioning – and bringing in impressive results, both in the way of arrests and information, as a result – under Detective Inspector Henry Dowswell, who had been awarded a particularly well-merited George Medal for his actions during the Balcombe Street siege in 1975. However, DAC Powis disagreed with the existence of the Dips Squad, saying that they had outrun their usefulness and that they should be disbanded; if, he added, there was a sudden upsurge of pickpocketing, then the squad could be reformed.

It was exactly this type of imbecile logic that was anathema to seasoned detectives, and it would happen time and again in the years that followed, when senior uniformed officers who commanded full-time occupations by sitting on working parties, suggested that the Flying Squad could be dissolved and the officers sent to divisional duties. Then, they added brightly, if there was a sudden upsurge in robberies, the divisions could form their own, little – you know – sort of mini-Flying Squad.

What Powis (and the other uniformed officers) was unable to comprehend, was that to keep on top of a particular type of crime, whether it be robbery, drugs, or pickpocketing, there must be a dedicated team tasked to address that type of crime. Nothing else will do.

Henry Dowswell's downfall stemmed from the fact that he was a real detective, who knew who was who and what was what, so what with being the head of the Dips Squad and supporting an officer who was under investigation, it took very little for Powis to kick Dowswell off the Flying Squad.

As detective inspector at Bexley Heath police station, Dowswell investigated a case where a little girl had died, having suffered horrific burns from an electric fire. At the completion of the court case, Dowswell was so incensed with the social services and the circumstances which brought about the child's death, he showed the police photographs to members of the press, who published them. Powis hit the roof and Dowswell (who had already been selected for the rank of chief inspector) was told that he would be transferred to King's Cross police station as a uniform inspector. It caused such a furore amongst Dowswell's contemporaries that this course of action was later rescinded, but it was sufficient for his wife to describe him as 'a broken man'.

When Dowswell investigated a fire at Deptford where a number of black youngsters had lost their lives, Powis turned up. Pointing to Dowswell, Powis told another officer, in a voice loud enough for Dowswell to hear, 'You've got to watch him.'

Referring to the Balcombe Street siege, Dowswell told his wife, 'I can dodge bullets being fired at me from the front,' and added sadly, 'but not when I'm being shot at from behind.'

Quite suddenly, Dowswell died from a massive heart attack whilst he was on holiday with his wife in 1981; he was just forty-one. Tributes poured in, not only from his colleagues but also from the parents of the youngsters who had been killed in the Deptford fire, who commented on Dowswell's tact, kindness and professionalism. His funeral at Sidcup was so well attended that loudspeakers had to be erected outside for those unable to enter the church. His widow had one, unequivocal direction as to the funeral: 'I don't want Powis within a hundred miles of it.'

Rightly or wrongly, the blame for Dowswell's demise was laid at Powis' door; and anybody on the Squad who had not already loathed Powis (and there were not many), did now.

So with the famous Dip Squad disbanded, the twelve sets of handcuffs which had been issued to them in 1976, specifically for their duties, were put to other uses. But the Squad at the Yard soldiered on and brought in impressive results, not only of armed robbers but also high-class burglars and receivers of stolen goods. Their capabilities as a dedicated team of detectives, ready to go anywhere in a hurry, armed or unarmed, were in no doubt whatsoever, after they were called to head the hunt for David Ralph Martin, a highly dangerous escaped prisoner, who had shot and seriously wounded an unarmed police officer. Detectives from C11 and 'D' Division had shot an innocent man, Stephen Waldorf, who was sitting in a yellow Mini at Earl's Court, in the mistaken belief that he was Martin. They were off the investigation and the Squad was in; and after eleven days, culminating in an exciting chase through London's Underground system, Martin was caught. Thought to be armed, he wasn't. 'Take it easy, guys,' he told the late Detective Sergeant Nicky Benwell QPM, from the Squad, 'you've got me!'[1]

The Squad had got Martin, but who had got the Squad? When the Securicor robbery at Curtain Road, Shoreditch, East London, was carried out on Easter Bank Holiday Monday, 1983, in which armed raiders poured petrol over the staff and stole £5,961,097 in cash, it was a team of fifty detectives made up from the Walthamstow office and bolstered by officers from 10 &

---

[1] For a full account of this case, see *Rough Justice – Memoirs of a Flying Squad Detective* (Merlin Unwin Books, 2001).

12 squads, who tackled the case, leading to the eventual arrest and imprisonment of Ronnie Knight, Freddy Foreman and six others. And in November that year, resources were really stretched when raiders stole gold valued at £26 million from the Brink's-Mat warehouse, near London Heathrow Airport. The Barnes office took over the investigation, but again their numbers were supplemented with Squad officers from the Yard. Whilst these investigations were being pursued, on 1 August 1983, the remaining teams at the Yard were formed into No. 5 Central Robbery Squad, to investigate armed robberies committed in the inner London divisions. Over the next three years, this squad was also dissolved, their officers mainly bolstering the staff at the four area Robbery Squad offices. Left at the Yard were the commander, the operational detective chief superintendent and the two detective superintendents, one of whom supervised the offices at Walthamstow (later Rigg Approach) and Finchley, the other the offices at Rotherhithe (later Tower Bridge) and Barnes – plus the civil staff.

So was there a case for keeping dedicated teams of detectives on squads at the Yard, to run their own informants, carry out their own cases and yet be ready to supplement any of the area Robbery Squads when necessary? Yes, of course there was. And the information which was acquired by these officers, unfettered from the investigation of crime, could be passed on to the requisite area office, to supplement their knowledge or to provide them with the impetus to take on a whole new, previously unknown, gang of armed robbers. But no more.

Never again would a Flying Squad officer on the fourth floor, in receipt of some red-hot information, excitedly telephone to the drivers' room on the ground floor, with the terse instruction to bring the Squad car up to the concourse in front of the Yard: 'Get it up!'

No. The Squad would continue to 'swoop' – but now, it had flown from the Yard.

Bibliography

ADAMSON Iain, *The Great Detective* (Frederick Muller Ltd, 1966)

BALL John, CHESTER, Lewis & PERROTT Roy, *Cops and Robbers.* (Andre Deutsch, 1978)

BERRETT James, *When I was at Scotland Yard* (Sampson Low, Marston & Co. Ltd, 1932)

BEVERIDGE Peter, *Inside the CID* (Evans Bros. Ltd, 1957)

BOOTH Nicholas, *ZigZag* (Portrait Books, 2007)

BROWN D., *The Rise of Scotland Yard* (Greenwood Press, 1956)

BUNKER John, *From Rattle to Radio* (KAF Brewin Books, 1988)

BURT Leonard, *Commander Burt of Scotland Yard* (Heinemann, 1959)

CAPSTICK John (with Jack Thomas), *Given in Evidence* (John Long, 1960)

CATER Frank (with TULLETT Tom), *The Sharp End* (Bodley Head, 1988)

CHALLENOR Harold & DRAPER Alfred, *Tanky Challenor – SAS and The Met* (Leo Cooper, 1990)

CHERRILL Fred, *Cherrill of the Yard* (George G. Harrap & Co. Ltd, 1954)

CLARKSON Wensley, *Killing Charlie* (Mainstream Publishing, 2004)

CORNISH G.W., *Cornish of the Yard* (John Lane, the Bodley Head, 1935)

COX Barry, SHIRLEY John & SHORT Martin, *The Fall of Scotland Yard* (Penguin Books, 1977)

DARBYSHIRE Neil & HILLIARD Brian *The Flying Squad* (Headline Book Publishing plc 1993)

DONNELLY Mark, *Britain in the Second World War* (Routledge, 1999)

DU ROSE John, *Murder was my Business* (W.H. Allen, 1971)

FABIAN Robert, *Fabian of the Yard* (Naldrett Press, 1950)

FABIAN Robert, *London After Dark* (Naldrett Press, 1954)

FIDO Martin & SKINNER Keith, *The Official Encyclopedia of Scotland Yard* (Virgin Books, 1999)

FIRMIN Stanley, *Scotland Yard: The Inside Story* (Hutchinson & Co., 1948)

FISH Donald *Airline Detective* (Collins, 1962)

FORBES Ian, *Squadman* (W.H. Allen, 1973)

FORDHAM Peta, *The Robbers' Tale* (Hodder and Stoughton, 1965)

FRASER Frank (with MORTON James), *Mad Frankie* (Little, Brown & Co., 1994)

FROST George, *Flying Squad* (Rockliff, 1948)

GOSLING John, *The Ghost Squad* (W.H. Allen, 1959)

GOSLING John (with Dennis CRAIG), *The Great Train Robbery* (W.H. Allen, 1964)

GRANT Denis, *A Fragmented History of the Flying Squad, its transport, Drivers and Detectives* (Boxing Programme Notes, 1976)

GREENO Edward, *War on the Underworld* (John Long, 1960)

HAMBROOK Walter, *Hambrook of the Yard* (Robert Hale & Co., 1937)

HART E.T., *Britain's Godfather* (True Crime Library, 1993)

HATHERILL George, *A Detective's Story* (Andre Deutsch Ltd, 1971)

HIGGINS R.H., *In the Name of the Law* (John Long, 1958)

HILL Billy, *Boss of Britain's Underworld* (Naldrett Press Ltd, 1955)

HINDS Alfred, *Contempt of Court* (Bodley Head, 1966)

HOGG A., McDOUGLE J. &. MORGAN R., *Bullion* (Penguin Group, 1988)

HONEYCOMBE Gordon, *The Complete Murders of the Black Museum* (Leopard Books, 1995)

HOSKINS Percy, *No Hiding Place!* (Daily Express Publications, undated)

HOUGH Richard, *Winston & Clementine – The Triumph of the Churchills* (Bantam Press, 1990.)

HOWE Sir Ronald, *The Pursuit of Crime* (Arthur Barker Ltd, 1961)

INWOOD Stephen, *A History of London* (MacMillan, 1998)

JACKETT Sam *Heroes of Scotland Yard* (Robert Hale Ltd, 1965)

JACKSON Sir Richard, *Occupied with Crime* (George G. Harrap & Co. Ltd, 1967)

KIRBY Dick, *The Squad – A History of the men and vehicles of the Flying Squad at New Scotland Yard, 1919–1983* (Unpublished manuscript, Metropolitan Police History Museum, London 1993)

KIRBY Dick, *Rough Justice – Memoirs of a Flying Squad Detective* (Merlin Unwin Books, 2001)

KIRBY Dick, *The Real Sweeney* (Constable & Robinson, 2005)

KIRBY Dick, *You're Nicked!* (Constable & Robinson, 2007)

KIRBY Dick, *Villains* (Constable & Robinson, 2008)

KRAY Reg, *Villains we have known* (Arrow Books, 1996)

LANE Brian, *The Murder Guide* (Robinson Publishing, London 1991)

LEE Christopher, *This Sceptered Isle* (BBC Worldwide Books, 1999)

LUCAS Norman and SCARLETT Bernard, *The Flying Squad* (Arthur Barker Ltd, 1968)

LUCAS Norman, *Britain's Gangland* (W.H. Allen, 1969)

MACINTYRE Ben, *Agent Zigzag* (Bloomsbury Publishing plc, 2007)

MARK Sir Robert, *In the Office of Constable* (Collins, 1978)

MASSINGBERD Hugh (Ed.), *Fourth Book of Obituaries* (Macmillan, 1998)

McCALL Karen (Ed.), *London Branch NARPO Millennium Magazine* (Orphans Press, Leominster, 1999)

McKNIGHT Gerald, *The Murder Squad* (W.H. Allen, 1967)

McNEE Sir David, *McNee's Law* (William Collins, Sons & Co. Ltd, 1983)

MILLEN Ernest, *Specialist in Crime* (Harrap, 1972)

MORTON James, *Gangland – London's Underworld* (Little, Brown, 1992)

MORTON James, *Bent Coppers* (Little, Brown, 1993)

MORTON James, *Supergrasses & Informers* (Little, Brown, 1995)

MORTON James, *East End Gangland* (Little, Brown, 2000)

MORTON James & PARKER Gerry, *Gangland Bosses* (Time Warner Books, 2005)

MOYLEN J.F., *Scotland Yard and the Metropolitan Police* (G.P. Putnams & Sons Ltd, 1929)

MURPHY Robert, *Smash & Grab* (Faber & Faber, 1993)

NARBOROUGH Fred, *Murder on my Mind* (Allan Wingate, 1959)

O'FLAHERTY Michael, *Have you seen this Woman?* (Corgi Books, 1971)

PEARSON John, *The Profession of Violence* (Weidenfeld & Nicolson, 1972)

PROGL Zoe, *Woman of the Underworld* (Arthur Barker, 1964)

RAWLINGS William, *A Case for the Yard* (John Long, 1961)

READ Leonard (with MORTON James), *Nipper* (MacDonald, 1991)

READ Piers Paul, *The Train Robbers* (W.H. Allen, 1978)

REYNOLDS Bruce, *Autobiography of a Thief* (Bantam, 1995)

ROSE Andrew, *Stinie – Murder on the Common* (The Bodley Head, 1985)

SAMUEL Raphael, *East End Underworld* (Routledge & Kegan Paul, 1981)

SAVAGE Percy, *Savage of the Yard* (Hutchinson & Co., 1934)

SCOTT Sir Harold, *Scotland Yard* (Andre Deutsch, 1954)

SELLWOOD A.V., *Police Strike 1919* (W.H. Allen, 1978)

SHARPE F.D., *Sharpe of the Flying Squad* (John Long, 1938)

SHORT Martin, *Lundy* (Grafton Books, 1991)

SIMPSON Keith, *Forty Years of Murder* (Harrap, 1978)

SLIPPER Jack, *Slipper of the Yard* (Sidgwick & Jackson, 1981)

SPARKS Herbert, *The Iron Man* (John Long, 1964.)

SWAIN John, *Being Informed* (Janus Publishing Co., 1995)

THOMAS Donald, *An Underworld at War* (John Murray, 2003)

THOMAS Donald, *Villains' Paradise* (John Murray, 2005)

THORP Arthur (with A. Noyes THOMAS), *Calling Scotland Yard* (Allan Wingate, 1954)

TULLETT Tom, *Strictly Murder* (Bodley Head, 1979)

WENSLEY F.P., *Detective Days* (Cassell & Co., 1931)

WICKSTEAD Bert, *Gangbuster* (Futura, 1985)

WILLIAMS Frank, *No Fixed Address – The Great Train Robbers on the run* (W.H. Allen, 1973)

WOFFINDEN Bob, *Miscarriages of Justice* (Hodder & Stoughton, 1987)

WYLES Lilian, *A Woman at Scotland Yard* (Faber & Faber Ltd, 1952)

YOUNG Filson (Ed.), *The Trial of Bywaters and Thompson* (William Hodge & Co, 1923)

Index

Abbreviations

ACC	Assistant Chief Constable
AC(C)	Assistant Commissioner Crime
CC	Chief Constable
CC(CID)	Chief Constable CID
Comm.	Commissioner
DAC	Deputy Assistant Commissioner
DCC	Deputy Chief Constable
DCI	Detective Chief Inspector
DCS	Detective Chief Superintendent
DDI	Divisional Detective Inspector
Dep. Comm.	Deputy Commissioner
DC	Detective Constable
DI	Detective Inspector
DS	Detective Sergeant
Det. Supt.	Detective Superintendent
Insp.	Inspector
PC	Police Constable
PS	Police Sergeant
SPS	Police Station Sergeant

About the Author

Born in the East End of London in 1943, Dick Kirby joined the Metropolitan Police in 1967. He spent over half of his service with the Serious Crime Squad and the Flying Squad until 1993 when he was medically discharged.

He saw the toughest slice of police-work and was described by a Judge at the Old Bailey as 'one of the best detectives at Scotland Yard'. A senior police officer in Belfast called him 'a good man to have in an explosive situation,' and Kirby was commended on forty occasions for catching criminals by Commissioners, Directors of Public Prosecutions, Trial Judges and Magistrates by displaying courage, determination and detective ability.

Dick Kirby is the author of *Rough Justice – Memoirs of a Flying Squad Detective* (Merlin Unwin Books, 2001), *The Real Sweeney* (Constable & Robinson, 2005), *You're Nicked!* (Constable & Robinson, 2007), *Villains* (Constable & Robinson, 2008) and *The Guv'nors* (Pen & Sword Books, 2010). He has contributed to four anthologies and six other true crime books and contributes to magazines and national newspapers on a regular basis. He appears on radio and television, provides talks for groups on 'the golden age of policing', is a member of the Crime Writers' Association, an international member of the American Police Writers and is a former member of the Special Forces Club.

From his village home in Suffolk, Dick Kirby lives with his wife Ann – they have four children and five grandchildren – at a somewhat more leisurely pace than before. He writes, corresponds with friends all over the world, listens to music and tends his garden.

DICK KIRBY
has also written

Rough Justice

'He treats criminals the only way they understand. His language is often shocking, his methods unorthodox.' NATIONAL ASSOCIATION OF RETIRED POLICE OFFICERS MAGAZINE.

'His style of writing pulls no punches and he tells it like it is. Highly recommended.' POLICE HISTORY SOCIETY JOURNAL.

'Real *Boys' Own* stuff, this. Tinged with a wry sense of humour makes this an excellent read.' METROPOLITAN POLICE HISTORY SOCIETY.

'*Rough Justice* is a fast-paced, amusing and enjoyable read, full of absorbing crime stories.' SUFFOLK JOURNAL.

'The continuing increase in violent crime will make many readers yearn for yesteryear and officers of Dick Kirby's calibre.' POLICE MAGAZINE.

'An exciting and fascinating insight into a highly experienced and effective detective's approach to some of the most difficult areas of policing.' LONDON POLICE PENSIONER.

The Real Sweeney

'Everyone's talking about *The Real Sweeney* ... Tough, fast-paced and funny, this one's a must.' LONDON POLICE PENSIONER.

'His reflections on the political aspect of law enforcement will ring true for cops, everywhere.' AMERICAN POLICE BEAT.
'Its no-nonsense portrayal of life in the police will give readers a memorable literary experience.' SUFFOLK JOURNAL.

'A Scotland Yard legend ... has had a second hard-hitting volume of memoirs published.' ILFORD RECORDER.

'A must for the true-crime bookshelf.' METROPOLITAN POLICE HISTORY SOCIETY.

'These are the real-life accounts of a tough London cop.' DAILY EXPRESS.

You're Nicked!

'Dick Kirby ... gives a gruelling, gritty, yet funny look at life on the front line against crime.' ROMFORD RECORDER.

'It's full of dark humour, tense busts and stand-offs. As crime rates rocket, this book will go down well.' DAILY SPORT.

'A great read with fascinating stories and amusing anecdotes from a man who experienced it all.' SUFFOLK NORFOLK LIFE MAGAZINE.

'*You're Nicked!* is a gritty series of episodes from his time in the Met – laced with black humour and humanity.' EAST ANGLIAN DAILY TIMES.

'In *You're Nicked!* he describes his hair-raising adventures ... with an equal measure of black humour and honesty.' NEWHAM RECORDER.

'Once again, Dick Kirby has produced an exciting, entertaining and readable account of his exploits and I would strongly urge its perusal at an early opportunity.' THE PEELER.

Villains

'Kirby is all too happy to spill every metaphorical bean ... your reviewer's favourite section looks at the so-called toffs abandoning their fine-living backgrounds and falling victim to the long arm of the law.' BARKING & DAGENHAM RECORDER.

'All of the stories are told with Dick Kirby's acerbic, black humour in a compelling style, by a detective who was there.' AMERICAN POLICE BEAT.

'I'm a huge Dick Kirby fan … this is a fast-paced, riveting read, made even more enjoyable by Kirby's trademark humour.' TANGLED WEB WEBSITE.

'The humorous and lively telling keeps the reader enthralled. Tales of escapees and con after con keep the reader engaged and Mr. Kirby's stories have a flavour of *Life on Mars* and *The Sweeney*.' BURY FREE PRESS.

'Kirby's style is strong and energetic … the humour and honesty keep the pages turning, while the reader can't help but dream up characters befitting the television hit show, *Life on Mars*.' NEWHAM RECORDER.

'This is magic. The artfulness of these anti-heroes has you pining for the bad old days.' DAILY SPORT.

The Guv'nors

'Chief constables could learn a great deal from how these old-time detectives tackled crime'. JOHN BEADLE, PRESIDENT OF THE EX-CID OFFICERS' ASSOCIATION OF THE METROPOLITAN POLICE.

'It takes a great detective to recognise and explain the craft of others. Dick Kirby's latest endeavour, The Guv'nors is an informed and thrilling account of the work of these great men.' PAUL MILLEN, AUTHOR OF CRIME SCENE INVESTIGATOR.

'Fred Wensley, Nutty Sharpe, Hooter Millen, Fabian and other colourful New Scotland Yard legends are vividly brought to life by a man who has walked the walk, the Flying Squad's own Dick Kirby. What a brilliant TV series this would make!' JOSEPH WAMBAUGH, AUTHOR OF THE CHOIRBOYS AND HOLLYWOOD MOON.